Foundations of Early Childhood Education

LEARNING ENVIRONMENTS AND CHILD CARE IN CANADA

Beverlie Dietze

Loyalist College

with
Ken Pierce

PEARSON

Prentice
Hall

Toronto

Library and Archives Canada Cataloguing in Publication

Dietze, Beverlie, 1957–
    Foundations of early childhood education : learning environments and child care in Canada / Beverlie Dietze.

Includes index.
ISBN 0-13-127460-0

    1. Early childhood development—Canada—Textbooks. I. Title.

LB1139.3.C3D53 2006   372.21'0971   C2005-905631-2

ISBN 0-13-127460-0

Vice President, Editorial Director: Michael J. Young
Executive Editor: Dave Ward
Marketing Manager: Toivo Pajo
Supervising Developmental Editor: Suzanne Schaan
Production Editor: Kevin Leung
Copy Editor: Colleen Ste. Marie
Proofreader: Reena Kreindler
Senior Production Coordinator: Peggy Brown
Composition: Janet Zanette
Permissions Research: Susan Wallace-Cox
Art Director: Julia Hall
Cover and Interior Design: Anthony Leung
Cover Image: J. A. Kraulis, Masterfile

For permission to reproduce copyrighted material, the publisher gratefully acknowledges the copyright holders listed on page 279, which is considered and extension of this copyright page.

Statistics Canada information is used with the permission of the Minister of Industry, as Minister responsible for Statistics Canada. Information on the availability of the wide range of data from Statistics Canada can be obtained from Statistics Canada's Regional Offices, its World Wide Web site at http://www.statcan.ca, and its toll-free access number 1-800-263-1136.

13 14 15 16 17   14 13 12 11

Printed and bound in Canada.

I dedicate this book to my late mother,

Eileen Lucy Arthurs, and my late father,

William Christie Arthurs, who together provided

me with an environment that allowed me to

explore, seek answers to my questions, and

celebrate my quest to wonder and explore—all of

which are true gifts to lifelong learning.

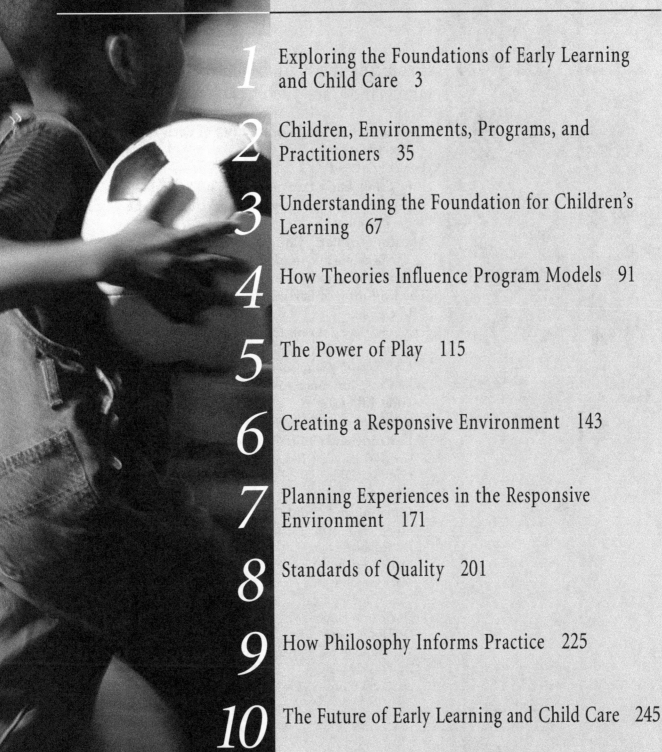

Brief Contents

Table of Contents

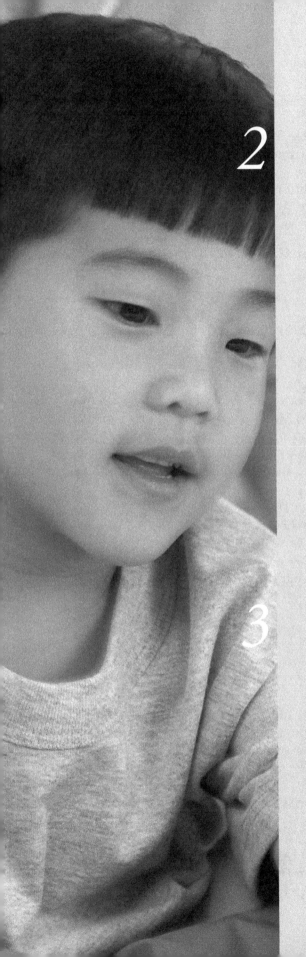

4 How Theories Influence Program Models   91

5 The Power of Play   115

6   Creating a Responsive Environment   143

8   Standards of Quality   201

9   How Philosophy Informs Practice   225

10 The Future of Early Learning and Child Care   245

Preface

If you're reading this book, you probably have an interest in children and are embarking on an educational journey that will support you in launching or enhancing a career that is child focused.

When I began writing this text, I reflected on my career initially with children and later as an educator. I soon recognized that never before has there been such momentum in government and Canadian society to support children and families in having access to quality early learning and child care programs. It is an exciting time to be entering this area of study because so many initiatives are charting the way for early learning and child care to evolve to new heights. Early learning and child care is an up-and-coming profession that will probably have as much impact on the fabric of Canadian society as business-related careers.

Foundations of Early Childhood Education: Learning Environments and Child Care in Canada is a direct outgrowth of my educational and work experience with children, parents, and early childhood practitioners. No matter which group I work with, the rich learning opportunities have been the impetus for me to explore and wonder about how children learn and what environments are most conductive to supporting a child's sense of curiosity. I continually am inspired by the knowledge I gain from early childhood practitioners about ways to facilitate and create children's environments that are rich with language, exploration, laughter, and wonderment.

The presentation of this book has been influenced by my own learning style. Looking at theory and then examples of how theory informs practice, followed by discussion points, helps me to visualize how these concepts transfer to practice. As a result, each chapter features "Points to Ponder," "Conversation Café," and "Parenting Portrait." Through this combination of theory and practice, I envision that you will acquire a comprehensive introduction to the study of early learning and child care. The text provides a framework for understanding the complexity of early learning and child care environments by exploring the who, what, where, how, and when of early childhood. It emphasizes the importance of becoming an active member of your learning community, and it encourages you to develop partnerships with children, families, and communities. This approach is intended to actualize that familiar African proverb, "It takes a village to raise a child." You are entering one of the most important fields of practice—guiding children through their foundation stages of life. You can make a difference in the lives of our children. Welcome to our learning community!

Organization of the Text

This text is organized into three major sections. The first section (Chapters 1–4) provides the foundation knowledge of early learning and child care. These chapters outline the importance of practitioners studying about early child care. The roots, the framework, and the principles of early learning and child care are high-lighted. As well, how children learn and how their environments support learning are explored.

In the second section (Chapters 5–8), you will explore the power of play and the importance of children's environments to play, exploration, learning, and development. Chapter 8 highlights the concept of quality and how benchmarks, assessments, and evaluation elevate the standards of quality for children and prac-titioners.

The third section (Chapters 9–10) focuses on how an individual's philosophy informs practice, followed by a discussion on the future of early learning and child care. Here you will explore the key trends that may emerge in an early childhood professional's life.

Approach of the Text

This text was designed to be reader-friendly. It provides theory with application examples as a way to support you in making sense of how theory informs practice. Throughout the text, you will encounter opportunities to read about early learn-ing and child care in practice.

Foundations of Early Childhood Education: Learning Environments and Child Care in Canada is unique in several ways.

- First, many of the examples focus on presenting children's programming outdoors. Although some other texts present information on planning outdoor programs for children, this book clearly emphasizes the impor-tance of viewing outdoor play and indoor play as equal environments in which children play and learn.

- A second unique feature of this book is that a large percentage of the research studies cited are Canadian based, helping the reader examine the content from a Canadian perspective.

- Third, this book introduces the concept of a learning community. Together, both in the classroom setting and as a practitioner, by working and learning together, we engage in a richer learning experience.

- Another key feature of this book is the emphasis on partnerships among early learning and child care staff, children, and families.

- The final attribute of this book that differs from other texts is the per-spective on responsive environments, room design, and programming. A strong emphasis is placed on examining the environment and adjusting it accordingly to support the interests, needs, and developmental levels of children.

Features of the Text

The pedagogical features of the text are designed to support the theory presented and encourage an active, participatory learning environment.

- *Learning Objectives:* Each chapter begins with a series of learning outcomes that focus attention on the core concepts presented in the chapter.
- *Chapter-Opening Vignettes:* At the beginning of each chapter, "A Day Begins in an Early Learning and Child Care Centre" sets the stage for you to become familiar with some of the typical experiences and challenges faced by early childhood practitioners, children, and parents.
- *Points to Ponder* and *Conversation Café:* These questions encourage you to look beyond the text and can be used for personal reflection or group discussion.
- *Parenting Portraits:* Real-life examples help you understand the issues parents face and how you can work with them as partners.
- *Key Terms with Definitions* and *Glossary:* Throughout the text, key terms are shown in boldface, with definitions provided in the margins. All the key terms and definitions are also gathered in a glossary at the end of the text for easy reference.
- *Chapter Summary:* This review of the chapter summarizes key points, focusing on the core concepts outlined in the learning objectives.
- *Further Opportunities for Enrichment:* These end-of-chapter exercises provide suggestions for research, group work, and exploring your role as an early childhood practitioner.
- *Additional Reading* and *Weblinks:* The listed resources can be used for further study and research.

Student Supplement

Companion Website (www.pearsoned.ca/dietze): This website, created specifically to accompany *Foundations of Early Childhood Education: Learning Environments and Child Care in Canada*, offers self-grading quizzes to test your understanding of basic concepts, additional Weblinks to help you with further study, and other resources.

Instructor Supplements

Instructor's Manual: This manual offers case studies, teaching and learning methods for consideration, and other resources.

PowerPoint Presentations: These PowerPoint slides provide faculty with the core concepts from each chapter to help learners explore and assimilate the theory and application of the foundations of early childhood education. In addition, there is a variety of additional materials, or resources for both instructors and students.

These instructor supplements are available for download from a password-protected section of Pearson Education Canada's online catalogue (vig.pearsoned.ca). Navigate to the book's catalogue page to view a list of those supplements that are available. See your local sales representative for details and access.

Acknowledgments

I would like to thank the reviewers whose feedback has helped to shape the development of this project, including the following people:

Katherine Bonell, College of the Rockies
Cathy Smey Carston, Mount Royal College
Deborah Collins, St. Lawrence College–Kingston
Gail Hunter, George Brown College
Dale Long, Seneca College
Donna Mese, Cambrian College
Diane Nyisztor, Vanier College
Marian Pickton, North Island College
Robynne Smith, Durham College

I would like to sincerely thank the Pearson staff who guided and contributed to the content and presentation of this book. In particular, I would like to acknowledge and thank Suzanne Schaan for her support, guidance, direction, and most of all patience throughout the development of this book. In addition, I would like to thank the children, families and early learning and child care staff who have allowed me to use their photos to emphasize key elements throughout the book. Their photos add richness to each of the chapters. I would like to acknowledge the support and contributions that my friend and colleague Barbara Crossley made to this project. As always, her ability to ask questions, stimulate my thought process, and provide guidance when necessary increased the quality of the project. Thank you to Amy Chamberlain, Julie Colasante, and Maureen Brown, graduates of the Early Childhood Education Program at Loyalist College. I appreciate you allowing me to combine elements of your philosophy statement into this publication.

I would like to thank my brothers, sisters, aunt, and extended family for being curious about this project and offering me the encouragement to proceed. Finally, I would like to thank Peter for providing me with the love, support, time, and encouragement that allowed me to engage in this incredible learning experience.

I will be forever grateful to all of you who became part of my learning community and who contributed to this phase of my lifelong learning journey.

Beverlie Dietze

A Great Way to Learn and Instruct Online

The Pearson Education Canada Companion Website is easy to navigate and is organized to correspond to the chapters in this textbook. Whether you are a student in the classroom or a distance learner, you will discover helpful resources for in-depth study and research that empower you in your quest for greater knowledge and maximize your potential for success in the course.

Companion
Website

[www.pearsoned.ca/dietze]

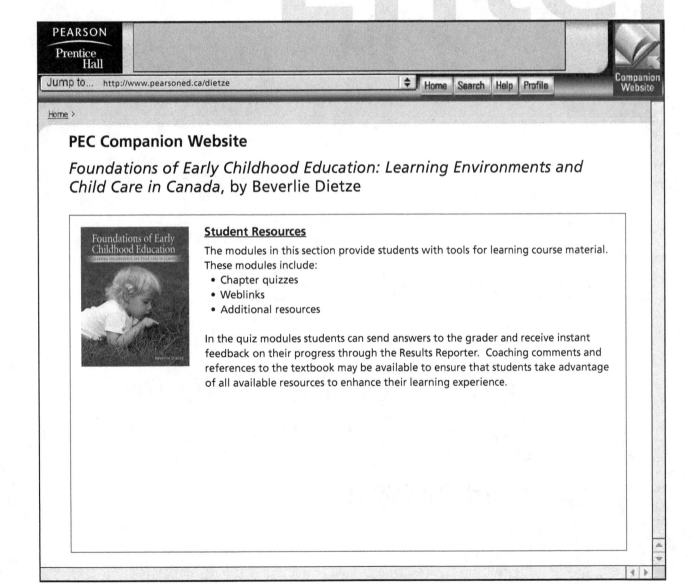

PEARSON
Prentice
Hall

Jump to...   http://www.pearsoned.ca/dietze   ⬍   Home | Search | Help | Profile

Companion
Website

Home >

PEC Companion Website

Foundations of Early Childhood Education: Learning Environments and Child Care in Canada, by Beverlie Dietze

Student Resources

The modules in this section provide students with tools for learning course material. These modules include:
- Chapter quizzes
- Weblinks
- Additional resources

In the quiz modules students can send answers to the grader and receive instant feedback on their progress through the Results Reporter. Coaching comments and references to the textbook may be available to ensure that students take advantage of all available resources to enhance their learning experience.

"Early Learning and child care learning communities plant the seeds, weave the ideas, nurture the growth, and collectively reap the harvest."

Dr. Beverlie Dietze, 2005

1

Exploring the Foundations of Early Learning and Child Care

A Day Begins in an Early Learning and Child Care Centre

A family vehicle comes to a complete stop directly in front of an early learning and child care centre, and a child unbuckles from her seat and gets out of the car. Not waiting for Mom, and with jacket open to the winter cold and hat and mittens in hand, the little girl races to the door of the preschool centre. An early childhood practitioner opens the door and greets her with a warm smile. Before the practitioner is able to say hello, the young child says excitedly, "Jennifer, I saw them, I saw them, I saw the little birds, the little chickadees! I saw the happy little birds."

Jennifer crouches down to the young child's eye level. Remaining still and ignoring the outdoor clothing flung to the floor she replies, "How exciting for you, Annie." Jennifer maintains eye contact and listens attentively to the child's words. Then she asks, her tone soft and engaging, "Where did you see the winter birds?"

Annie sits on her jacket on the floor and puts on her indoor shoes. She responds quickly in the same elated manner. "I saw them in the park," she says. "Daddy and I walked there and they were in the trees and on the ground just like you said they would be."

The conversation continues. "Were you able to see the colours of the birds?" "I did see some black, some white, and a yellow kind of tummy. Daddy says we can make the chickadee house and put it in the park so the birds can be warm in the winter. I need to find soft things for the birdhouse." The child gets up from the floor, places her clothing in her cubbyhole, and returns to the still-crouching Jennifer.

Jennifer states, "I think there is some soft stuff around the centre that you could use for your birdhouse. Where could you look first?" With a sudden pop of her head as she nods, the young child then bounds off, knowing exactly where to look. A smile spreads across Jennifer's face.

Building a Learning Community of Early Childhood Practitioners

The fundamental purpose of this book is to teach you, the learner, the student practitioner, about children, children's environments, and early childhood services. Becoming an active member of a learning community offers you, the student practitioner, a number of benefits, all of which help your academic success and prepare you to become an early childhood practitioner, including:

1. The discovery of new information about children and families.
2. The development of new perspectives and ideas that influence your knowledge, skills, and attitudes on topical issues related to children and families.
3. The development of relationships with children and families, peers, mentors, early childhood practitioners, and other professionals. Such interactions and relationships will help you to develop a sense of community and will provide the foundation for learning partnerships.
4. The recognition of how you can play an active role in your learning and how you can contribute to others' learning. For when learning is active, when learning is shared with others, and when you reflect on new information, you will enhance your understanding of that information and its application.
5. The acceptance of being part of a learning community so that you contribute to creating a learning environment that values diversity and multiple perspectives. You recognize the strengths of your peers and build upon those strengths. This allows you and your peers to ask difficult questions, define problems, and lead conversations to support your areas of exploration.

We have chosen to share insights into aspects of the early childhood field through our chapter features: "A Day Begins in an Early Learning and Child Care Setting," "Parenting Portrait," "Conversation Café," and "Points to Ponder." As educators, we have learned that these types of insights provide new early childhood practitioners with a starting point for discussion, debate, exploration, reflection, and for making connections to the early childhood learning community. We hope that the chapter features will help you recall information about the diverse issues that comprise the early childhood field. We envision that you will develop an understanding of some of the concerns,

Children and practitioners build healthy, respectful environments.

decisions, and challenges that parents face. By speaking with others and sharing your learning, you will become a reflective observer and you will make choices and form opinions about your beliefs and practices. Together, these actions will allow you to construct new knowledge and become a contributing member of the early childhood learning community.

Throughout this book, we emphasize the impact that children's experiences have on their learning and development. We discuss how nurturing occurs and how children require stimulating environments to flourish. We highlight the important role of the early childhood practitioner in the process. We encourage you to enjoy your learning journey.

Children are the reason for early learning and child care environments.

Looking Ahead

In this chapter, we introduce you to the foundations of the field of early childhood. We examine why we study early childhood, and we outline the roots of early childhood services and present selected theorists who have influenced early childhood services and programming. We highlight how family and culture affect early childhood services, and we identify the role of government and how it shapes the structure of early childhood services. As you explore each area, you will examine your own beliefs, ideas, and opinions about particular issues and you will begin to understand the broad components that encompass early learning and child care. By examining various perspectives, you will begin to acquire knowledge and an understanding of the field. This will enable you to determine your philosophical beliefs about how children learn and what types of play environments and learning experiences best support children's development.

Why Study Early Learning and Child Care?

In "A Day Begins in an Early Learning and Child Care Setting" at the beginning of the chapter, Jennifer exhibited many developmentally appropriate early learning and child care strategies, such as greeting Annie, getting down to Annie's eye level, using a soft and engaging voice when posing a question to Annie, and then encouraging Annie to locate some soft material for the birdhouse. How did

Jennifer know these strategies, and how was she able to use them effectively? Like you, Jennifer studied early learning and child care.

Since the turn of the 21st century, interest in early learning and child care has surged among provincial governments, territories, and the federal government. Since 2003, "there has been unprecedented recognition of early learning and child care in national policy initiatives" (Childcare Resource and Research Unit, 2005, p. 1). Interest has evolved for two reasons: policy-makers now recognize that access to quality early learning and child care can strengthen the foundations of lifelong learning for all children; and there is "a keen international interest in it as an important foundation for achieving societal goals" (Childcare Resource and Research Unit, 2005, p. 1).

As a result of the public's interest in establishing a national system of early learning and child care, the provinces, territories, and the federal government are negotiating roles, responsibilities, and policies that will influence expanding access to and the quality of non-parental care for children. The establishment of a pan-Canadian early learning and child care system is sure to affect the role of early childhood practitioners. Employment options, salary levels, program standards, and minimum educational standards will change as governments revise policies and financial commitments to early childhood services. New research, program models, and policies are continually evolving. As ongoing development occurs, it is indeed an exciting time to be entering the field.

Post-secondary programs prepare students for careers with children by integrating theoretical perspectives from various sciences. These theoretical perspectives provide a body of information that guides program philosophies and practices. The present-day delivery of early childhood services draws on diverse disciplines, including health, neuroscience, cognitive science, developmental psychology, and education. Research advances will continue to influence best practice in the early childhood sector and will change the emphasis of early childhood programs.

Throughout history, there have been shifts in thinking about child rearing, the importance of play, how children learn, and the roles of family and community. Each shift impacts practice. For example, Plato (c. 428–348 BCE) argued that children should be removed from their parents early and placed in state-run schools so that experts would guide children's educational experiences, maximizing their inborn potential (Mayfield, 2001). Conversely, Comenius (1592–1670) viewed the family, especially the mother and the home environment, as the most important venue for providing educational experiences for children under the age of six (Mayfield, 2001). In the 20th century, people debated which experience was better for children—being home with a primary caregiver or being in some form of group care. More recent research, such as the groundbreaking U.S. study conducted under the auspices of the National Institute for Child Health and Human Development (NICHD) (2000), found that high quality, non-parental care generally has important positive effects on children from all backgrounds and that "good quality early childhood programs together with parental care at home is better than parental care on its own" (p. 3). Cleveland and Krashinsky (2001) suggest children benefit when they have both rich experience within a family setting and access to *quality* community early childhood services.

In partnership, families and early childhood practitioners provide the experiences, opportunities, and environments that foster the development of the child and the acquisition of life skills necessary to function and flourish in our complex society.

Early childhood student practitioners benefit from studying early learning and child care because it helps them to understand the relationship of family to child development, of child development to play, and of play to early childhood services, each of which directly affects the child and the role of early childhood practitioners. Early childhood practitioners require this information so that they can effectively create environments that respect, nurture, and support children in their growth and development. Throughout this text, we will present information to build your knowledge about how each of these components affects your role as a student practitioner and later as a practitioner.

Early childhood student practitioners. Individuals who are enrolled in early childhood studies in a college certificate, diploma, or university degree program.

Beginning Your Journey . . . Understanding the Terminology

Many terms are used to describe the people, the positions, the concepts, and the diverse issues associated with the early childhood sector. Like most other areas of study, this one is under continual construction and refinement, enabling the field

Early childhood student practitioners learn about the concept of scaffolding by constructing a scaffold.

Early learning and child care. A comprehensive system of early learning and child care programs for children from infancy to 6 years based on principles of inclusion, affordability, accessibility, quality, and parental choice. In these environments, early childhood practitioners create safe, interesting, innovative play opportunities that are responsive to children's needs, interests, and abilities, while supporting the needs of families.

Early childhood education and care. Programs that support the healthy development of all children by providing each child with access to quality programs that are developmentally and culturally appropriate regardless of choice of service, age, or developmental needs of children, or residence of family.

Canadian Child Care Federation. A bilingual, non-profit, national, member-based organization established in 1987. There are more than 11 000 members, including early learning and child care practitioners, academics, parents, and policy-makers.

Early childhood education. The study of theories and practices that support the implementation of programs and services that support the healthy development of all children.

to evolve. Think of it as a scaffold used in construction. The scaffold has a platform connected with poles, planks, and ties, but that platform must be solid before additional sections may be added. You too will need to build a foundation of knowledge about children before adding new layers of information. The more solid the foundation, the easier it will be for you to make connections with new information and research.

Because the terminology associated with the early childhood sector is continually being redefined, most terms, such as *early childhood education,* do not have universal definitions. Nor is there a common term used to describe those individuals who pursue a career in early childhood. Yet without common terminology, developing an identity for this field of study would be challenging. Throughout this book, you will be introduced to new terminology. As you prepare for your role as an early childhood practitioner, it is beneficial for you to become familiar with the current terms and to use them with other student practitioners and with early childhood practitioners. In many documents, the terms *early learning and child care* and *early childhood education and care* are used interchangeably. There are also similarities among some of our definitions. However, the wide variety of terms used to describe the sector and employees causes confusion among those working in the field, as well as among the general public. Since no professional body regulates the early childhood sector, the terms are open to personal interpretations, which allows regional and personal flexibility and choice but also contributes to confusion.

Following are some of the most common key terms.

Early learning and child care. Refers to a comprehensive system of early learning and child care programs for children from infancy to 6 years that are based on principles of inclusion, affordability, accessibility, quality, and parental choice. The programs provide positive stimulation and nurturing to children, which lay the foundation for learning, health, and behaviour for a person's life (*A Canada Fit for Children*, 2002, p. 17).

Early childhood education and care (ECEC). The Organisation for Economic Co-operation and Development (OECD) (2001) defines *early childhood education and care* as "all arrangements providing care and education for children under compulsory school age, regardless of setting, funding, opening hours or program content" (p. 14). Beach et al. (2004) define ECEC as "programs that support the healthy development of all children; provide additional supports to children with disabilities, and to those living in conditions of risk; and enables parents to participate in the labour force, in training and education, and in the community" (p. 3). The **Canadian Child Care Federation** (1991) describes ECEC as "developmentally and culturally appropriate for each child in its service. Quality care encompasses all types of care provision available to all families in Canada, regardless of choice of service, age or developmental needs of children, or residence of family" (p. 2).

Early childhood education (ECE) and early childhood educator. Morrison (2003) uses *early childhood education* to describe "the services provided by early childhood professionals" (p. 22). Others use terms such as *early childhood educator, early childhood practitioner, teacher, daycare* or *child care worker,* or *child care provider*. Statistics Canada uses the term *early childhood educator* to describe employees in the sector with or without training, whereas Beach et al. (2004) suggest that *early childhood educator* is most often used to describe an individual with a post-secondary ECE credential.

Early childhood practitioner. As identified by Ferguson (2004), Funk and Wagnall's (1976) defines a practitioner as "one who practices an art or profession." In early learning and child care, *practitioner* encompasses the variety of positions within this sector.

Early childhood services. Programs provided for children in child care settings, homes, institutions, recreational facilities, or other group settings. In these environments, early childhood practitioners create safe, interesting, innovative play opportunities that are responsive to children's needs, interests, and abilities, while supporting the needs of families.

Early childhood. Refers to the period from birth to 8 years of age.

Child care. Refers to child care offered in centres and family child care homes that are regulated by provincial/territorial governments.

Community programs. Refers to nursery schools/preschools and resource programs that are regulated by provincial/territorial governments.

The Roots of Early Childhood Services

Students frequently ask why it is important to explore the roots of early childhood services and how historical perspectives impact current practices (see Figure 1.1). Exploring those roots is essential because the historical perspective gives practitioners insight into the beliefs, ideals, and concepts impacting current practices. Exploring previous practices and determining which ones, according to our belief system, are appropriate to use in a given situation leads to "new knowledge."

This new knowledge, combined with a practitioner's own beliefs, influences standards of practice. For example, Montessori, Froebel, and Waldorf each determined that young children benefit from outdoor play. Why would this be important? Each of these theorists recognized that outdoor play provides children with rich learning experiences about nature and the environment while contributing to physical development. Children who have hands-on experiences with our natural environment develop a respect for living things and a curiosity about how things grow and why our environment is important. At the same time, children are learning to move their bodies, develop balance, and strengthen their kinesthetic awareness. As obesity increases among children, and as we try to support children in learning about their environment, there is a renewed interest in early childhood practitioners' increasing the amount of outdoor play and the options for children to explore and discover (Crossley & Dietze, 2004).

Examining the roots of early learning and child care helps practitioners understand how the field has developed over time. Equally important is gaining an understanding of how and why current standards of practice have evolved. Examining theories provides early childhood student practitioners with a structure to understand how learning occurs; a tool to examine, evaluate, and predict children's learning needs based on identified benchmarks; and a reference point to

Early childhood educator. A term used to describe individuals who work with children and hold a post-secondary ECE credential.

Early childhood practitioner. Individuals who have completed early childhood studies in a college certificate, diploma, or university degree program, and who participate in continuous learning about young children.

Early childhood services. Programs provided for children in child care settings, homes, institutions, recreational facilities, or other group settings. In these environments, early childhood practitioners create safe, interesting, innovative play opportunities that are responsive to children's needs, interests, and abilities, while supporting the needs of families.

Early childhood. Refers to the period from birth to 8 years of age.

Child care: Government-regulated child care offered in centres and family child care homes.

Community programs. Nursery schools/preschools and resource programs that are regulated by provincial/territorial governments.

Conversation Café

What's in a name? Should there be one specific name used to identify individuals working with children from infancy to 6 years of age? If so, what should it be? Why? Should there be one name used to identify the field? If so, what should it be? Is it best to use a broad name, such as early learning and child care, or should a more focused name be used? Why or why not?

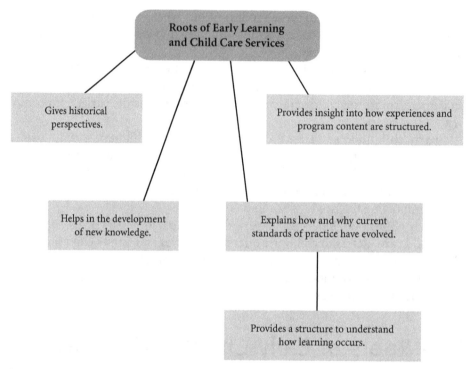

Figure 1.1 *Why Examine the Roots of Early Childhood Services?*

communicate to others how children develop. These elements eventually influence how experiences and program content are structured. However, before we discuss programming we will present 12 selected theorists and their insights into how children learn, how early childhood practitioners support children in their development, and how the environment impacts the development of children.

The Beginning Roots of Early Childhood Services

Before the 14th century, children made the transition from childhood to adulthood by the age of 7 (Mayfield, 2001). Between the 5th and 13th centuries, childhood was extremely short, often lasting barely beyond infancy. The only available education was religious instruction and training for the priesthood at monastery schools. Children learned survival skills by working side by side with their families or employers.

During the latter part of the Dark Ages, the policies of Charlemagne of France strongly influenced societal direction. He proclaimed that the nobility should know their letters. At the same time, craft guilds and apprenticeship programs were being developed and expanded across the country. Learning became important to society (Gordon & Brown, 1989).

In the years of transition from the Dark Ages to the Renaissance in the 14th century and the Reformation in the 16th century, society evolved from one of survival to one of sophistication. Several economic, political, social, and religious movements began to work together as a way to support the development of society. For example, young boys were provided with opportunities to learn specific skills from a male adult that prepared those boys to become contributing members of society. At the same time, Germany established a school system, leading other European societies to do the same. As more educational programs were established, the infant mortality rate declined (Mayfield, 2001), and there was a pronounced shift in how people viewed children. Societies began to recognize that children required educational programs early in life, rather than as adults. Children educated in their early years would be better equipped to help families improve their position in society. European societies developed an appreciation of the value of creating specific environments to foster a child's development (Mayfield, 2001). Hence, the concept of early childhood education was born.

The first written documentation referencing early childhood education is found in the writings of the ancient Greeks and Romans (Mayfield, 2001). Plato (c. 428–348 BCE) and Aristotle (384–322 BCE) determined that the early years (prior to formal schooling) had more of an impact on a child's development than any other life period. For example, Plato suggested that the early years were critical for developing healthy bodies and formulating the blueprint for one's character. This belief continues to prevail in early childhood theory even today.

Plato advocated for children to be educated initially by nurses and then by their parents during the first six years in a home setting. He believed that in the home environment children could participate in games, stories, music, and literature, activities essential for the development of interpersonal skills and later academic skills. He also indicated children 3 to 6 years old required play opportunities with other children of similar ages under the guidance of adults, such as nurses. Plato concluded that formal education in a school-like setting was most appropriate after the age of 6.

Aristotle expanded the discussion on the importance of the early years to include the relationship between early childhood experiences and lifelong learning. He, like Plato, suggested children up to the age of 7 should be taught at home by their mothers and/or nurses. Leaving the care and nurturing of children to adults other than the parents was unacceptable. Aristotle also made connections between prenatal development and later development. He suggested that women exercise and eat a nutritionally balanced diet during pregnancy (Mayfield, 2001). Aristotle recognized that individual children have different needs and strengths, a principle that continues to influence many early childhood programs today.

The Modern Roots of Early Childhood Services

Europeans who immigrated to Canada have long influenced Canadian society. Although many other cultures have made significant contributions to early childhood services, because of the European influence on Canadian society overall this introductory text focuses mainly on European theorists.

In the late 19th and early 20th centuries, there were at least 12 theorists who contributed fundamentally to the body of literature on early childhood. Each discovered new ideas and new knowledge by concentrating either on how children

Developmentally appropriate programs offer children experiences indoors.

develop, how children learn, or how early childhood services in communities advance child development. An introduction to their theories follows in Table 1.1. We have selected these theorists primarily because their work continues to impact current early childhood philosophies and practices. We present two key points about their contributions to learning about children, followed by how their work impacts practices today. This is intended to help you become familiar with their names and, briefly, their work. (You will learn more about these theorists in upcoming chapters and in other courses.) For ease of presentation, we have listed the theorists in chronological order.

The theories of Erik Erikson, Howard Gardner, Abraham Maslow, Jean Piaget, and Lev Vygotsky contribute to understanding child development. Their works help us to understand how children learn and develop. John A. Comenius's, John Dewey's, Friedrich Froebel's, John Locke's, Maria Montessori's, Johann Pestalozzi's, and Jean-Jacques Rousseau's theories and beliefs help us to understand about how children learn and how people and environments influence learning. Early childhood practitioners combine their understanding of how children develop and how they learn to create optimal learning environments that foster curiosity and exploration.

Developmentally appropriate programs offer children experiences outdoors.

Table 1.1 Historical Contributors and Their Influence on Early Learning and Child Care

Contributor	Key Ideas	Impact on Practice
John A. Comenius (1592–1670)	• Children should have access to education and in own language. • Families, especially mothers, impact learning.	• Active learning is essential for learning. • Make reading a core of school curriculum.
John Locke (1632–1704)	• Children are born as blank tablets. • Children's experiences determine who they are.	• Children require many learning experiences early in life. • Children learn acceptable societal behaviours through role modelling.
Jean-Jacques Rousseau (1712–1778)	• There are natural consequences to child rearing. • Children have an innate timetable and will develop accordingly.	• Educational environments need to be homelike, such as family groupings. • Children flourish best in authentic environments.
Johann H. Pestalozzi (1746–1827)	• Effective education is based on sensory experiences. • Mother is the child's first and best teacher.	• Family-centred groupings enhance development. • Incorporate sensory experiences into programming.
Friedrich Froebel (1782–1852)	• Child development is an "unfolding" process. • Initiated the first kindergarten—i.e., "Garden of Children."	• Provide materials that support children in discovering about specific concepts both indoors and outdoors. • Practitioner's role is to provide "seeds of ideas" to children.
John Dewey (1859–1952)	• Children's interests are more important than subject content. • Children learn best when involved in problem-solving activities with peers and practitioners.	• Integrated experiences provide children with a wider scope of learning. • A child-centred philosophy and curriculum guides the role of practitioners.
Maria Montessori (1870–1952)	• Child development occurs in stages. • Children are interested, receptive, and successful to certain learning during these stages, or "sensitive periods."	• Provide progressively more difficult, self-correcting materials, real-life activities. • Children benefit from being in mixed-age groupings.
Abraham Maslow (1890–1970)	• Children have basic needs—food, safety/security; belonging/love; achievement/prestige; and aesthetic needs. • Having needs satisfied is essential for individuals to achieve their fullest potential.	• Children require their basic needs to be met before they are able to participate in cognitive learning. • Practitioners support children in developing a sense of "belonging" and self-esteem.

continue **Table 1.1**

Contributor	Key Ideas	Impact on Practice
Lev Vygotsky (1896–1934)	• Children's mental, language, and social development is enhanced by social interactions. • Children's learning is magnified when they interact with positive role models in their environment.	• Relationships between the early childhood practitioner and the child impact children's engaging in higher-level learning. • Co-operative learning enhances development.
Jean Piaget (1896–1980)	• Children learn most effectively when they have active, hands-on involvement in learning. • Hands-on experiences are the foundation for being able to think and learn.	• Children construct knowledge by interacting with materials and others. • Provide programs that offer a variety of manipulative materials that support problem-solving skills.
Erik Erikson (1902–1994)	• Cognitive and social development cannot be separated. • Children's personalities develop within the context of family, society, and culture.	• Practitioners provide children with comfortable environments that trigger children to explore, play, and discover. • Environments are rich in language and social relationships.
Howard Gardner (1943–)	• Children have multiple intelligences. • Children learn differently.	• Practitioners provide experiences that support all nine intelligences. • Practitioners provide experiences appealing to all learning styles.

The Evolution of Early Learning and Child Care in Canada

The beginning of early childhood services in Canada dates back to 1850, when the first crèche opened in Montreal (Schulz, 1978) to serve children of poor working mothers. Seven years later, a group of wealthy women in Toronto opened a crèche as a way to care for the increased number of children being left home alone while their mothers worked or for those children whose mothers were unable to care for them. In 1857, the Grey Nuns in Montreal operated the first educational program (Gestwicki & Bertrand, 1999) known as "*salle d'asile Saint Joseph*." It provided care for children aged 3 to 7, most of whom were from poverty-stricken homes.

The crèches were typically funded by private charities. Women volunteers from churches, missions, or settlement houses for new immigrants generally raised the funds required to offer the services. Mothers paid a small fee to use the services. The *salle d'asile* was funded by a combination of monies from the Quebec government, charitable donations, and parent fees (Gestwicki & Bertrand, 1999).

In 1873, the Toronto public school system established the first kindergarten programs for 5-year-olds. In 1926, the first nursery school in Canada, St. George's School for Child Study (now known as the Institute of Child Study), opened its doors at the

University of Toronto. Other specialized early childhood service programs have developed throughout the decades and continue to evolve today as family and community needs change. These programs will be discussed in more detail in Chapter 2.

The Second World War had the greatest impact on the need for early childhood services in Canada. Women of all ages, single and married, contributed directly to the war effort, leaving few women at home to care for the children. As a result, some parents were forced to place children in orphanages, while others left younger children in the care of siblings or extended-family members, such as grandmothers. In an effort to build the workforce that was needed during the war, the federal government passed an order-in-council in 1942 authorizing the minister of labour to establish a cost-sharing program with those provinces interested in establishing daycare centres. This agreement, known as the Dominion-Provincial Wartime Day Nurseries Agreement, was signed only with the provinces of Ontario and Quebec. Soon after the war, the federal government decided that there was no need to continue to financially support daycare and the cost-sharing program was suspended in 1946.

Following the Second World War, most women with children returned to their previous roles as full-time mothers. Federal financial support for daycare remained suspended until 1966, when the federal government introduced the Canada Assistance Plan (CAP). Known as the national welfare plan, the CAP was intended to restructure society to support families in poverty. The CAP program was administered by the federal government, which entered into 50–50 cost-sharing agreements with provincial governments for welfare services that included child care. The cost-sharing conditions "stipulated that federal funds were available to pay only for services of the needy, or potentially needy, families, and that to be eligible for funding as a welfare service, child care had to be regulated and public or not-for-profit" (Friendly & Beach, 2005, p. xvi). Because Canada's social service programs are provincial- and territorial-government responsibilities, it took nearly a decade for all of the provinces to sign on to the CAP agreement and to become eligible for cost sharing of child care. As identified by Friendly and Beach (2005), it was the CAP program that influenced the development of regulated child care in Canada. However, because the funding formula for child care was under the umbrella of the welfare system rather than education or health, policy-makers, politicians, and the business sector have long been negligent in acknowledging the importance of child care to the fabric of Canadian society.

In 1970, the Royal Commission on the Status of Women made history by calling for a national daycare act—this was the first time there was national recognition of the need for child care to evolve if women in Canada were to gain equality in society. During the late 1970s and 1980s, large numbers of women with young children entered the workforce, many of whom were middle class. These middle class families demanded access to child care that previously only serviced children from economically deprived families. This demand led to the expansion of child care services across Canada, and at the same time provinces developed more operational regulations and funding-allocation policies. By the end of the 1980s, provinces began to recognize the need for child care and for funds separate from subsidies to be injected into the system.

At the same time that provincial social service departments struggled with devising a child care system, most provincial and territorial education departments were establishing kindergarten programs for 5-year-olds, most of which were part-time, which put further pressure on child care programs as parents needed access to child care for part days.

Part of Jean Chretien's 1993 Red Book election campaign was a renewed pressure to recognize the importance of the early years and to establish a national child care strategy. This renewed interest was short-lived, however, due in part to the increasing tensions between the federal and many provincial governments that appeared to escalate by mid-decade.

In 1996, the federal government eliminated the Canada Assistance Plan and devised a new strategy for transferring funds to the provinces. Under the umbrella of the Canada Health and Social Transfer (CHST) program, block funding for health, education, and welfare occurred. This block-funding model was not without controversy as there was concern that accountability was limited and that provinces might use the money in ways that would compromise social policies.

Recent Developments Influencing the Early Learning and Child Care Agenda

The Canadian government plays a significant role in early childhood services—its role is unique from that of the other levels of government. The policies and funding made at a national level shape the health and social fabric of Canadian society. The federal government does, however, work closely with provincial and territorial governments to develop strategies and policies.

There are a number of federal/provincial/territorial agreements that have a direct bearing on the structure of early childhood services in Canada: the *Social Union Framework Agreement* (SUFA); the *Early Childhood Development Agreement* (ECDA); the United Nations Special Assembly on Children Declaration, *A World Fit for Children*; and *A Canada Fit for Children*. In addition to these agreements, individual provinces are negotiating or have signed agreements in principle for early learning and child care. For example, on April 29, 2005, the Government of Canada and the Province of Saskatchewan signed their agreement entitled *Moving Forward on Early Learning and Child Care*. Table 1.2 provides a snapshot of the most recent developments that are influencing the early learning and child care agenda.

The National Children's Agenda (NCA) In January 1997, the two (federal and provincial/territorial) levels of government agreed to work together to develop a strategy that would recognize the importance of children and their well-being. In June 2000, the *National Children's Agenda* (NCA) was released. The NCA identified four core vision statements:

1. That children be loved and thrive.
2. That children be valued and have the opportunity to develop their unique capacities.
3. That they be respected and protected and in turn respect and protect others.
4. That they belong and contribute to caring communities.

Table 1.2 Recent Developments Influencing Early Learning and Child Care

January 1997	Federal and provincial/territorial levels of government agreed to work together.
February 1999	*Social Union Framework Agreement* signed.
June 2000	*National Children's Agenda* released.
September 2000	*Early Childhood Development Agreement* signed.
May 2002	United Nations Declaration, *A World Fit for Children* signed.
April 2004	*A Canada Fit for Children* signed.
February 2005	Federal and provincial/territorial levels of government negotiating and/or signing moving forward on early learning and child care agreements.

The *National Children's Agenda* further identified four goals to support the vision:

1. Physical and emotional health, including strong self-esteem, life skills, and healthy lifestyles.
2. Safety and security, such as meeting basic physical and emotional needs and protecting children from abuse, neglect, and other harmful situations.
3. Success at learning, including physical, emotional, and social development, language skills, literacy, numeracy, and general knowledge.
4. Social engagement and responsibility, such as forming stable attachments and supportive relationships, valuing diversity, and understanding the rights and responsibilities of a citizen.

The Social Union Framework Agreement (SUFA) The *Social Union Framework Agreement* (SUFA) was signed on February 4, 1999, by the federal government, nine provinces, and two territories. (The Province of Quebec did not sign on to SUFA.) Its main purpose is to improve the social policies and programs developed by various levels of government in Canada.

Under this agreement, each level of government made two commitments: the first is to work together to build a framework that will adjust and modernize social programs, and the second is to work together to develop social programs.

The SUFA may not visibly impact early childhood services because the provincial and territorial governments continue to have control over how to spend funds from the federal government for social programs. However, SUFA guarantees access to comparable services for all Canadians and advocates for citizen participation in social-policy development. For example, all Canadians should have access to and be able to take advantage of social programs on the same terms as their neighbours, regardless of how long they have lived in a particular province or territory.

Early Childhood Development Agreement (ECDA) The *Early Childhood Development Agreement* (ECDA), signed on September 11, 2000, was a $2.2 billion social program designed to support the early development of children in Canada. This agreement builds on the SUFA agreement as a way of improving social programs for Canadians. The objectives of the ECDA are to promote early childhood development and support families and communities so that children will reach their fullest potential—physically, emotionally, socially, and intellectually.

The ECDA requires the provinces and territories to spend the ECDA funds/transfer payments on any or all of the following areas: promoting healthy pregnancy, birth, and infancy; improving parenting and family supports; strengthening early childhood development, learning, and caring; or strengthening community supports.

United Nations Declaration—A World Fit for Children The *A World Fit for Children* declaration was signed on May 10, 2002. All countries belonging to the United Nations (except for the United States of America and Somalia) signed on to the 10-year plan of action for children, which contains four priorities:

1. To promote healthy lives.
2. To provide quality education.
3. To protect against abuse, exploitation, and violence.
4. To combat AIDS.

The plan outlines how to create a world fit for children through specific goals, strategies, and actions. It also identifies how to mobilize resources and examine results.

Paragraph 59 of *A World Fit for Children* calls upon governments of the world to develop national plans of action by 2003 that will facilitate the implementation of the commitments identified in *A World Fit for Children.*

A Canada Fit for Children Canada's national plan of action, *A Canada Fit for Children*, was developed with input from every sector of society and all levels of government, including our children. *A Canada Fit for Children* contains the following:

> [a] declaration of Canada's commitment to children, a Canadian vision for children that highlights Canadian governments' strong agenda for children, and a plan of action that reflects a consensus on goals, strategies and opportunities for action on key priorities within four central themes: supporting families and strengthening communities; promoting healthy lives; protecting from harm; and promoting education and learning.
> (Government of Canada, 2004, p. 4).

A Canada Fit for Children calls for strategies that are child-centred, multi-sector, forward-looking, and collaborative. It is intended to include everyone in Canada who cares about or is responsible for children.

A Canada Fit for Children recognizes that every child living in Canada deserves a healthy start in life. Early childhood to age 6 is a critical period for growth and development. Building on the research that identifies that quality early learning and child care have a positive impact on child development, researchers suggest that governments support communities in the development and implementation of a comprehensive system of early learning and care. Early learning and care programs should be based on "principles of inclusion, affordability, accessibility, quality and parental choice" (Government of Canada, 2004, p. 17).

A Canada Fit for Children represents a roadmap to guide Canada's efforts in developing support systems, services, and strategies for children.

These agreements and the UN Declaration provide the framework for the commitments that federal and provincial/territorial governments make to their citizens. The challenge occurs when federal or provincial/territorial governments change. Often program priorities and initiatives may be revised or cancelled or new ones implemented.

Early Learning and Child Care Agreements

In February 2005, provincial and territorial ministers responsible for social services recognized the need to proceed with developing a national early learning and child care program. Since that time, provinces and territories (excluding Quebec) have been negotiating agreements-in-principle with the federal government.

Provincial and Territorial Government Roles Most early learning and child care programs are regulated by the provincial and territorial governments through a ministry of social, community, or family services. These include child care, preschool programs (half-day programs), and **family child care.**

Each province and territory has established regulations that outline the minimum standards required to operate early learning and child care programs. Generally, the regulations outline specific requirements for staff qualifications, adult–child ratios, maximum number of children allowed in the facility by age group, physical space required for each child both indoors and out, daily routines, health and safety, and programming. These regulations and programs will be further explored in Chapter 2.

All provinces provide parents with low incomes with some form of subsidy for regulated child care. The amount of subsidy varies from region to region, and the guidelines for qualifying for subsidy also differ. Often the difference between the actual cost of regulated child care and the amount of subsidy allotted prohibits parents from accessing regulated child care. Quebec is the only province that has set goals for families to have access to affordable child care and hence has invested substantial public funding to support this social program. Some provinces provide regulated child care programs with grants to support special initiatives, such as wage enhancement for centre staff. All provinces/territories have established kindergarten programs for 5-year-olds as part of the public education system, whereas child care, including school-aged care, is generally operated by community boards of directors, specialized institutions, or by an owner/operator. The

Family child care. Child care offered on a full- or part-time basis for small numbers of children and provided by a non-relative caregiver, in a home setting. This may or may not be government-regulated.

exception is Quebec, where school-aged child care is under the auspices of the *ministère de l'éducation*.

In Ontario, most boards of education also offer a junior kindergarten program for 4-year-olds. Kindergarten programs may be part-day, part-time, or full-time, depending on the province and in some cases the region. Note, however, that there are different policies and regulations that govern child care and kindergarten. As a result, a 5-year-old child who attends kindergarten for half the day and child care the other half-day will be subject to different programming. For example, at school the teacher–child ratio is approximately 1 teacher for every 22 children (depending on the province), whereas the ratio at child care is approximately 1 early childhood practitioner for every 12 to 15 children (again, depending on the province). Children in a regulated child care are required to have a specific number of hours of their program outdoors in all types of weather, while kindergarten children have recess and some outdoor play after lunch, depending on the weather. There are other major differences between the two systems as well, some of which you will be introduced to throughout this book.

At the time of the writing of this book, the federal government and most provinces (excluding Quebec) are either negotiating or have signed early learning and child care agreements.

Why Governments Should Invest in Early Learning and Child Care

Across Canada, there are inequalities in program quality, accessibility, educational requirements, and in compensation in salaries and benefits for early childhood practitioners. In New Brunswick, for example, the community college early childhood training program is a 10-month certificate program. In Prince Edward Island, however, the community college early childhood program is a two-year diploma program. In Ontario in 2003 the average annual salary for a full-time ECE working in a not-for-profit child care centre in Toronto was $29 000 (Cooke, Keating, & McColm, 2004), while nationally in 2000, the overall average income was just over $19 000 (Beach et al., 2004). British Columbia operates culturally specific programs, such as the Chinese Presbyterian Nursery School and Vancouver's Multicultural Resource Centre. And Saskatchewan provides many specialized programs for its Aboriginal families. Meanwhile, Quebec provides a universal, publicly funded child care program.

Provincial governments use the federal government's transfer payments for early childhood services and development in different ways. It appears as though the financial allocations to government programs are based on what will benefit the government in power. If there are limited advocates for children and families at government policy meetings and at cabinet tables, then how are governments hearing about the needs of Canadian families, and in turn how are their needs being addressed? Research confirms that early childhood services support the formation of human and social capital. For example, Coffey (2004) indicates that "the development of human capital at an early age is central to a thriving economy."

Cleveland and Krashinsky (2003) maintain that economists estimate a two-dollar return on every dollar invested in quality early childhood programs and services. As early childhood student practitioners, it will be important for you to advocate for families to have access to quality early learning and child care programs.

Points to Ponder

We can assume that by the year 2015 more than half of Canada's post-secondary students entering early childhood education programs will have experienced some form of early childhood service, either as a child or through community work. Some may have been young children enrolled in regulated child care programs, others in non-regulated (depending on the jurisdiction). Some students may have experienced nursery schools or before- or after-school care. How will this affect the needs of students studying early childhood? Why?

As identified by the Government of Saskatchewan, "of all the investments a society can make for its future, the nurturing of young children is perhaps the most crucial" (2005, p. 2). Given the current research from various sectors that unequivocally shows that the quality of a child's development during the first six years affects health, lifelong learning, earning potential, and the advancement of society, without question children in Canada require commitments from all levels of government to develop and implement services that will support a strong early learning and child care sector.

The Influence of Family and Culture on Early Learning and Child Care Services

The fabric of Canadian culture has changed dramatically over the last 40 years. One of the most significant changes has been the increased ethnic diversity among Canadian citizens and landed immigrants. As new Canadians settle in both our urban and rural communities, there is a shift in our demographics. As communities change, early learning and child care requirements also change. For example, in many eastern Ontario communities, more primary caregivers are returning to the workforce when their children enter school. As a result, there is an increased need for school-aged child care programs. In another example, many families with young children are establishing homes in Quispamsis, New Brunswick. The demand for families to have access to licensed early learning and child care programs is probably the highest it has been in that area, whereas other communities may be noticing a decline.

Canada's Families Today

According to the 2001 census, Canada's population is more than 30 million. As of 2003, there were 4 804 405 children between 0 to 12 years of age residing in Canada (Friendly & Beach, 2005). The Inuit and First Nations groups make up just

Single-female–parent families are most prevalent in Canada.

Two-parent families are headed by a mother and father or couples parenting other people's children, such as nieces and nephews.

over 3 percent of Canada's population (Statistics Canada, 2002a). In Canada, a bilingual nation, 59.1 percent of the population reported English as their mother tongue and 22.9 percent indicated French was their first language (Statistics Canada, 2002b). Twelve percent of Canadians report a mother tongue other than French or English.

Canada's Immigrant Population Canada's society has changed dramatically since the 19th century. Initially, our immigrant population comprised individuals from European countries, such as France and Great Britain. Statistics Canada

Other types of families include new Canadians whose first language is neither English nor French.

Blended families occur when two adults bring children from previous relationships together to live as a newly formed family.

(2003a) reports that in the 1990s, 58 percent of Canada's immigrants were from Asian and Middle Eastern countries, while only 20 percent were from Europe. This societal change has led languages such as Chinese, Italian, German, Punjabi, and Spanish to dominate many parts of Canada's larger urban areas. In cities such as Toronto, Vancouver, and Montreal, more than 50 percent of kindergarten children were born outside of Canada or are from recently immigrated families (Larose et al., 2001). As a result, early childhood practitioners must understand various cultures and respect diversity, because children's values, communication processes, and needs are highly influenced by family culture, beliefs, and family support systems.

Canada's Aboriginal Families Canada has approximately 33 000 children between the ages of 0 and 4, and 37 000 between the ages of 5 and 9, living on reserves (Statistics Canada, 2003a). The child population continues to increase in the Aboriginal community, whereas in other parts of Canada there has been a steady decline since the 1990s. Many Aboriginal children live in poverty in substandard housing, and a high percentage of these children have poor physical and mental health (*A Canada Fit for Children*, 2004). The remote communities have difficulties accessing health, social, and educational services, and parents have higher rates of unemployment than other groups living in Canada. Aboriginal children are overrepresented in the child welfare and youth justice systems.

Changes to Family Structure Societal changes, cultural influences, and exposure to global perspectives on family values and issues are influencing the values and structures of Canadian families. Following, we give an overview of today's family structure and family units. As well, we identify the common societal factors influencing families, which in turn impact early childhood services. As we note in Table 1.3, the number of mothers in the workforce has influenced changes to the family unit and to society.

Table 1.3 *Mothers in the Workforce*

- In 2003, there were 4 804 405 children in Canada between the ages of 0 and 12 years. Of these, 3 051 900 had mothers in the paid workforce (Friendly & Beach, 2005).

- There were 1 005 275 children between the ages of 0 and 2 years. Of these, 588 100 had mothers in the paid workforce (Friendly & Beach, 2005).

- There were 1 040 730 children between the ages of 3 and 5 years. Of these, 635 000 had mothers in the workforce (Friendly & Beach, 2005).

- There were 2 758 400 children between the ages of 6 and 12 years. Of these, 1 828 800 had mothers in the workforce (Friendly & Beach, 2005).

- In 2002, 47% of lone mothers with a child under 3 were employed, compared with 62.3% of mothers in two-parent families (Statistics Canada, 2002c).

Family Unit. Families today may be described in various ways:

- Lone-parent families, headed by mothers or fathers.
- Teenage parents living on their own with their children or teenage parents and children living with the teenagers' parents.
- Blended families, where children born into previous family units are united in a new family unit, usually with either the biological mother or father and a new partner.
- Single-parent or two-parent families headed by gay or lesbian parents.
- Two-parent families headed by a mother and a father.
- Two-parent families with no children of their own but providing support to other people's children, such as nieces and nephews.
- Parents caring for their children and their parents.
- Grandparents caring for their grandchildren.
- New immigrant families whose first language is neither English nor French.

Societal Changes. As society changes, the family unit and the community are affected. Following are some of the more common societal impacts on early childhood services:

- More parents work full-time outside of the home.
- More parents work a variety of hours, including part-time and shift work.
- More parents work longer hours.
- More women and children live in shelters on a temporary basis.
- More young children are cared for by non-family members.
- More children with special needs are remaining with their family unit.
- Less time is available for families to support each other.
- Less low-income housing is available, increasing the number of families living on the streets or in shelters.
- More parents are caring for their children *and* their parents.
- More immigrant families without family or community support are trying to establish new lives in Canada.

As family and societal needs change, the types of early childhood services required also must change. Families require different early childhood services at different phases of early childhood. For example, an increased service industry coupled with societal demands for many round-the-clock services has led to an increase in non-traditional work hours. In 1999, 41 percent of women working outside the home were employed in jobs with non-traditional hours (*Background Report of Canada*, 2003). Predominately, new immigrant women work these non-traditional hours. Many communities require early childhood services beyond the traditional Monday-to-Friday daytime delivery mode. Each family has different needs, values, and resources, so options in early childhood services become important to families.

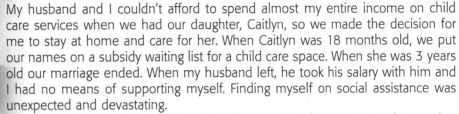

PARENTING PORTRAIT

My husband and I couldn't afford to spend almost my entire income on child care services when we had our daughter, Caitlyn, so we made the decision for me to stay at home and care for her. When Caitlyn was 18 months old, we put our names on a subsidy waiting list for a child care space. When she was 3 years old our marriage ended. When my husband left, he took his salary with him and I had no means of supporting myself. Finding myself on social assistance was unexpected and devastating.

I wanted to get back to work to be able to support the two of us right away but couldn't afford to put my daughter in full-time care at either a private home daycare or at a child care centre. My name was on a subsidy waiting list at a centre for three years. I wanted a "hand-up" not a "hand-out." Thanks to a quality, affordable child care space that finally opened up, I was able to get retrained, get back to work, and get my life back. Today, Caitlyn and I have a bright future ahead of us. And, as an aside, I did a quick calculation recently. I have paid more taxes back into the system in the last three years than I took from it being on social assistance for five.

Would a national early learning and child care program have helped Caitlyn and her mother start a new life? Why or why not? What alternatives do parents have if they don't have access to quality, accessible, affordable child care?

Context, Culture, and Ethnicity

In order to effectively examine the relationship of culture to early childhood services, we must consider three important concepts: context, culture, and ethnicity. A **context** refers to the environment in which development occurs. The environment is influenced by historical, economic, social, and cultural factors (Santrock, 2002). These environments include home, early childhood setting, schools, peer groups, and neighbourhood. Every child's development is influenced by these factors.

Culture refers to the underlying beliefs, patterns of behaviour, and assumptions of a group that are passed on from one generation to the next. Culture is developed from the society's key values. What people do and say in a particular culture is usually consistent with what they believe and value (Cole, 1999; Shiraev & Levi, 2001; Valsiner, 2000). Knowing people's cultural beliefs and values enables early childhood practitioners to know, understand, and to some degree predict behaviour.

Ethnicity refers to cultural heritage, nationality characteristics, race, religion, and language. Canada has numerous ethnic groups represented in our communities, including Asian Canadians, Italian Canadians, Polish Canadians, and so on. And within each ethnic group is diversity. Often, however, we fall into the trap of

Context. Refers to the environment in which development occurs.

Culture. The underlying beliefs, patterns of behaviour, and assumptions of a group that are passed on from one generation to the next.

Ethnicity. Refers to cultural heritage, nationality characteristics, race, religion, and language.

stereotyping ethnic groups or regions of our country by assuming that everyone within a particular grouping or community is alike. Eccles (2001) and McLoyd (2000) encourage us to think of ethnic groups and communities as portraying diversity rather than conformity.

The culture and ethnicity of any society influences parenting practices and places a particular value on the early childhood period of a lifespan. For example, during a recent visit to Norway we participated in preschool programs located totally outdoors, year-round. Children came dressed to play and learn in the forest for their five-hour-per-day program. During the February visit, the temperatures were similar to parts of Canada, with the high being about minus 24 degrees Celsius. Campfires were lit, children cooked their lunch, and they played in the natural landscape. The children moved freely from one experience to another. They balanced on rope structures made by students in the early childhood program. They climbed on icy rocks, they sledded down hills, they rolled in the snow, and they climbed trees. Norwegian culture values outdoor life and freedom to explore. How many Canadian families would feel comfortable registering their children in an outdoor preschool program during the winter months? How would the government regulations for preschool programs deal with open campfires or children climbing trees? Currently, our society emphasizes safety to the point that children are at risk of losing the freedom to take safe risks (Crossley & Dietze, 2003).

Parental practices reflect cultural and ethnic backgrounds, which in turn influence early childhood experiences and the types of early childhood services required. Not all communities require the same types of services. For example, in farming communities extended child care is necessary during the planting and harvesting periods. In communities close to manufacturing plants, where shift work is required, 24-hour child care is necessary to accommodate families. Families require access to flexible, supportive services.

Changes to the family structure, the increase of new Canadians, demographics, and family mobility are all shifting Canadian culture. These changes will continue to impact the types of early childhood services that communities need.

In order to offer all children living in Canada access to early childhood services, programs "need to be universally available, of high quality, and affordable. Parents, especially in the early years, need supports in accommodating work and parenting. Embedding a unified early learning and care system along with integrated referral and services in the community as an institution is key" (Keating, 2004). As you prepare to enter the field of early childhood, you must continue to examine government roles and commitments to early childhood services.

Contemporary Canadians Influencing Early Learning and Child Care

Several Canadians have been instrumental in advocating that provincial and territorial governments and the federal government recognize the importance of the early years and develop strategies to ensure families have access to high quality programs for their children. Following, we introduce 10 Canadians who have made major contributions to developing new knowledge and advancing issues related to early learning and child care, either directly or indirectly, at a national level. This overview is not intended to be exhaustive, but rather to introduce you to some of the people who have contributed or are contributing to the advancement of programs and services for children in Canada. These individuals have been chosen because of their research, their discoveries of new knowledge, and their commitment to diligently advocate to all levels of government to move ahead in developing policies and programs that contribute to the development of healthy children and families.

Rosemary Brown (1930–2003)

Rosemary Brown, known for her work as a social activist, educator, politician, and author, contributed greatly to advancing women's rights and gender equality. She was concerned about the shortage of money for women's issues because she believed that if society addressed poverty, economic independence, and violence prevention, then women and girls would be better able to achieve their full potential and build a healthier society and economy.

In 1972, Ms. Brown became the first Black woman in Canadian history to hold a seat in a Canadian legislature. She also served as the chief commissioner of the Ontario Human Rights Commission for three years in the 1990s. An unwavering feminist, Ms. Brown campaigned to remove sexism in school textbooks, increase female representation on community and government boards, and remove discrimination based on sex or marital status.

Dr. Gillian Doherty

Dr. Doherty is one of Canada's leaders in early childhood research. She was the project director and a principal investigator for the national *You Bet I Care!* project, which identified predictors of quality in child care centres and family child care homes and continues to influence the framework for quality child care. Dr. Doherty was also the principal investigator for the Canadian Child Care Federation's *Partners in Quality* and its *Training for the Delivery of Quality Early Childhood Development, Learning and Care Services* projects. She has also published many policy and research articles related to early childhood development, programming, and service delivery.

Martha Friendly

Martha Friendly is well recognized as one of Canada's leading early childhood researchers. She has authored and co-authored numerous articles and reports on issues related to child care and child care policies. Much of her work has contributed to identifying the state of early childhood across Canada and has provided data and recommendations necessary for policy development. Her advocacy work on behalf of children and the early childhood sector has influenced the advancement of services and policies for children.

Mary Gordon

Mary Gordon has been a teacher of children, a teacher of parents, and a teacher of teachers both nationally and internationally. She has developed a number of programs that support children and family development. For example, in 1981 Ms. Gordon developed the first and largest school-based parenting and family-literacy program. In 1996 Ms. Gordon founded *Roots of Empathy*, a not-for-profit, groundbreaking, evidence-based classroom program that focuses on reducing levels of aggression and violence among school-aged children by raising children's social and emotional competence and empathy. This program is offered in classrooms across Canada in English and in French and in Aboriginal communities.

Ms. Gordon has served on provincial, federal, and international government committees affecting policies on education, the young child, and the family. She has also consulted on the U.S. government's Early Childhood Development Research Agenda-Setting Committee on parental engagement through schools, and she was a member of the groundbreaking Ontario *Early Years Study*, chaired by Dr. Fraser Mustard and the Honourable Margaret Norrie McCain.

Dr. Clyde Hertzman

Dr. Hertzman has been instrumental in examining the relationship of prenatal and early childhood experiences to lifelong health, well-being, and competence. He has created a framework that links population health to human development, emphasizing the special role of early childhood development as a determinant of health. Dr. Hertzman's research is contributing to international, national, provincial, and community initiatives for healthy child development and is starting to affect a number of policies for children across Canada.

Dr. Sharon Hope Irwin

Dr. Hope Irwin, the founder and director of SpeciaLink, a non-profit organization, has long been an advocate of supporting parents of children with disabilities to have the same level of access to inclusive early learning and child care programs as children with typical development.

Dr. Hope Irwin has been involved in research, policy development, and leadership in supporting inclusion of children with atypical development in community programs. She advocates that all children and society benefit from being in inclusive environments.

Dr. Donna Lero

Dr. Lero has made many contributions to new knowledge on issues related to work-life and families, as well as to a national evaluation of the impact of changes to Canada's parental-leave legislation. She has researched, authored, and co-authored a number of articles, many with Martha Friendly and Dr. Gillian Doherty.

The Honourable Margaret Norrie McCain

The Honourable Margaret Norrie McCain has been active in organizations that promote women's rights, social equality, education, and the arts across Canada. She is the founding member of the Muriel McQueen Fergusson Foundation in New Brunswick. This foundation's mission is to eliminate family violence through public education and research. In 1994, Mrs. McCain was appointed the first female lieutenant-governor of New Brunswick. She has been involved in many educational and youth-oriented pursuits, such as Ontario's *Promise*, a non-partisan initiative for children and youth.

Mrs. McCain is well recognized for co-chairing, with Dr. Fraser Mustard, the highly regarded Ontario study the *Early Years Study: Reversing the Real Brain Drain* (1999). This study has provided a blueprint for action for the future direction of early learning and child care in that province.

Dr. Fraser Mustard

Dr. Mustard has made significant contributions to the early childhood sector by examining the socio-economic determinants of human development and health. He has placed a great deal of emphasis on the importance of early childhood and the role of communities in supporting children and their development. He co-chaired a report with the Honourable Margaret Norrie McCain for the Ontario government, known nationally as the *Early Years Study*. Dr. Mustard continues to promote the importance of the early years as the foundation to developing a healthy and competent population.

Dr. Dan Offord (1933–2004)

Dr. David "Dan" Offord was founding director of the Offord Centre for Child Studies at McMaster University and was one the world's leading experts in child development and child psychiatry. His work has influenced child psychiatry and mental-health research and policy across many continents. He was particularly interested in children from disadvantaged backgrounds who are at risk for low self-esteem and emotional problems and in how such problems impact their potential and daily living.

Dr. Offord launched the *Ontario Child Health Study* (OCHS) in the 1980s. This landmark study revealed that one in five children has a serious mental health problem. This study continues to be one of the most important population-based studies on children's mental health conducted in the last three decades. It also continues to influence research today into the factors that cause children to be "at risk."

SUMMARY

Building a Learning Community of Early Childhood Practitioners

- Learning communities support student practitioners by helping them discover new information about children and families; developing new perspectives and ideas that influence practitioners' knowledge, skills, and attitudes on topical issues related to children and families; developing relationships with children and families, peers, mentors, early childhood practitioners, and other professionals; recognizing how students can play an active role in their learning and how they can contribute to others' learning; and personally contributing to creating a learning environment that values diversity and multiple perspectives.

Why Study Early Learning and Child Care?

- Early childhood student practitioners benefit from understanding the relationship of family to child development, of child development to play, and of play to early childhood services, and how each of these affects the role of the practitioner and the role of the child. Early childhood practitioners require this information so that they can effectively create environments that respect, nurture, and support children in their growth and development.

Understanding Terminology

- Terminology is constantly changing. Common terms are *early learning and child care, early childhood education and care, early childhood education, practitioner,* and *early childhood student practitioners.*

The Roots of Early Childhood Services

- The first written documentation referencing early childhood education is found in the writings of the ancient Greeks and Romans. Canada's early childhood programming has been influenced by European research and history. In the late 19th and early 20th centuries, there were at least 12 theorists who contributed to early childhood literature. They contributed to our knowledge about how children develop, how children learn, the types of environments that support learning, the impact of practices, how children's needs are satisfied, and the roles of parents and early childhood practitioners.

The Evolution of Early Learning and Child Care in Canada

- Early childhood services began in Canada to service children of poor working mothers. The services were funded through charity or church organizations. The federal government has influenced early learning and child care through initiatives such as the *National Children's Agenda*, the *Social Union Framework Agreement*, the *Early Childhood Development Agreement*, the United Nations Declaration *A World Fit for Children*, and *A Canada Fit for Children*. The provincial and territorial governments set the regulations and minimum standards for programs.

Why Governments Should Invest in Early Learning and Child Care Services

- Programs need to be universally available, of high quality, affordable, and to support parents in accommodating work and parenting.

The Influence of Family and Culture on Early Learning and Child Care Services

- Context, culture, and ethnicity affect the way in which a child's needs are accommodated, the value placed on the worth of the child, the understanding of the developmental phases of early childhood, and the role of parents and practitioners in supporting the child's development.

Features of Modern Canadian Families

- The family unit may consist of lone-parent families, teenage parents, blended families, single- or two-parent families headed by a mother and a father or gay/lesbian parents, grandparents caring for grandchildren, or new immigrant families. Societal changes have seen more parents working outside the home, more children being cared for by non-family members, children with special needs remaining part of their family unit, and more women and children living in temporary housing.

Canadian Contributions to Early Learning and Child Care in Canada

- The selected Canadians advocate for children. Their research and knowledge has advanced our understanding of how children develop and how children learn. Their work has contributed to the development of policies and practices that support creating early learning and child care environments for children and families.

FURTHER OPPORTUNITIES FOR ENRICHMENT

Research

1. Examine the documents *A Canada Fit for Children* at **www.phac-aspc.gc.ca/dca-dea/publications/ncd-jna/canada_fit_for_children.pdf** and *A World Fit for Children* at **www.iin.oas.org/declaracion_sesion_especial_ingles.htm**. Determine how the content of each of these documents impacts the future direction of a national plan of action for children living in Canada. Discuss what Canada's commitment to children is. How will this affect early childhood services? Why is the document *A Canada Fit for Children* important to early childhood practitioners?

2. Choose one of the contemporary Canadians who have influenced early learning and child care, and conduct further research on that person. Read about the work, examine articles or studies that have been published, and think about what your findings mean to you as you begin your studies.

3. Choose one of the historical contributors and conduct further research on that person. Identify five characteristics of the contributor's work with children, the contributor's philosophy, or the values that you believe are important to you as you begin to learn about early learning and child care. Discuss what intrigued you about the chosen contributor.

Group Investigation

1. Examine your provincial- or territorial-government ministry website responsible for children and families. List the key priorities related to children and family services. Then, examine the federal government Web site at **socialunion.gc.ca/ecd/2003/report1_e/ade.html**. Compare and contrast your findings. What are the similarities and the differences between the federal government's perspective and that of your province's government?

Making Connections

1. Conduct an interview with a person who is 20 to 30 years your senior. Ask the interviewee about the type of family structure he or she experienced growing up. Is it similar or different to the family structure that you are a part of? As a child, what types of early childhood services did your interviewee experience? Are they similar to what you experienced or what children today may experience? How? What does the interviewee predict will be the next phase of changes within Canadian society? Why? How might those changes affect early learning and child care?

2. According to *A Canada Fit for Children* (2004), a high percentage of Canada's Aboriginal families live in poverty. What are seven reasons that would contribute to the high percentage of poverty among Aboriginal families? How does living in poverty affect future physical and emotional wellness, opportunities for learning, and employment perspectives? Do new Canadians suffer poverty to the same extent? Are there particular groups of new Canadians that may have more challenges than others in getting a new start in Canada?

3. Review "A Day Begins in an Early Learning and Child Care Setting" at the beginning of the chapter. Outline five of the behaviours that Jennifer exhibited in her role as an early childhood practitioner.

4. Based on your learning in this chapter, do you think the federal government should proceed to develop a national early learning and child care strategy? Why or why not?

ADDITIONAL READING

Beach, J., Bertrand, J., Forer, B., Michal, D., & Tougas, J. (2004). *Working for Change: Canada's Child Care Workforce*. Ottawa, ON: Child Care Human Resources Sector Council.

Friendly, M. & Beach, J. (2005). *Early Childhood Education and Care in Canada 2004*. Toronto, ON: University of Toronto, Childcare Resource and Research Unit.

Government of Canada (2004). *A Canada Fit for Children*. Ottawa, ON: Government of Canada. Available at www.phac-aspc.gc.ca/dca-dea/publications/ncd-jna/canada_fit_for_children.pdf.

McCain, M. & Mustard, F. (1999). *Early Years Study: Final Report*. Toronto, ON: Publications Ontario.

WEBLINKS

www.phac-aspc.gc.ca/dca-dea/publications/ncd-jna/canada_fit_for_children.pdf: *A Canada Fit for Children*

www.childcarecanada.org: *Childcare Resource and Research Unit*

www.cccf-fcsge.ca: *Canadian Child Care Federation*

"Everyone acknowledges that investments in the early years provide enormous payoffs but community agencies and local governments have had little financial leeway to experiment in recent years....Only senior governments have the resources and the responsibility to make universal early learning and care a reality."

Dr. Charles Pascal, 2005

2

Children, Environments, Programs, and Practitioners

A Day Begins in an Early Learning and Child Care Centre

Marioe Using Clay

The bright May sunlight shines through the windows of the preschool. Marioe, a 3-year-old, stands by the table looking out the window while gently kneading the ball of clay in her hands. Several days ago, the children in this early learning and child care program visited a special display of face masks exhibited at a local art gallery. Since that visit, Marioe has been asking the early childhood practitioners and other children questions about masks. Yesterday she asked Jennifer, "What are the laughing masks used for?" She responded, "The laughing masks or happy masks were used in celebrations; we use them today for costume parties."

Today, Jennifer observes Marioe at the art table, but does not intrude on her thoughts. While helping another child carry blocks from one place in the centre to another, Jennifer notices that Marioe has flattened the clay. Intrigued, Jennifer remains nearby so that she can observe Marioe's efforts with the clay. Having flattened the clay, Marioe places it on her face, tips her face to the ceiling, and molds it to her features. She then gently removes the clay and places it on the table, where she stares at the image of her face. Sections of the clay are torn where she has pushed it against her face.

Marioe reshapes the clay, making it thicker in places. She flattens it and again molds it to her face. She removes the clay from her face and sets it on the table. Seemingly satisfied with the image, she takes the wooden cutting tool and shapes the mask into an oval. As she places the clay on the drying rack, Jennifer approaches her. Marioe announces to Jennifer, "I have made a laughing mask." Jennifer responds with a smile, "You certainly have!"

Marioe participates in a sequential process when creating her mask.

Looking Ahead

In this chapter, we present further foundation information about children, programs, and practitioners. We outline the physiological and psychological needs of children, and we discuss the learning process. As well, we introduce how play influences learning, and we discuss the effect environment has on learning. In the final phase of the chapter we introduce you to three categories of early childhood programs: foundation programs, specific program models, and support programs. We identify seven characteristics of early childhood practitioners as well as the characteristics of learning through a learning community model.

As you gain new knowledge from this book and from your studies, you will acquire the skills and tools needed to develop environments that provide children with the life space needed to offer the freedom to explore, wonder, and learn. Early childhood practitioners are encouraged to constantly examine, refine, evaluate, and adjust their ideas, beliefs, and practices to reflect current thinking, to ensure that children and their families have access to early childhood services that support their needs. We invite you to refer back to Chapter 1 to incorporate your learning from that chapter with the new information presented here.

Children's curiosity is affected by their environment, program, and practitioner.

Understanding the Framework of Early Learning and Child Care

There are many aspects of preparing to work with children. As we saw at the beginning of this chapter, Jennifer took on many roles while working with children. For example, Jennifer observed Marioe's intensity when working with clay and knew that she needed the time, space, and solitude to explore the clay. She observed Marioe proceed through the process of making a mask. Then, she chose an appropriate time to approach Marioe, providing Marioe with the opportunity to speak about her creation. Jennifer gained these vital skills by combining knowledge and experience about how children learn with observation skills, communication skills, and planning skills. As early childhood student practitioners, you, too, will learn about children and how they develop. You will learn how to support and work with parents, families, and community partners, and you will learn about cultures and ethnic backgrounds. And you will learn about working with children, planning for children, and assessing the development of children.

You have probably used the terms *who, what, where, how,* and *when* before as tools to organize important information. As Figure 2.1 shows, these terms are also useful in helping you understand the framework of early childhood. Think of the children as the *who* of early childhood. Think of child development as the *what* of early childhood. Learning about children's environments is the *where* of early childhood, while learning about the scope of children's needs and devising early childhood practices and services is the *how* of early childhood. Learning how to observe children as a way to determine needs and using that information to know when to plan curriculum, guide experiences, and offer experiences or materials that will expand optimal learning options is the *when* of early childhood.

Early childhood practitioner with child. Early childhood practitioners observe children and determine when to expand children's learning opportunities.

The child is the core focus of any early learning and child care program. Early learning and child care practitioners offer children experiences that are based on children's needs, abilities, and interests. In order to do this effectively, early childhood practitioners require a thorough understanding of the children, their development, and influences that affect their development. Each of these impact how the environment is designed, what types of experiences are offered, and where the experiences will be available. Children's needs are positively or negatively affected by their environments (Read, Sugawara, & Brandt, 1999). In this chapter, we will introduce you to the concept of a child's needs (the *who*) and how the environment (the *where*) supports those needs. We integrate elements of child development (the *what*) throughout this chapter.

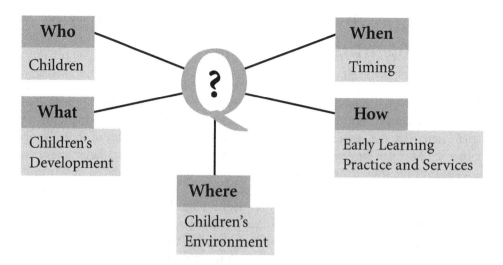

Figure 2.1 *Understanding the Framework of Early Learning and Child Care*

The Child—The *Who*

The Infant   *The Toddler*   *The Preschooler*   *School-age*

Early learning and child care encompasses children from infancy to school age.

Need. A lack of what is necessary for survival, health, or a feeling of well-being.

Physiological needs. Needs such as air, water, food, and rest needed for survival.

Each child begins development with a predetermined genetic program. This genetic information does not, however, form a blueprint of body and mind. Rather, it initiates a "developmental pattern." Locke identifies that the environment and experiences are key to human behaviour and development (Vasta, Miller, & Ellis, 2004). Children are individual, holistic beings who develop by interacting continuously with the environment as a way to meet their needs. Feelings of emotional arousal triggered by environmental conditions (e.g., tension, joy, a fast heartbeat) affect development (Bandura & Schunk, 1981). All children have similar needs, both physiological and psychological, although the degree of children's needs may vary, as does their ability to meet those needs.

There are many ways to describe the word *need*. Think about a need as the lack of what is necessary for survival, health, or a feeling of well-being. Needs are generally classified into two large groups: **physiological needs**—such as the need for air, water, food, and rest; and **psychological needs**—such as the need for freedom, power, love, and fun (Glasser, 1998). The gratification of both physiological and psychological needs is necessary to maintain a healthy equilibrium both physically and emotionally.

Physiological needs refer to the needs of the human body as an organism. These needs are hardwired into an individual's body to ensure survival and therefore do not require a lot of focused learning. We know instinctively how to breathe and how to rest, and we know what tastes good. Psychological needs, on the other hand, are human behaviours in which more choices are involved. The methods of satisfying our psychological needs are learned. Young children display four psychological needs:

1. The need to make choices (freedom).
2. The need to be valued and listened to (power).
3. The need to feel comfort and affection (love).
4. The need to explore, learn, and progress in their development (fun).

These needs are critical to children's survival, and all children are born with a drive to satisfy these needs. Understanding these needs forms the foundation for early childhood methodologies and practices. They guide the interactive roles of early childhood practitioners and provide the anchors for the development of quality services for young children.

The Child's Development—The *What*

Learning begins at conception, and then at birth the infant is born with a will to live and to learn. In fact, children are born with established learning processes. To help you understand the relationship between learning and adaptation and survival, we provide three examples. First, we highlight learning that occurs in utero. The developing fetus is learning while in the mother's uterus. This watery world protects the fetus but is not entirely silent, and as a result the unborn child's sense of hearing develops while in utero. The mother's physiological sounds, her heartbeat, her voice, her breathing, her digestion, as well as loud noises from the outside world, are all audible to the developing fetus. As a result, the newborn responds to noise with a startle reflex. As well, as the fetus grows she is capable of making herself more comfortable: if, for example, the fetus is resting against the mother's spine, as when the mother lies down, the fetus will turn to a more comfortable position.

We use the first movements of a newborn, sucking a thumb and thrashing arms and legs, as the second example of the relationship between learning and adaptation and survival. The infant has in fact rehearsed these movements in the uterus. Ultrasound images show the fetus sucking a thumb and closing and opening both eyes. The fetus moves sporadically, especially as she approaches birth size and weight. By the time she is born, she has learned to suck and swallow; she knows where her mouth is; she opens and closes her eyes; and she can hear. She can also make herself comfortable, if conditions permit, and she exhibits body reactions to

Psychological needs.
Human needs necessary to maintain a healthy equilibrium, both physically and emotionally.

the mother's movements. The emerging infant is a living being who has begun to learn and is now ready to commence the accelerated pace of learning that characterizes the first few years of life.

The prenatal ability to learn ensures the infant's adaptation to the environment outside of the uterus and, therefore, the infant's survival. This same motivation to learn helps individuals to adapt to personal and environmental changes throughout a lifetime.

During the first months of life, infants exhibit curiosity about most objects around them. Stimulating environments foster learning. When a 1-year-old decides to grasp, suck, and play with an unpredictable assortment of household articles and toys, this decision is one of the first links in the chain of learning.

The third example of the relationship between learning and adaptation and survival identifies the conditions children require for learning to continue. Figure 2.2 identifies three key roles of early childhood practitioners in supporting children's learning. Most children show their willingness to learn by their receptiveness to new experiences. Neuroscientists indicate that when children have new experiences and opportunities to repeat those experiences, wiring of the brain occurs, which results in learning (Nash, 1997). Children develop most easily in a stimulating and friendly environment known as a **responsive learning environment**. Children's learning is best supported in environments with adults who recognize the children' interests, know which experiences will meet the need to satisfy this curiosity, and provide situations in which children can play and learn, by themselves or with others.

Responsive learning environment. Includes people, ideas, objects, and places that support children by creating a stress-free and psychologically and physiologically comfortable place to play.

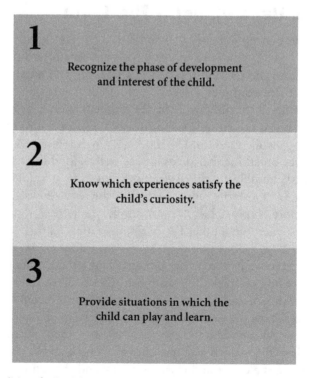

Figure 2.2 *Conditions for Learning*

Children are most intrigued and stimulated to learn about things that interest them. They want immediate satisfaction from their experiences. Curious by nature and having boundless energy, children want to be in environments that allow them the time, space, and freedom to explore and achieve—but not without guidelines and safety considerations. Rather, *freedom* implies opportunities to make decisions, perhaps try new things, and not be bound by unnecessary rules and regulations, such as having to complete a project because it is lunchtime or the end of the day. When children are placed in appropriate learning environments, they gain a sense of personal achievement and they develop personal autonomy, both necessary skills for later critical thinking and problem solving, which, in turn, support the development of children's psychological needs and abilities.

Many adults mistakenly equate learning with teaching (Hendrick & Weissman, 2006). That is, they think of learning as something that takes place in a formal setting. There is adequate research to identify that child's play sets the foundation for later academic achievement, social competence, and emotional competence (Catron & Allen, 1999). However, Cooke, Keating, and McColm (2004) indicate that educators, practitioners, and parents are downplaying the importance of play and instead are emphasizing academic skills. Early childhood practitioners "who respond to the pressure by bringing in increased adult-directed prescribed activities in an effort to enhance specific skills exacerbate behaviour problems" (Cooke, Keating, & McColm, 2004, p. 7). The absence of child-initiated play and guided play reduces children's abilities to develop the foundation skills that are later transferred to academic learning. Because parents spend a significant amount of time in their children's **life space,** they influence both what children learn and children's attitudes toward learning. As a result, Western psychologists attach considerable significance to the parent–child relationship (Vasta, Miller, & Ellis, 2004). Similarly, early childhood practitioners influence what children learn through the learning environment created. But the parents and the life space are children's first and primary teachers.

Psychiatrists, psychologists, and other professionals who work closely with children recognize their desire to learn in context with all their other needs. For example, Morrison (2003) indicates that "children need to be loved and feel that they 'belong' within their home and school in order to thrive and develop" (p. 80). Maslow's (1890–1970) theory of motivation, called **self-actualization**, is based on the satisfaction of human needs: basic needs of food, safety, and security are essential before higher-level needs, such as achievement and self-actualization, can be achieved. Children, therefore, thrive in environments where parents and early childhood practitioners recognize both their physiological *and* psychological needs, and children require a diverse range of experiences to enable them to meet those needs effectively.

Child's play is essential for learning. Knowing and understanding the importance of play allows parents and early childhood practitioners to fill a vital and enriching role in children's lives. *Play* can be described as "nature's learning tool." Play is intrinsically satisfying to all humans regardless of their age.

Children learn and adapt to family and community life through play. The more interesting and rewarding the play experience, the more opportunities children

Life space. Havinghurst and Neugarten describe *life space* as the physical space, the objects in the space, and the people in the space. Each affects children's behaviour.

Self-actualization. The process of realizing one's full potential.

have to engage in human interaction, relationship building, and risk taking. Adults who relax and honour children's needs for play effectively demonstrate an understanding of children's development. Children's sense of self, feelings of security, and pleasure in growing competence are all fostered by the relationship that the children establish with the people who play with them and take care of their needs.

Infants need rhythm and social play as much as they require food and sleep. Smiling and gurgling infants, reaching for a father's hand or a toy, send a clear signal of the need to play. Restlessness, crying, or fussing are infants' means of communicating that they are not interested in play at that moment in time. Rather, they more likely need to be loved and comforted.

Everything children do when playing is done with their entire beings. When something works, they smile or laugh, clap their hands, and feel good. When they are frustrated, they scowl, cry, or scream. Learning and emotions, thoughts and feelings are inextricably linked in children's play.

Adults can easily overlook the value of children's responsiveness, curiosity, and imagination. What children learn before school, they learn mostly through playful experimentation, discovery, and repetition—all in the secure setting provided by their parents or in early childhood services. Child's play is serious business and is vital to children's emotional and intellectual development. Because play is of such importance to the work of early childhood practitioners, Chapter 5 provides further discussion on play and learning.

The Child's Environment—The *Where*

Children's environments are the *where* of early childhood, with the home being the first physical and socio-cultural environment to which children are exposed and within which they interact. Children's physical environments are thought to have important effects on their behaviour. Bandura's model of learning and development (1986, 1998, 2000) suggests that children's learning is influenced by the significant people in their worlds and by the environments that are created for them to grow and learn in. Bandura indicates that each of these factors operates interactively, meaning that children's environments can influence their behaviour, or role models can influence their behaviour, and vice versa. In fact, children's environments are often described as their third teacher (Morrison, 2003). Through perception, children process knowledge and learn new skills. Children are active perceivers. They are motivated to discover, explore, and wonder. They examine information, extract information, and differentiate objects within their environment (Read, Sugawara, & Brandt, 1999). Recent studies that examine the relationship between children's development and their environmental space are almost non-existent (Read, Sugawara, & Brandt, 1999), although Nash (1997) indicates that the experiences within children's environments affect the neural connections that are formed early in life. We draw upon Havinghurst and Neugarten's (1967) seminal work to introduce the relationship of a child's life space to development. We also present the ecological model created by Urie Bronfenbrenner (1967) to illustrate how children's families and communities influence development.

As shown in Figure 2.3, Havinghurst and Neugarten (1967) describe the home-environmental determinants of children's behaviour as children's "life space." Life space involves three elements:

1. Physical space.
2. The objects in that space.
3. The people in that space.

To understand children's behaviour and needs, we examine these three elements.

Physical Space Children's physical life space is where they live and know their way around. The range of the physical space increases with the age of the child. For example, a 3-year-old is usually limited to the home and surrounding outdoor space. A 6-year-old's space expands to the street nearest the home and probably to the streets leading to school. A 12-year-old is familiar with the area around the home, and the physical life space may also be expanded to include stores, parks, recreational centres, and gathering places within the neighbourhood. Children's physical life space expands as their interests broaden and as experiences take them, physically or otherwise, away from the home setting or community.

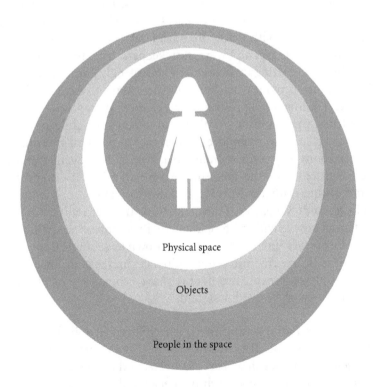

Physical space

Objects

People in the space

Figure 2.3 *Life Space*

The physical space is where children develop their minds as well as their bodies—i.e., learning about and developing physical exercises, such as walking, running, throwing, and jumping. And within this space, children take risks and try new things that they have not seen or tried before. Often, the physical space allows children to develop an appreciation of privacy and freedom from parents and others living in the home. Children learn about physical independence as they take responsibility for their own movements and actions.

Objects within Life Space   The second element of children's life space is the objects contained within that space. As children become older, the objects become more complex and are usually products of social living. Children learn to use the objects within the life space in ways that are defined by role models and society. Children's interactions with people and objects become more complex and varied with age and life experience. As children increase their ability to manipulate various objects, such as food utensils, clothes, and toys, they develop a sense of personal power and self-confidence.

People within Life Space   The third element that influences children's life spaces are the people who interact within the space. These people may be real or imaginary and may or may not live in the home, depending on the exposure children have to others in the home or in the community. The people in children's lives create the psychological and social life spaces in which children live. As children expand their interactions with family members, relatives, neighbours, early childhood practitioners, teachers, employers, storekeepers, etc., they form relationships that support them in meeting their needs in increasingly effective ways.

Positive life space provides children with the means to increase their levels of self-confidence. The degree of restraint or freedom placed upon children's life spaces varies from one family to another and affects how children use their life spaces. The social relationships children experience in the family setting determine the degree of freedom they perceive in the social world. Not all children have exactly the same life space or use the space in the same way. Life space and opportunities to interact within it impact learning and development.

Havinghurst and Neugarten (1967) identify the need to examine physical space, objects, and people within life space. Urie Bronfenbrenner (1967) developed an influential theory of human development known as **ecological theory**. He proposes that there are many environmental influences and systems that contribute to children's overall development. Bronfenbrenner's ecological model, as shown in Figure 2.4, is made up of five major systems.

Ecological theory. Bronfenbrenner's environmental-system theory of development. This theory emphasizes the role of social context through the five environmental systems: microsystem, mesosystem, exosystem, macrosystem, and chronosystem.

Microsystem.   This is the setting in which children live, including the home, school, and neighbourhood. It is in this system that the most direct interactions with social agents occur—such as parents, peers, and early childhood practitioners. These interactions and relationships, because they occur during children's early years, significantly impact children's development.

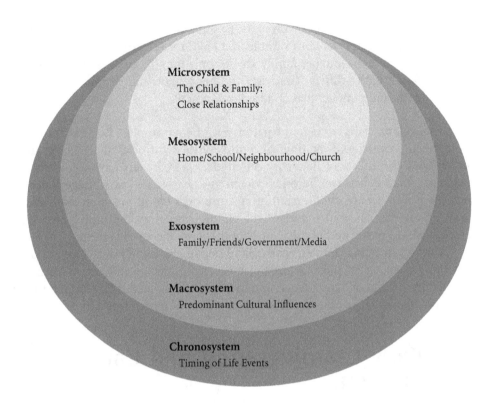

Figure 2.4 *Bronfenbrenner's Ecological Model of Human Development*

Mesosystem. The mesosystem surrounds the microsystem and involves the interactions and relationships or connections among the social agents. For example, the interactions and relationships between the parents and the early childhood practitioner positively or in some cases negatively impact children's development. If the parents and early childhood practitioner discuss children's strengths and needs and develop strategies to support one another in strengthening the areas of need, then the children benefit. Conversely, without a collective strategy children may not have as many opportunities or experiences to support areas requiring further development.

Exosystem. This system refers to experiences or influences from other social settings that impact development. Mass media, government, local services, or the parents' worksites would be considered influential. For example, many provincial governments have set new standards for playground apparatus in early learning and child care centres. As a result, many of the climbing experiences that provided children with challenges and physical-development enhancement have been eliminated from play areas, impacting children's physical development, wellness, and the confidence that develops with safe risk opportunities.

Macrosystem. This system involves the beliefs and ideologies of family, community, and country culture. For example, if a child moves from Japan to rural New Brunswick, where she and her family are not only the sole Japanese family but also the only family with a different ancestry, mother tongue, and customs, such a move would significantly impact that child's development.

Chronosystem. This refers to the patterning of environmental events, transitions over the life course, and the time since the events (Santrock, 2002). For example, in studying the effects of inactivity on children, researchers have found that the negative health effects can become evident at as early as 8 years of age. There are now high numbers of children suffering from high blood pressure, diabetes, and low self-esteem. The more overweight children become, the more their social, emotional, cognitive, and physical development are negatively affected.

Although meeting children's early childhood interests and needs does not ensure a happy and successful life, meeting those needs can prepare children to learn independently, to build self-confidence, and to take the calculated risks required to grow and develop and to become contributing members of our community.

The Early Learning and Child Care Environment

An early learning and child care environment outside of the home generally comprises three components: a planned physical space, the relationships among the people within the space, and the values and goals of the particular early childhood service, community centre, or school system. The environment is created by the interaction among these three components. Therefore, as shown in Figure 2.5, the early childhood environment can be described as consisting of a physical component, a human component, and an experiential component. The physical component includes features such as the space, room arrangement, equipment, and materials; the human component comprises the relationships and interactions among children and adults; and the experiential component includes activities supporting specific values and goals. Each component is considered in the design of any early childhood environment, and the environment is created through the interaction of these three components. The quality of these components makes each environment unique and frames the foundation for the role of the early childhood practitioner.

Early Learning and Child Care Principles

In Chapter 1, we outlined aspects of Canada's national children's agenda. The early learning and child care agenda identifies four core principles that are necessary to help advance a national vision (see Figure 2.6).

Quality High quality early learning and child care services support optimal child development opportunities.

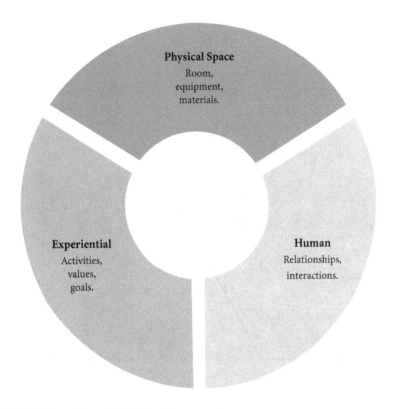

Figure 2.5 *Early Learning and Child Care Components*

Family child care. Child care offered on a full- or part-time basis for small numbers of children and provided by a non-relative caregiver in a home setting. This may or may not be government-regulated.

Centre-based child care. Care provided to children in a group setting, licensed by the provincial/territorial governments. Practitioners are usually not related to the children.

Preschool child care. Specialized group care for children from 30 months to 4–5 years of age.

Head Start programs. Centre-based programs designed and implemented for children who are generally from economically deprived environments and who are deemed to have social, emotional, or cognitive delays. Family support is offered through parenting programs and community resources.

Early intervention programs. Family- or centre-based programs for children who have been identified with atypical developmental patterns.

School-aged child care. Child care offered for children from kindergarten to approximately 10–12 years of age. The care is offered before school, at lunchtime, after school, and on school holidays.

Universal inclusiveness   All children, without discrimination, including children with special needs, Aboriginal children, and children with various cultural and linguistic backgrounds, have equal access to services.

Accessibility   All children and parents will have accessible and affordable early learning services and child care available to those who choose to use it.

Development   Early learning and child care services are child-centred and provide quality experiences that contribute to improved lifetime outcomes. The services encourage meaningful partnerships between parents and early childhood practitioners (Government of Canada & Government of Saskatchewan, 2005).

A number of different early learning and childhood services are available for families, including **family child care**, **centre-based child care**, nursery or **preschool child care, Head Start** or **early intervention programs**, **school-aged child care**, and **family resource centres**.

Although the early learning and child care agreements-in-principle state that all families should have equal access to services, in reality not all families living in Canada have access to the types of services presented. The quality also differs, with

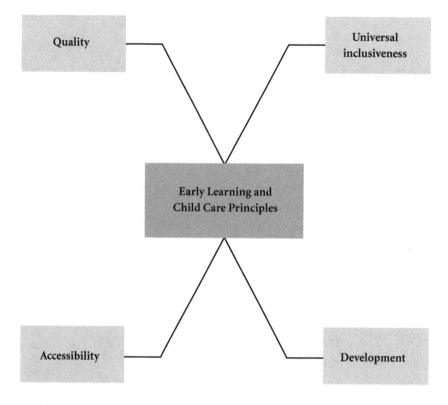

Figure 2.6 Early Learning and Child Care Principles

some offering high quality, while others barely meet a minimal standard. Some communities may have different names for similar services. And funding varies across communities, provinces, and territories. Moreover, each family has unique values, needs, and resources for its children. The Parenting Portraits section found later in this chapter clearly illustrates these points.

To introduce the array and scope of early learning and child care options, we have categorized them into three sections: foundation programs, contemporary program models with historical roots, and specialized support programs. Understanding the characteristics of each of these programs is important because each family will have different early learning and child care needs.

Foundation Programs

These programs are identified as the core early learning and child care programs and are widely known and used. All of the programs may have similar elements, but they also have differences that develop for a variety of reasons: they may be influenced by the philosophy of the providers, the sponsoring agency, parental requirements, financial resources, community, or any combination thereof.

Centre-Based Child Care Child care offered on a full- or part-time basis in a facility regulated by a provincial government department. It may include the following:

Infant–toddler child care. Specialized group care for children from 0 to 18 months and 19 to 30 months.

Preschool child care. Specialized group care for children from 30 months to 4–5 years of age.

School-aged child care. Child care offered for children from kindergarten to approximately 10–12 years of age. The care is offered before school, at lunchtime, after school, and on school holidays. In Quebec, school-age child care is the responsibility of the Ministry of Education.

Corporate child care. On-site child care set up at workplaces for the families of employees, which may also include children from the surrounding community.

Table 2.1 outlines the provincial/territorial- and federal-government program responsibilities and provides an introduction to the adult–child ratio and educational qualifications pertaining to children under the age of 6.

In-Home Child Care Child care offered either in a child's home or in the home of a relative or non-relative. This type of child care may be government-regulated or non-regulated. Table 2.2 highlights the family child care regulations.

Family child care. Child care offered on a full- or part-time basis for small numbers of children provided by a non-relative caregiver, in a home setting. This may or may not be regulated.

Nanny. Child care offered for one or more children in a child's home, by a trained or untrained person. This is non-regulated.

Full- or Half-Day Programs These programs may be full- or half-day programs, designed for children between 2 years of age and kindergarten age. These programs provide learning experiences that enhance children's social, emotional, and cognitive development and may include the following:

Parent co-operative. A program operated by a volunteer parent board of directors. Parent volunteers assist early childhood practitioners during the implementation of the program. Most of the centres are not-for-profit.

Kindergarten. Half- or full-day programs for children 5 years of age, generally offered as part of the school system, although there are also privately run kindergartens and kindergarten programs offered as part of centre-based child care. These programs focus on both social skills and academic skills.

Junior kindergarten. Half- or full-day programs, generally offered as part of the education system for children 4 years of age. Junior kindergarten is not offered in all provinces.

Demonstration programs. Full- or part-day programs, usually affiliated with a post-secondary educational institution. These programs provide college or university students studying about children with opportunities to observe, participate in placement experience, or collect data for specific assignments. These programs are often designated as demonstration programs by colleges and/or child care divisions operating in municipalities.

Contemporary Program Models with Historical Roots

Many families, most of whom live in urban areas, have access to program models that have been developed based on the interpretation of the philosophy of earlier theorists. These programs use a specific strategy to program design and implementation and have a stated philosophy based on the earlier theorist.

   The six most common program models in Canada are briefly described below, although some may only be available in specific regions of Canada. Chapter 4 provides further information on these programs.

Bank Street Programs Based on the work of Erik Erikson, Jean Piaget, and John Dewey, these programs focus on all aspects of child development. The programs encourage both interpersonal interactions and play experiences that support the cognitive, social, and emotional aspects of children's development.

Froebel Programs Based on the work of Friedrich Froebel, the founder of kindergartens, these programs have play as their focus, based on the child's level of development. The relationship of environment to learning and development is paramount.

High/Scope Programs Based on the theory of Jean Piaget and the work of David Weikart, classrooms are organized as interest centres. Children use a plan-do-and-review sequence as a way to focus their learning.

Montessori Programs Based on the philosophy of Italian educator Maria Montessori, these programs use specialized apparatus in a prepared classroom environment. Children participate in work-based learning experiences that are presented in sequential order, moving the child from simple to more complex tasks.

Reggio Emilia Centres This approach, adapted from programs in the city of Reggio Emilia, Italy, focuses on a community development model. It emphasizes the use of in-depth projects as a way for children to learn about their environment, their community, and themselves.

Waldorf Programs Based on the work of Rudolf Steiner, the curriculum draws on the natural nature of children, with emphasis on children's learning through imitation. Academic content is held to a minimum while art and movement are the core elements of the curriculum.

Specialized Support Programs

Family support programs are designed to address the changing needs of families and communities. Although each community may not use the same title for the programs, generally the program goals are similar. The list below offers you a sampling of the types of family support programs that may be found in our Canadian communities. Not all communities have access to these programs. Other communities may offer all of the types of support programs listed, plus others.

Aboriginal Head Start These are centre-based programs designed for First Nations families. They offer families early childhood experiences and health-promotion services.

Children's Health Services These are programs designed by health units to support children's health, wellness, and development.

Drop-in Programs These programs are designed to provide children with care for short periods of time while their parents participate in a particular activity or service. Such programs are often located in shopping malls, resorts, and fitness centres.

Early Intervention Programs These are family- or centre-based programs for children who have been identified with special needs. Information, support, and specialized programming or activities are usually provided to the child, families, and non-family caregivers. Children with atypical developmental patterns are integrated with children with typical developmental patterns.

Family Resource Centres These are community-based centres that offer child and parenting programs. Resources such as play materials, parent-support materials, toy-lending libraries, and workshops are available.

Head Start Programs "Head Start" programs are centre-based and are designed and implemented for children who generally are from economically deprived environments and who are deemed to have social, emotional, or cognitive delays. Family support is offered through parenting programs and community resources.

Play Therapy Programs These are play-based treatment programs designed for young children who have been identified with emotional or psychological problems.

Success by 6 Programs "Success by 6" are community-based programs championed by community business leaders. The programs are designed to help children by the age of 6 to be healthy and prepared for success in school and life.

Supervised Access Programs These refer to settings where children visit with a parent/parents required by law to see their children only in a supervised, neutral environment.

Teen Parent Programs These are centre-based child care programs for children from infancy to school age, usually located in or near high schools. Support services specific to teen parents, including parenting classes, parent–child conferences, and program participation may be offered.

Child Life Programs Child Life programs refer to programs located in hospital settings to encourage the physical and psychological care of children while recuperating from illness or injury.

Childminding (LINC—Language Instruction for Newcomers to Canada) These are informal, unlicensed arrangements for children of newcomers, while their parents attend language instruction.

Community Action Program for Children (CAPA) These programs serve children and their families who live in conditions of risk. Funds are available for community coalitions who provide information, education, and support services to families.

Some provinces have developed specialized programs to meet the needs of their children's families. For example, in Ontario early years centres have been established in every provincial riding. Parents and children have access to early

Table 2.1 *Provincial/Territorial and Government of Canada Program Responsibilities*

Early Learning Child Care	
Provincial and Territorial Responsibility	**Government of Canada Responsibility**
Social Services • Centre-based child care • Family child care • School-aged child care (excluding Quebec) • Nursery or preschool programs (some provinces) • Family Resource Centres • Early Years Centres (Ontario) • Kids First (Saskatchewan) • Early Intervention programs Education • Kindergarten • Junior kindergarten (some provinces) • School-aged children (Quebec)	• Aboriginal Head Start (on- and off-reserve) • Family Head Start (New Brunswick) • First Nations and Inuit child care • Military Family Resource Centres • Childminding (LINC) Programs

learning and literacy programs, and parents may participate in programs that support parents in understanding all aspects of child development, pregnancy, and parenting. Manitoba has a program entitled Healthy Child Manitoba that supports children in high-risk situations by providing a home-visiting program. Saskatchewan has a KidsFirst program that is a partnered program with school and health districts, First Nations, Metis, and community organizations. Information on child care and parenting is provided, and home visiting and prenatal outreach is conducted.

Early Learning and Child Care Program Regulations

Each province and territory across Canada establishes regulations for early childhood programs that provide guidelines for the minimum standards for health and safety, as well as guidelines for staff qualifications, child-to-adult ratios and group size, accommodation of children with special needs, and the overall physical environment. Table 2.2 provides an overview of ratios and staff training requirements for child care centres. Table 2.3 provides an overview of ratios and staff training requirements for family child care.

Table 2.2 *Child Care Centre Regulations*

Province or Territory	Age	Ratio	Group Size	Staff Training Requirements
Alberta	0–12 months	1:3	6	One year ECE certificate required for one-quarter of staff. All other staff require a 45-hour course. The centre director requires a two-year ECE diploma.
	13–18 months	1:4	8	
	19–35 months	1:6	12	
	3–5 years	1:8	16	
	5–6 years	1:10	20	
British Columbia	0–36 months	1:4	12	For children under 36 months, each group of four children or fewer requires one infant/toddler teacher. Five or more children require an infant/toddler educator and an early childhood educator. For children from 30 months to school age, staff are required to have a basic early childhood education tranining program and 500 hours of supervised work experience for one staff per group.
	30–72 months	1:8	25	
Manitoba	Mixed age groups			Two-thirds of staff working with children from 0–6 years are required to have a two-year ECE diploma. One-half of staff require an ECE diploma for school-age and nursery-setting programs. Directors are required to have a post-diploma continuing-education certificate or a degree and one year experience.
	12 weeks to 2 years	1:4	8	
	2–6 years	1:8	16	

continue **Table 2.2**

Province or Territory	Age		Ratio	Group Size	Staff Training Requirements
Newfoundland and Labrador	0–24	months	1:3	6	The centre director requires a two-year ECE diploma and two years experience. One staff per group requires a one-year ECE certificate and one year experience.
	25–36	months	1:5	10	
	37–69	months	1:8	16	
New Brunswick	0–23	months	1:3	9	The director or one in four staff is required to have completed a 10-month ECE training program or equivalent. Other staff do not require training.
	24–36	months	1:5	10	
	37–48	months	1:7	14	
	49–60	months	1:10	20	
Nova Scotia	0–17	months	1:4	10	The director and two-thirds of staff require training in early childhood education or its equivalent.
	18–35	months	1:6	18	
	36–60	months	1:8	24	
	18–60	months	1:12	24	
Northwest Territories	0–12	months	1:3	6	There are no specific staff training requirements.
	13–24	months	1:4	8	
	25–35	months	1:6	12	
	3	years	1:8	16	
	4	years	1:9	18	
	5–11	years	1:10	20	
Nunavut	0–12	months	1:3	6	There are no specific staff training requirements.
	13–24	months	1:4	8	
	25–35	months	1:6	12	
	3	years	1:8	16	
	4	years	1:9	18	
	5–11	years	1:10	20	
Ontario	0–17	months	3:10	10	Supervisors and one person with each group of children must have a two-year ECE diploma or its equivalent. Supervisors require a minimum of two years experience.
	18–30	months	1:5	15	
	31–60	months	1:8	16	
	61–72	months	1:12	24	

continue **Table 2.2**

Province or Territory	Age	Ratio	Group Size	Staff Training Requirements
Prince Edward Island	0–24 months	1:3	6	Supervisors and at least one full-time staff member must have an ECE diploma from a one- or two-year program, combined with experience. (One-year diploma requires three years experience; a two-year diploma requires two years experience, a university degree in child studies or related field with additional ECE courses and experience.) All staff are required to complete 30 hours of in-service training every three years.
	25–36 months	1:5	–	
	37–60 months	1:10	–	
	61–72 months	1:12	–	
Quebec	0–18 months	1:5	–	Two-thirds of staff in non-profit centres are required to have an ECE college diploma or a university degree. One-third of staff in commercial centres are required to have a college diploma or university degree in ECE.
	19–47 months	1:8	–	
	48–71 months	1:10	–	
Saskatchewan	Infants	1:3	6	All staff employed for 65 hours or more per month are required to have completed a 120-hour community college child care orientation course or equivalent.
	Toddlers	1:5	10	
	30–72 months	1:10	20	
Yukon	0–17 months	1:4	8	20% of staff require a two-year ECE training program or equivalent; 30% must have a one-year ECE training program. All other staff require the completion of a 60-hour child care orientation.
	18–24 months	1:6	12	
	3–6 years	1:8	16	

(Source: Adapted from Friendly, Beach, & Turiano, 2002.)

Points to Ponder

If the federal government continues to provide funding to the provinces for early learning and child care without specific guidelines for the use of those funds, how will Canada provide all children and families with equal access to quality early learning and child care services? Conversely, do all regions in Canada need the same types of services? Why or why not?

Table 2.3 *Family Child Care Regulations*

Province or Territory	Number of Children That May Be Cared For	Education Requirements
Alberta	Up to six children under age 11 (including provider's children). No more than three children under the age of 3 and no more than two children under the age of 2.	No training required.
British Columbia	Up to seven children under the age of 12 (including provider's children). No more than five of the children may be preschoolers and no more than three children under the age of 3. Only one child under the age of 1 is allowed.	A course on child care is recommended or relevant work experience.
Manitoba	Up to eight children under the age of 12 (including provider's children). No more than five children may be under the age of 6, and no more than three may be under the age of 2. If there is a second adult present, there may be up to 12 children under the age of 12 (including provider's children). Up to three children may be under the age of 2.	An approved 40-hour course is required within the first year of operation.
Newfoundland and Labrador	Up to six children under the age of 6 (including provider's children). No more than three children may be under 36 months and no more than two of these children may be under 24 months.	An orientation course of 30 to 60 hours, depending on the age of the children. 30 hours of professional development every three years is required.
New Brunswick	Up to six children of mixed ages (including provider's children) under the age of 12. Only three infants and only five children age 2 to 5 are permitted.	No training required.
Nova Scotia	Up to six preschool-aged children of mixed ages (including provider's children), or up to eight school-aged children (including provider's children).	No training required.
Northwest Territories	Up to eight children under the age of 12 (including provider's children). No more than six children may be 5 or under, and no more than three children may be under the age of 3. No more than two children may be under the age of 2.	No training required.

continue **Table 2.3**

Province or Territory	Number of Children That May Be Cared For	Education Requirements
Nunavut	Up to eight children under the age of 12 (including provider's children). No more than six children may be 5 or under, and no more than three children may be under the age of 3. No more than two children may be under the age of 2.	No training required.
Ontario	Up to five children (including the provider's) under the age of 6. No more than two children may be under the age of 2, and no more than three children under the age of 3.	No training required. Agencies are required to hire a home visitor for every 25 homes. Home visitors are required to have post-secondary education in child development/family studies and two years of experience.
Prince Edward Island	Up to seven children of mixed ages (including provider's children) under the age of 12. No more than three children under the age of 2 are permitted.	A 30-hour course. An additional 30 hours of professional development required every three years.
Quebec	Up to six children (including provider's children) under age 9. No more than two children may be under the age of 18 months. If there is a second adult present, there may be up to nine children (including provider's children) under age 9. No more than four children may be under the age of 18 months.	Completion of a 45-hour course on child development, health, safety, and nutrition, and organization of physical environment.
Saskatchewan	Up to eight children (including provider's children) under the age of 13. Only five may be younger than age 6 and only two may be younger than 30 months. If there is a second adult present, there may be up to 12 children (including the provider's). Only 10 may be younger than age 6 and only two may be younger than 30 months.	Completion of a 40-hour introductory ECE course within the first year of operation. If more than one adult, the primary caregiver must complete a 120-hour ECE course within the first year of operation. Six hours of professional development each year is required.
Yukon	Up to eight children (including the provider's) under the age of 6. No more than four infants or eight preschoolers. If there is a second adult present, four additional children may be cared for.	Completion of a 60-hour ECE course within the first year of operation.

(Source: Adapted from Friendly, Beach, & Turiano, 2002.)

PARENTING PORTRAIT

Two Families: Two Different Perspectives

Two mothers, Brenda and Karen, provide their perspectives on childhood and family. The interviewer asks Karen, the mother of a 4-year-old and a 7-year-old, and Brenda, the mother of a 10-year-old and a 7-year-old, to share their views about today's children and the type of childhood they envision for their children.

Karen begins. "My husband and I want our children to have as many options for learning and stimulation as we can possibly provide. We believe that it is our role to encourage our children to participate in extracurricular activities such as dancing, skating, gymnastics, and skiing. We are prepared to make the financial commitment and time needed to offer our children these options. Yes, this is difficult for us because my husband works and lives in Toronto during the week. This means that when I leave work, I am required to ensure that the children get to their activities. This is important to us."

Brenda provides a different perspective. She says, "What is wrong with children today is that they have too many options. Our family is so busy driving the children to activities that we don't spend time or have the energy to offer our children quality experiences in their own home. We are programming our children to be stimulated most of the day. Can they ever relax and just be?"

Karen responds to Brenda. "It is essential as parents today that we begin to prepare our children for the workplace. We can best do this by offering children recreation, exposure to information technology, and experiences that introduce them to the global work, teamwork, and competition. If we don't do this, our children will not have the competitive edge needed to compete in society when they are ready to enter the workforce."

Brenda thinks for a moment and then suggests to Karen, "We are programming our children too much. We have specific schedules for computer play, enrichment programs, socialization events. We have them in child care or preschool programs. Where is the time for 'free play' and leisure? I believe this need for activity promotes hurried lives for children. Because Wayne and I want a more relaxed environment for our children, we often feel guilty when other parents ask what kinds of extracurricular activities we have our children enrolled in. Who is robbing the children—us, because we only have them in a couple of activities, or parents who have them continuously involved in activities?"

Karen cautions Brenda, "Parents today must realize that children need more stimulation and opportunities for learning. Children don't know how to play as we did. Activities and community experiences set the benchmarks for childhood today."

Over the past two decades children's enrolment in programs or experiences outside of the family home has changed the way children play. As a result, early childhood services need to change to meet the changing needs of children, and the study of early childhood services must change as well, by drawing attention to the new developmental needs of children, the environmental impacts influencing children, the emergence of technological processes, and the family socialization process.

The concerns expressed by parents such as Karen and Brenda, combined with observations of children entering early childhood programs, suggest that today's young children and families have a different set of needs from children accessing services in the early 1980s.

Earlier in the chapter, child's play was identified as essential for children because they experiment and discover through play, which is vital to a child's emotional and cognitive development. How do you respond to Karen's and Brenda's perspectives? What do you think is best for young children today?

Exploring Characteristics of Early Childhood Student Practitioners

Now that you have read about, discussed, and explored information related to the foundation of early learning and the types of early childhood services, you are ready to visit and participate in one or more aspects of an agency offering an early learning and child care service. As you do so, it is of value to explore the expected personal characteristics of early childhood student practitioners.

A **personal characteristic** describes how an individual thinks, communicates, relates to others, and conducts daily life (Gestwicki & Bertrand, 1999, p. 141). By exploring personal characteristics, you will understand how your personal characteristics impact others. As a way to explore key characteristics, think about an early childhood practitioner or teacher whom you fondly remember. Record three positive memories you have of that person. Then explore those memories from the perspective of personal characteristics. What would you describe as the core characteristics this individual displayed? Next, identify where, in your own life, you have exhibited these same traits, but perhaps in a different form. For example, if you ascribed *dedication* to your teacher, maybe your "dedication" is to your best friend or your favourite hobby. Then, identify three of this person's traits that you wish to display more often in your own career. Next, list your first action step to increase this trait in your work.

Go back now to the beginning of Chapters 1 and 2 and read about Jennifer's role with the children. As you reread these vignettes, record the characteristics that Jennifer demonstrates with each child. Think about the values, beliefs, and techniques she displays.

More than 30 years ago, Haim Ginott (1972) made the following statement, which continues to provide a valuable reminder to us today about how our characteristics, role modelling, and personality impact children:

> I have come to a frightening conclusion. It is my personal approach that creates the climate. It is my daily mood that makes the weather. As an [early childhood practitioner], I possess tremendous power to make a child's life miserable or joyous. I can be a tool of torture or an

Personal characteristic. Describes how an individual thinks, communicates, relates to others, and conducts daily life.

instrument of inspiration. I can humiliate or humour, hurt or heal. In all situations it is my response that decides whether a crisis will be escalated or de-escalated, a child humanized or de-humanized.(p. 13)

The more we know and understand about our personal characteristics, the better we are at exhibiting respect and support for children and families.

A number of traits, qualities, and behaviours are of particular importance to early childhood practitioners. Over years of working with children, student practitioners, and practitioners, and based on various readings and discussions among those in our learning community, we have identified seven essential characteristics desirable in an early childhood practitioner (see Figure 2.7). We encourage you to strive to achieve each of these characteristics.

Respect

The practitioner demonstrates respect for self and others. This is reflected in skills like compassion, patience, co-operation, support, and challenge, and is based on the belief that each person, including oneself, is entitled to be respected for who they are.

Self-Confidence

The practitioner has confidence in one's ability to learn and evolve, with the same consideration given to all those around, including children, parents, and the community. An early childhood practitioner demonstrates self-confidence by being willing to explore new ideas, experiences, and techniques.

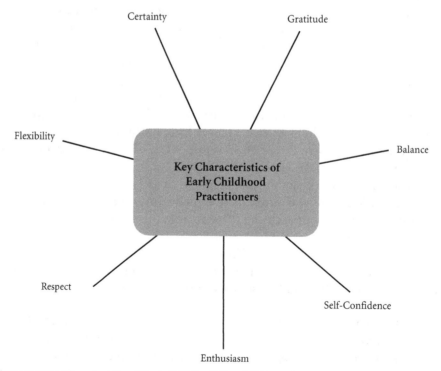

Figure 2.7 *Key Characteristics of Early Childhood Practitioners*

Balance

An early childhood practitioner demonstrates balance in all seven areas of life, including spirit, health, family, social life, career, finances, and mind. Recognizing your responsibilities as an early childhood student practitioner, you practise and strive to model a balanced lifestyle.

Gratitude

A practitioner appreciates this wonderful opportunity to create and implement environments that nurture children in a manner that respects their unique characteristics. Early childhood practitioners reflect gratitude in their commitment to continuous, lifelong learning and in a humble pride in their work.

Certainty

Practitioners are aware of the importance and impact of their work on the future of individual children and their families, and also on community and society in general.

Flexibility

An early childhood practitioner adapts to the continuing evolution of not just the children, but also the program, the field, the community, and society. Practitioners' flexibility is evident in their ability to adapt to change and direction.

Enthusiasm

Practitioners are able to connect work with who they are as people. This self-reflection generates the passion and commitment needed to attract children to the learning environment, and is a personal and shared process where practitioners think analytically from several perspectives about the concepts learned through the lifelong learning process. Through self-reflection, early childhood practitioners explore how their newly acquired knowledge impacts both their personal and professional relationships as well as their work.

Learning through a Learning-Community Model

Learning community. Groups of people, such as students, who come together to examine their knowledge, skills, and visions for their learning and set forth a collaborative plan to support themselves in gaining new knowledge that is transferable to early childhood service settings.

In addition to the seven characteristics highlighted above, we believe that it is important for you to see yourself as a learner and as part of a **learning community**. By participating in a learning-community process, both during your current studies and as you launch your career, you enrich your continuous learning. When you share your learning, when you contribute to others' learning, and when you learn with a group that is committed to exploring a subject matter, you have more options and insights into the subject. Whenever you acquire a variety of perspectives, you develop openness to new knowledge and skills.

Early childhood student practitioners learn most effectively and efficiently when groups of students come together to examine their knowledge, skills, and visions for their learning and set forth a collaborative plan to support them in gaining new knowledge that is transferable to early childhood service settings.

Learning communities are intended to enhance collaboration and expand learning. When early childhood practitioners adopt the learning-community philosophy, they commit themselves to continuous learning and to supporting each other in the learning cycle. Participants share their gained knowledge as well as the excitement and the challenges that come with learning difficult material. They discuss and reflect on ways to transfer their newly acquired knowledge and skills to the early childhood setting, and they develop strategies that will support them in determining how to measure success. Generally, members of effective learning communities exhibit the following characteristics:

1. **Collective inquiry.** Early childhood student practitioners seek new information, methods, and ideas. They test their methods and reflect on the results to determine if further inquiry and processes are required.

2. **Collaborative teams.** Early childhood student practitioners focus on a willingness to work together to gain new information and to understand how theory transfers to application.

3. **Continuous improvement.** Early childhood student practitioners work together by engaging in discussions, self-reflection, and assessment as a way to prepare for the transfer of knowledge and skills to the workplace (Dietze, 2002).

Learning communities value the experiences and knowledge of their members. The learning-community group expects to learn from everyone present and to form a nurturing, caring environment through the camaraderie of learning together, which in turn promotes the celebration of cognitive diversity among team members.

SUMMARY

Understanding the Framework of Early Childhood

- Children are the *who*; child development is the *what*; learning environments are the *where*; children's needs, early childhood practices, and services are the *how*; and knowing when to guide and provide experiences is the *when* of early childhood.
- According to Havinghurst and Neugarten (1967), children's environments encompass physical space, objects in that space, and people in that space. This is known as *life space*. Urie Bronfenbrenner's (2000) ecological theory identifies environmental influences and systems, known as the microsystem, mesosystem, exosystem, macrosystem, and chronosystem, that contribute to children's development.
- Early learning and child care environments consist of physical space, experiential components, and human components that interact to support children and their development.
- The national early learning and child care agenda identifies quality, universal inclusiveness, accessibility, and development as the core principles.
- Children learn and adapt to family and community life through play.

Types of Early Childhood Services

- The three types of early childhood services are foundation programs, specific program models, and support programs.
- Provincial and territorial governments are responsible for establishing minimum standards for health and safety, staff qualifications, child-to-adult ratios, physical space, group size, and accommodation of children with special needs.

Characteristics of Early Childhood Student Practitioners

- The seven key desirable characteristics of early childhood student practitioners are respect, self-confidence, balance, gratitude, certainty, flexibility, and enthusiasm.

Learning through a Learning-Community Model

- Learning-community members are committed to collective inquiry, collaborative teams, and continuous improvement.
- Learning communities value the experiences and knowledge that members share.

FURTHER OPPORTUNITIES FOR ENRICHMENT

Research

1. Choose a program identified from the foundation, program models, or support programs listed. Examine three new sources of information that will provide further insight into the program's philosophy, how the program supports children and families, and if there is specialized staff training necessary to work in the program. Cite your sources.
2. Examine the history of early childhood services in your province. When was the first child care centre established? When were the first nursery school/preschool and kindergarten programs established? Are specialized programs available, and if so, what types are available? What are the newest programs?

Group Investigation

1. Examine your local community resources to determine the types of early childhood services available to families. Decide which one of those early childhood services you would like to visit. Before making your visit, make a list of five questions that would help your group gain insight into the type of early childhood service that is being offered. Devise questions that will help you understand the services to the families, the roles of early childhood practitioners, and the guiding principles or philosophies of the facility. Categorize the service into one of the three categories presented in this chapter. Share your findings with other members of your learning community.

Making Connections

1. Examine the photos at the beginning of this chapter of the child making the mask. What do these photos tell you about the process Marioe used to learn about making masks and about connecting previous learning with new information? What steps do children go through to complete a learning episode? What do the photos communicate to the early childhood practitioner? Would there be a particular celebration that might trigger children to become intrigued with masks?
2. In the Chapter 1 and Chapter 2 vignettes, "A Day Begins in a Learning and Child Care Centre," Jennifer exhibits important practices when working with Annie and Marioe that are inherent in being an effective early childhood practitioner. Review each vignette and list three important practices that you feel are essential as a practitioner. Then, examine how Jennifer's practice supports children's learning.
3. Examine this chapter's Parenting Portraits. What is your response to Karen? Do you believe that children today need more stimulation and opportunities for learning than children of your generation? Why or why not? What is your position on Brenda's comment, "We are programming our children too much." Do you agree or disagree with Brenda? Justify your response.

ADDITIONAL READING

Beach, J. & Bertrand, J. (2000). *More Than the Sum of the Parts: An Early Childhood Development System for Canada*. Toronto, ON: University of Toronto, Childcare Resource and Research Unit.

Doherty, G., Lero, D. S., Goelman, H., LaGrange, A., & Tougas, J. (2000). *You Bet I Care! A Canada-Wide Study on Wages, Working Conditions, and Practices in Child Care Centres*. Guelph, ON: Centre for Families, Work and Well-Being, University of Guelph.

Edwards, C., Gandini, L., & Forman, G. (Eds). (1998). *The Hundred Languages of Children: The Reggio Emilia Approach—Advanced Reflections* (2nd ed). Grennwich, CT: Ablex Publishing.

Fraser, S. (2000). *Authentic Childhood: Experiencing Reggio Emilia in the Classroom*. Toronto, ON: ITP Nelson.

Hohmann, M. & Weikart, D. P. (1995). *Educating Young Children: Active Learning Practices for Preschool and Child Care Programs*. Ypsilanti, MI: High/Scope Press.

Montessori, M. (1914). *Dr. Montessori's Own Handbook*. New York: Frederick A. Stokes.

Varga, D. (1997). *Constructing the Child: A History of Canadian Day Care*. Toronto, ON: Lorimer.

WEBLINKS

www.bankstreet.edu/about: *Bank Street programs.*
www.cccf-fcsge.ca: *Canadian Child Care Federation.*
www.froebel.com: *Froebel programs.*
www.acf.hhs.gov/programs/hsb: *Head Start programs.*
www.highscope.org: *High/Scope programs.*
www.Montessori.org: *Montessori programs.*
www.infed.org/thinkers/et-pest.htm: *Johann Heinrich Pestalozzi.*
www.ericdigests.org/2001-3/reggio.htm: *Reggio Emilia centres.*
www.philosophypages.com/ph/rous.htm: *Jean-Jacques Rousseau.*
www.uwbg.org/initiatives/successbysix: *United Way: Success by 6.*

"Listen to the desires of your children. Encourage them and then give them the autonomy to make their own decision."

Dr. Denis Waitley

3

Understanding the Foundation for Children's Learning

Learning Objectives

In this chapter you will:

1. Discuss how environments support learning.

2. Explain the three ways that observation informs practice, and discuss the seven steps of the observation process.

3. Discuss how the five levels of being, thinking, and learning can be used to enhance children's development.

4. Discuss how the seven guidelines for practice support children's learning and the practitioner's role.

5. Highlight the importance of intergenerational relationships in influencing children's learning.

A Day Begins in an Early Learning and Child Care Centre

Jennifer Uses Her Observation Skills to Support Marcdon's Learning

Marcdon appears interested in the blocks, carpet cylinders, and boards that were placed near the alligator pond prop. Jennifer observes as Marcdon tries to stack the carpet cylinders four high and then the boards across. Each time Marcdon puts the boards on the cylinders, the cylinders tumble. Then, he places the large blocks on the cylinders. This time the cylinders collapse.

Suddenly, Marcdon starts to move away from the blocks toward the sand area. At that moment, Jennifer realizes she should have explored with Marcdon his idea for using the blocks, carpet cylinders, and boards.

Jennifer quickly moves toward Marcdon. Bending down, she makes eye contact with Marcdon and asks him, "May I assist you with your construction?" Marcdon says, "I want to build a bridge. I can't 'cuz the boards keep falling off the cylinders."

Jennifer replies, "Come show me. Perhaps together we will be able to think of another way to build a bridge." As Jennifer and Marcdon approach the area, Jennifer asks, "Did you try building the bridge using the large blocks for the foundation?" Marcdon looks at Jennifer and says, "No, I used the cylinders. Should we try the large blocks?" "What do you think will happen if we use the large blocks for the foundation, rather than the cylinders?" "Let's try," replies Marcdon.

As Jennifer and Marcdon decide where to place the blocks, Jennifer says, "The boards are very heavy. They need something solid with even edges to help them be stable." Then she says, "Which is heavier, the blocks or the cylinders?" Marcdon replies, after lifting one of each, "The blocks are heavier." Then Marcdon builds his bridge while Jennifer remains nearby for support.

Looking Ahead

In this chapter, the focus is on children and learning and on what they require to maximize their learning. We present a process for conducting observations to highlight how observations guide practitioners in determining children's interests and needs. We present the concept of being, thinking, and learning, and we also offer an introduction to the seven guidelines for practice that support children's development. The chapter concludes with an overview of how intergenerational influences support children's learning.

Lifelong Learning

Children require interesting and different experiences.

Learning is a lifelong process with many steps. Children, during their early years, require learning options and choices—ones that best meet their needs. A practitioner's role is to nurture children in environments so that their potential is maximized. Becoming a successful practitioner, however, does not come without challenge, effort, research, observation, exploration, and experience. For the beginner practitioner, learning about children is achieved through research, study, and observation, and through mentoring from experienced practitioners who have gained knowledge and skills in nurturing children.

Practitioners use their understanding of child development and learning to guide their practice. Understanding how children think and learn and what they require to maximize learning is a complex phenomenon that will challenge practitioners for their entire careers and, in fact, their entire lives. There is much we still do not know about early learning and child care, so each practitioner is on a lifelong journey in the pursuit of newer ideas and skills that will enhance his effectiveness with children.

Creating Supportive Environments

Teachable moment. That point in a learner's development where a keen observer intervenes in some way to build on the learning that is occurring, thereby maximizing the learner's evolution.

The field of early childhood is about nurturing children. How we create an environment for children and how we as early childhood practitioners nurture children dramatically influences their learning and development. As you will note in the opening vignette of this chapter, Jennifer recognized the need to support Marcdon in satisfying his interest in combining boards and cylinders in his block play. Through observation, Jennifer noted her need to offer Marcdon assistance. Had she missed this **teachable moment**, Marcdon may have neglected to continue to try to combine the two materials together.

Friedrich Froebel (1782–1852) was among the first theorists to identify the importance of adults who consciously nurture children. He recognized that children require adults to guide them in developing knowledge and skills that are useful through their lifespan. Froebel indicated the environment has many facets to it, all of which must be examined and understood by adults to effectively support children's development.

Many educators today echo Froebel's perspective on the important role of the adult and the environment in nurturing children. For example, Jalongo and Isenberg (2004) advocate that "caring for children, enjoying their company, respecting them as individuals, and treating them equitably form the cornerstone of early childhood practice" (p. 16). In order to flourish, children require **developmentally appropriate environments,** and to effectively create these environments early childhood practitioners must continually examine children's development and their needs associated with their growth process. Jalongo and Isenberg (2004) also contend that early childhood practitioners require an understanding of their own professional goals in order to link the knowledge and skills necessary to complement their application to practice.

Developmentally appropriate environments. Environments designed to support and challenge children with age-appropriate play experiences.

How Observation Informs Practice

As we noted above, children require supportive environments to reach their optimal development. Abraham Maslow (1987) suggested that individuals must first satisfy their basic needs before higher-level growth needs can be addressed. He described these basic needs as including the physiological needs for food and water, as well as physical and psychological security. The higher-level growth needs include the feelings of love and belonging. As needs are met, individuals intuitively seek higher needs. William Glasser (1998) supports this view of human development and, like Maslow, contends it is of particular importance to children during their preschool and adolescent years.

As a way to determine what children's needs are, practitioners become keen observers. "Observation is essential for understanding and responding to children" (Jalongo & Isenberg, 2004, p. 85). Practitioners gain information about children's needs, interests, strengths, and areas requiring further development through direct observation. Observations guide the early childhood practitioner in the following:

1. Understanding children's interests.
2. Identifying the types of materials children are interested in.
3. Determining the skills or knowledge children currently have or are working toward.

Conducting useful observations requires diligence and effort on the part of the practitioner. And throughout your studies, you will learn observation methods and you will practise your observation skills. Collecting useful data requires practitioners to carefully observe children's behaviours, what types of play they participate in, what materials they use, and with whom they interact. Observing children provides early childhood practitioners with new insights about children's support requirements. These supports can take many forms, including a comment, a question, a word of encouragement, an acknowledgment of an effort, a smile, or even some humour to lighten the moment.

The Observation Process

Learning to observe efficiently and effectively is a process and an acquired skill. New early childhood student practitioners require not just an introduction to the process but also lots of practice. The steps that follow are a brief introduction to a generic observation process used to gather information about a child that can later be used to inform practice (see Figure 3.1). Observation techniques will be studied in more detail in other phases of your studies.

1. The Preparation Component. *What do I already know about this child?* This component requires practitioners to determine what they already know about a child and where they think that child may need to extend his learning.

2. The Planning Component. *What do I need to know about this child?* This component requires practitioners to make a list of what else they want to know about the child. The observer may have questions related to such

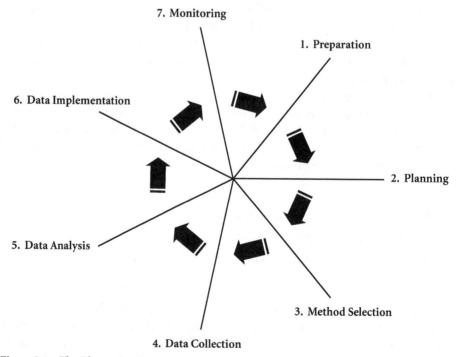

Figure 3.1 *The Observation Process*

things as the type of experiences the child prefers, the child's developmental characteristics, current language skills, the types of interactions between the child and his peers and also between him and adults.

3. The Method Selection Component. *What observation method will obtain the best informational data?* This component requires practitioners to determine the most efficient observation method and to prepare the resources required.

4. The Data Collection Component. *What data will I collect?* This component requires practitioners to carefully search out and record the pertinent behavioural information needed, such as which experience-centres a child predominantly plays at and with whom. The practitioner observes the child and records what he sees and hears.

5. The Data Analysis Component. *What information does the data provide?* Here, practitioners examine the information collected. They interpret the data in terms of their knowledge of child development and learning pedagogy and determine how the data can inform future practices with this child and other children.

6. The Data Implementation *Component. What new information does the data provide that guides me in the types of experiences I provide the child with?* According to this component, practitioners use the data to guide them in determining appropriate experiential challenges needed to support and nurture the child.

7. The Monitoring Component. *How do I monitor how the interventions are impacting the child?* In this component, practitioners continue to observe the child and evaluate the impact of their interventions on the child's learning and development. And in so doing, practitioners may adjust their interventions as required to ensure an ongoing evolution of this child's learning and development. In this way, their observations inform the practice of their professional skills.

There are a variety of observation methods. Intentional observation, for example, is a useful, informative, and powerful strategy for guiding children's learning experiences. Practitioners use observation to gain insight into children's being, thinking, and learning. Knowing that life will provide children with a variety of experiences later on, during the preschool years practitioners shrewdly support nurturing children's sense of self. Supportive environments build on each child's strengths, culture, interest, and abilities. Observation is pivotal to creating environments that support children's thinking, learning, and evolving.

Practitioners need to make the time to observe children carefully.

PARENTING PORTRAIT

The Third Parent

Mabel is a widow with two adult children, James and Patricia, both of whom are married. James lives in western Canada, while Patricia lives three blocks from her mother. Recently, Patricia and Sean, her husband of 10 years, divorced. Patricia and Sean now share custody of their two children: Nathan, aged 6 years, and Sarah, aged 3 years. Sean is employed full-time in a manufacturing plant, working daily from 8:00 a.m. to 5:00 p.m. Patricia works full-time at a local call centre, with rotating shifts every six weeks.

Nathan is in grade 1. Patricia and Sean require after-school care for Nathan and full-day child care for Sarah when Patricia is on the day shift. Patricia approached her mother for assistance.

Mabel wanted to help but was concerned that her arthritis might interfere with her ability to care for the children. However, because the children did not need child care daily, Mabel agreed to try to care for them. Mabel, Sean, and Patricia worked out a six-week schedule. Sean cares for the children when Patricia works evenings or nights. Mabel provides child care when Patricia works days.

As a result, Mabel provides child care every two weeks in a six-week cycle. She was nervous at first, but said, "The children are pleased to be with me and I really enjoy them. It gives me something to look forward to in my day." Sean and Patricia both feel that "We are lucky that Grandma is interested in helping us out and offers the children such a calming, nurturing environment. And it is so great to have her as the third parent raising our children. She shows love and respect to each child and provides them with an unhurried environment. We are so fortunate."

In past generations, grandparents were a common sight in many households, living with their adult children because their own economic situation was so precarious. Today we are seeing it again, and often because of the economic situation of the adult children. What are some of the inherent costs and benefits for children in their development? And how does the situation impact the adults, both the grandparents and their adult children?

Grandparents and other seniors can play a significant role in a child's development.

Being, Thinking, and Learning

Human beings are the only species that think about thinking. As a result, we are the only species that can consciously imagine the future and prepare for it. We have the ability to take concrete objects or experiences and, by representing them with symbols or abstractions, generalize them to other past, present, and future applications. This ability, combined with our adaptability, is responsible for our evolution to date. One way to conceptualize this phenomenon is to view humans as having the ability to be, think, and learn at five distinct levels, as shown in Figure 3.2.

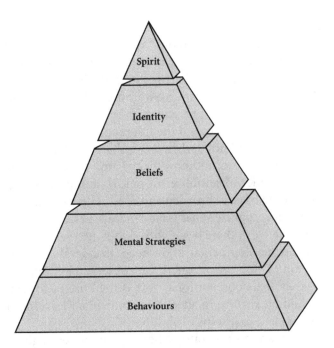

Figure 3.2 *Hierarchy for Being, Thinking, and Learning*

These levels move up from the more concrete to the more abstract. The higher the level of learning that occurs, the greater its application. The higher the level at which someone operates, the greater that person's ability to generalize or use the information in other contexts. The behavioural level refers to those actions that people display toward self or others. The mental-strategy level refers to how people organize their thoughts to determine a behaviour. The belief level refers to the significant filters that people use to view their lives. The identity level refers to the general overall perception people have of themselves. And the spirit level relates to how people see themselves connected to the universe or cosmos in general.

The behavioural level at the base is considered concrete, while the spirit level at the top is more abstract in nature, but each level is connected to the previous one. So, children's spirits have developed from their identities, which arose from their beliefs, which came from their mental strategies, which in turn arose from their behaviours. Conversely, children's spirits determine their identities, which create their beliefs, which initiate their mental strategies, which ignite their behaviours. Children operate at all these levels—as a result, having an awareness of the levels can be useful in facilitating children's development and evolution.

Let's look at an example. Isaac is an energetic 4-year-old who is playing with his friend Ben at the sand and water table. They are chatting while they scoop sand and pour water in a variety of interesting ways. Observing Isaac, Jennifer, the practitioner, notes his behaviour of sharing his play tools with Ben. Raising her awareness to the next level of Isaac's being, thinking, and learning, Jennifer interprets that Isaac realizes that sharing his play tools helps build friendships, which would suggest that he is operating at the next level—i.e., the mental-strategy level.

Jennifer listens intently to the children's exchange as a way to confirm her perspective. Isaac says to his companion, "You are my friend, right, Ben?" Jennifer notes that Isaac is now functioning at the even higher belief level. To facilitate Isaac's integration of the role of sharing in his life, Jennifer might ask him, "Isaac, what does it feel like sharing your toys with a friend like Ben?" This challenges Isaac to move to an identity level. His response, "I feel all nice inside," suggests he is now functioning at this level. To expand the full range of his learning around this concept, Jennifer adds, "You know, when I can share what I have with my friends it helps me appreciate me, too, and how lucky I am." Isaac responds, "Yeah, me too."

So, through Jennifer's keen observations, skilful questions, and comments to Isaac, she has assisted Isaac to broaden and deepen his awareness of the importance of sharing. Jennifer recognized that Isaac can learn at five distinct levels and can be assisted to move between these levels with skilful interventions. Jennifer has facilitated Isaac in his developmental knowledge of the value of sharing and in his overall evolution. Thus, practitioners can observe children to determine their functioning levels. This observational data is then useful to identify the types of experiences children require to meet their individual learning needs. This same process is also applied to groups of children.

Let's consider as a second example how a practitioner might use the concept of *a garden* with a group of children as a developmental learning tool. At the behavioural level, the practitioner might explore with the children the behaviours involved in creating a space for a garden, selecting the appropriate tools, and the watering or fertilizing required for a healthy garden. At the mental strategy, level, the practitioner and the children could discuss what they specifically wish to plant in their region, when is the best time to plant, how to maximize exposure to the sun, and other strategies to maximize the harvest. If the practitioner limits the learning to only these two levels, then the children miss being exposed to the full potential of learning of which they are capable. At the belief level, for example, is a vast range of ideas that various people and cultures in both the past and present believe about the role that gardens play in their lives. The practitioner could introduce this level by including various perspectives, such as the role of gardens in survival and family life. At the identity level, the practitioner could explore the role of gardens in assisting people to develop their culture—including customs, music, and dance. And at the spirit level, the children could learn about the role that gardens can play in connecting people with nature and the spirit of the land, the earth, the planet, and so on.

Then, if the children express an interest in exploring the topic even further, the practitioner could offer resources and experiences that lead them to examine important personal, cultural, and community perspectives that are prevalent

Children develop skills in being, thinking, and learning by developing interpersonal skills with others.

around them. For example, children could be engaged in creating their own gardens or visiting local public and private gardens. They might wish to plant vegetables for food and flowers for their beauty or some combination of both. The children could also explore the process of planting, nurturing, cutting, and arranging flowers. These types of experiences impact children's connection to nature.

When children have the opportunity to experience all five levels of being, thinking, and learning, they expand their potential learning value many times over. So a practitioner's awareness and use of these five levels and decision to offer a variety of experiential activities augments children's knowledge and skill development in significant and often dramatic ways at all levels of their being, thinking, and learning.

If an environment focuses only on one or two of the levels of children's being, then those children have more difficulty achieving depth, scope, or retention of their learning. The practitioner, then, must create opportunities for children to move beyond the behaviour and strategy levels of being, thinking, and learning to the higher levels. This in-depth process of child development maximizes children's potential to learn from any experiential activity in which they are engaged.

This developmental process complements Lev Vygotsky's (1978) **zone of proximal development (ZPD)** theory. He maintains that one of the primary roles of early childhood practitioners is to assist children in moving to higher levels of thinking and experiencing in their development. To achieve this, practitioners encourage children to explore their interests and engage in activities that are slightly more difficult than children can master alone. Practitioners support children by exploring and role modelling strategies that help them in completing these challenging experiences, thereby encouraging them to gain the self-confidence to engage in the experience independently.

Zone of proximal development (ZPD). A concept developed by Vygotsky (1978) that suggests that children require activities that both support past learning and encourage new learning at slightly more difficult levels.

When practitioners think about planning an experience for children, they have numerous options in their approach. For one, they could go to a book and select an experience and implement it. This experience may or may not be developmentally appropriate for a particular child. As new practitioners, how can you know if or how the experience supports children's interests or the scope of their levels of learning? How do you determine what you might consider doing as a follow-up experience next time?

Now, consider this next approach. Practitioners examine their knowledge about how to nurture children's learning. They engage in specific observations to determine children's phases of development and interests. They also observe how their mentors prepare the environment and support children in expanding their interests. Practitioners discuss their interpretation of their observations with one or more of their mentors. They discuss potential options and variations for implementing a specific experiential activity that they have selected. They implement the idea and receive coaching and guidance throughout the process. After the experience they solicit feedback from both the children and their colleagues, and make note of their learning for future reference.

Which experience requires practitioners to engage in a higher level of thinking? Which will assist practitioners in gaining the self-confidence needed to engage in planning and implementing developmentally appropriate experiences with

Conversation Café

There is an African saying that "it takes an entire village to raise a child," reflecting the belief that each child in a community is the responsibility of every person in that community. From your personal experiences and your professional studies, is Canada a good village to be born in today? Would you rather be parenting your child or seeking professional employment in Quebec or Alberta? Or does it really matter in which province or territory you reside?

children next time? When we, too, engage at all the levels of being, thinking, and learning, we challenge ourselves to question and to build upon our previous knowledge and to learn from others. We then make the connections necessary for learning and development to occur for all concerned.

Ed Labinowicz (1980), in his study of the work of Jean Piaget, provides another example of how higher thinking and learning occur. He suggests that children develop their intelligence by interacting with natural materials, such as sand, water, blocks, etc. He maintains that learning about mathematics is not just about addition, subtraction, multiplication, and division. Rather, each number reflects a relationship between other things. For example, the number five is based on the relationship of "one more than four and one less than six." The numbers represent both the amount of things as well as the relationship between things in the natural world. To consider the number five in this manner encourages children to engage in a much deeper and pervasive understanding of the concepts.

The **hierarchy of being, thinking, and learning** can thus form the practitioner's foundation for planning and implementing experiences in early childhood settings. Children require exposure to materials and experiences that trigger their curiosity and interest. The practitioner provides children with the tools, the environment, and the support necessary to develop knowledge and skills. Further discussion on program planning occurs in Chapters 6 and 7.

Hierarchy of being, thinking, and learning. A conceptual paradigm that outlines five levels at which children's learning can be focused to maximize the potential impact of a specific activity or environment.

Quality indicators. A predetermined set of criteria used to identify the degree of program excellence available to children and families.

Guidelines for Practice

Knowledge, observation, research, and experience inform and guide our practice. The essential environmental and interpersonal conditions that children require to learn become the practitioner's reference points when examining **quality indicators.** We outline seven factors to guide readers in their practice (see Table 3.1). As you read and explore them, think about how each informs and guides our practice. Make a point of identifying what we should see, hear, and feel in developmentally appropriate environments.

1. Respect Children's Self-Esteem

Self-esteem. The feelings of self-worth developing from an individual's beliefs about being valuable, capable, lovable, and worthwhile.

Self-concept. A term used to describe the collection of beliefs that people have developed about themselves through their experiences.

There are a number of ways to define **self-esteem**, but here we define it as the feelings of self-worth developing from an individual's beliefs about being valuable, capable, lovable, and worthwhile. This collection of beliefs that the child has of him- or herself is referred to as the *self-concept*. High self-esteem and a positive **self-concept** are essential characteristics of children's well-being (Harter, 1999). By the time children are 6 years old, their self-concept is established. Children's reactions to the challenges in their world will be directly determined by the beliefs and attitudes they hold about themselves. B. S. Heathington (1980) has noted that "no other time is as critical as childhood for establishing positive self-concepts."

Comenius (1592–1670) outlined that children's development evolves in a natural way and that early childhood experiences are like an "unfolding." Children have an innate desire to seek and ingest nourishment from their surroundings so that

Table 3.1 Guidelines for Practice

Guideline #1	Respect children's self-esteem.
Guideline #2	Honour children's uniqueness and curiosity.
Guideline #3	Nurture children's need for movement.
Guideline #4	Nurture children's need for supportive and challenging activities.
Guideline #5	Recognize children's innate multi-sensory learning modalities.
Guideline #6	Respect children's need to have choices.
Guideline #7	Honour children's need to scaffold their learning experiences.

they may grow and unfold, a process that requires continuous nourishment for growth to occur. This inborn belief in self is crucial to survival. Without it, children will not blossom. If children's "will to live" is stifled by their environment, the damage can be overwhelming. For example, there were many children in post-war Germany and in wartorn countries today that exhibit "failure to thrive" syndrome. These children become lethargic and lose their will to live. When children's environments do not provide sufficient resources to meet their physiological and psychological needs, then children may give up this "will to live, then wither and die."

Children's self-esteem is the basis for what is often called **motivation** and is critical to children's survival. Perhaps what is most important about self-esteem is that it is learned (Pierce, 1990). As well, self-esteem is not constant; rather, it may change, especially in response to family, community, or individual life situations. Furthermore, self-esteem and respect are interrelated. Respect for children, which is interrelated with self-esteem, is often a misunderstood principle in a learning environment.

Montessori (1914) wrote that "respect for the children is of the greatest importance and must be observed in practice" (p. 113). She advocated respect for each child and his individuality. In order for children to learn respect for others, they need to experience it from their role models—i.e., the adults in their lives. Children require adults to treat all children with the same level of respect in all interactions, regardless of age, gender, race, personality, or any other idiosyncrasy.

When children exhibit signs of low self-esteem, further observation is required to determine their sources of self-esteem. And focusing on the causes and severity of the level of self-esteem (Harter, 1990) helps to facilitate planning an environment conducive to children's needs. Children's self-esteem is developed in environments and through experiences whereby they gain emotional satisfaction, social approval, achievement, and coping strategies. Children will retain a higher level of self-esteem in environments that provide them with the freedom to participate in activities and experiences that they will be successful with, which leads to confidence-building and competence.

Motivation. A biological drive that each person is born with to live, learn, and evolve.

Children's self-esteem is the basis for self-motivation and is critical to their learning.

2. Honour Children's Uniqueness and Curiosity

As the word implies, *uniqueness* means being the only one of its kind among a larger group. All children are born with a unique genetic makeup that reflects their parents and ancestors. Current research contributes to our interest and discussion of our uniqueness. For example, the research completed on the human genome map—the identification of the role or purpose of every gene in human DNA—reinforces that each person is unique. Studies of twins who share the same DNA confirm there will be unique differences between how each adjusts and adapts to his environment (*Discovery*, April, 2004). This principle of uniqueness is fundamental in nature and is demonstrated in a variety of ways. For example, each snowflake is a unique quartz-crystal configuration; each blade of grass is a unique shade of green; each grain of sand is a unique shape; and our fingerprints, footprints, and retina prints are unique in the world.

In the same way, each child is born into a unique family environment with its own special culture, customs, and experiences, which are like no other's. As noted by Driscoll: where uniqueness is honoured, "early childhood programs reflect the cultural values of the children and families they serve, so they must look different from place to place" (Jalongo & Isenberg, 2004, p. 52). When children's uniqueness is honoured, their curiosity flourishes. And curiosity triggers learning.

Curiosity. A child's desire to explore, discover, question, and wonder.

Curiosity is the desire to explore, discover, question, and wonder, and is instrumental to children's learning and survival. Practitioners and other adults actually increase children's chances for survival by responding constructively to children's every curiosity.

Children express curiosity in different ways. Some children in some situations may explore more with their minds, while others explore more physically. Some children exhibit higher levels of risk taking, while others are more timid. And both timid children and exuberant children are curious: timid children may require encouragement from adults, whereas children who are more exuberant may act on curiosity triggers with or without adult support.

Perry (2001) identifies that children have higher levels of exploration, discovery, and learning when they are in environments where curiosity is honoured. For example, if a 3-year-old child discovers how to blow small bubbles and then larger and larger bubbles, the discovery provides a sense of pleasure. As shown in Table 3.2, when the child has gained pleasure, the act will be repeated. In essence, pleasure leads to repetition. As the child continues the repetitive actions, mastery of bubble blowing occurs, which leads to confidence. And as a child's self-esteem and confidence are built, the child will expand his interest in acting on other

Table 3.2   *How Curiosity Leads Children to Learning*

Curiosity	Results in	Exploration
Exploration	Results in	Discovery
Discovery	Results in	Pleasure
Pleasure	Results in	Repetition
Repetition	Results in	Mastery
Mastery	Results in	New Skills
New Skills	Result in	Confidence
Confidence	Results in	Self-esteem
Self-esteem	Results in	Sense of Security
Security	Results in	More Exploration

(Source: Dr. Bruce Perry, *Curiosity: The Fuel of Development*, 2001.)

elements of curiosity. When the child has a peer or an adult to share his discovery with, positive reinforcement occurs and esteem building occurs. Curiosity, if encouraged, is most powerful in early childhood (Perry, 2004).

Children need practitioners who assume that each child knows innately what he needs to learn and how he can most effectively learn. Practitioners support children in their quest for learning by being supportive and by nurturing them within the scope of their safety and with available resources.

When children are exposed to environments that constrain curiosity, the results can be devastating and lifelong. Perry (2004) says, "Curiosity dimmed is a future denied. Our potential—emotional, social, and cognitive—is expressed through the quantity and quality of our experiences. And less-curious children will make fewer new friends, join fewer social groups, read fewer books, and take fewer hikes" (p. 1). Curious children have enthusiasm and motivation, while less-curious children lack these elements; as a result, their learning potential is impaired.

3. Nurture Children's Need for Movement

Movement is life, and the human body is the perfect motion machine. The human body begins movement at conception, and does not stop moving in some way until death. Movement, therefore, is the tool for survival and development.

Children use movement to explore and experience a sense of self and the environment. Children who move efficiently and easily develop feelings of self-confidence and competence, which promote positive social interactions. The popularity of sports in all forms is a testament to the vital role of movement in human development.

You may have heard the saying that to ask children not to move is like asking them not to breathe. This applies to all human beings, regardless of age. Let us check to see if this is true—stop reading right now, and be still in every part of your body for 30 seconds, including your limbs, neck, shoulders, eyes, mouth, etc. Go ahead, do it right now! How long did it take before you moved something? And this challenge was only at a muscular level. What if your respiratory or your cardiovascular systems had been added? Was it uncomfortable? Movement is one of life's primary tools for life and learning.

The merit of movement activities in early childhood programs has long been recognized. Crossley (2000) indicates that "current studies in the field of developmental, educational and physiological psychology suggest the child's earliest learning is based on movement and so too is the collection of subsequent knowledge" (p. 1). For example, when a child masters how to play within specific space allocations, he has also learned about concepts of space, shape, and abstract thought.

New research in the development and function of the human brain is encouraging early childhood practitioners to revisit the importance of encouraging movement activities for young children. The more movement experiences children have, the more efficient their brains become at processing motor responses. Developing and using nerve tissue is a mutually enhancing process, and using the neural muscular mechanism facilitates development (Crossley, 2004).

Children's brains exercise three major steps when formulating movement plans. Initially, the brain selects an appropriate cue for the desired outcome and then forms a mental picture of the body's movement that should achieve the desired result. This information is then integrated with past experience so that children may decide and select an appropriate strategy. Then, the brain develops a pathway that gives feedback information about the appropriateness of the mental image and the selected plan. Once the image of the task is clear and a plan is in place, an opportunity to practise the skill is necessary to increase the efficiency of the action. Although this sounds time-consuming and complicated, when children are given the freedom to move, the brain becomes efficient in processing the steps.

As you just experienced, it is difficult to not move—to be still. Inactivity goes against our very nature—it is unnatural

Movement is one of a child's primary tools for learning.

not to be moving and active. Self-confidence is sustained through movement. Children require activities that support them in building control over their own bodies and the freedom to manipulate objects in their environment. This builds children's sense of security and predictability in the environment, which contributes to maintaining a measure of self-confidence.

Movement impacts motor skills, and motor skills influence movement. Gallahue (1993) describes the importance of motor movement. He says that "movement is at the very center of young children's lives. It is an important facet of all aspects of their development, whether in the motor, cognitive, or affective domains of human behavior" (p. 24). The movement component of early childhood programs requires it to be as carefully planned as the social/emotional, language, and cognitive experiences. The movement experiences are necessary for the evolution of all other aspects of children's development. Recognizing the importance of movement, early childhood practitioners seek out unique and interesting ways to introduce and encourage movement experiences as a way to expand children's sense of well-being.

4. Nurture Children's Need for Challenging and Supportive Activities

Daily living challenges children in a variety of ways. Children require practice in dealing with the unforeseen and the unexpected, and they build the skills and abilities to deal with life challenges through active learning experiences (Driscoll & Nagel, 2005). These experiences can take many forms, customized to each child and each situation.

Children require both challenging and supportive activities. **Challenging activities** are described as experiences that provide children with new areas of growth and are slightly more difficult than what children have previously experienced. **Supportive activities** are repeated experiences that affirm children's past learning and enhance their self-confidence. A balance of both supportive and challenging activities is necessary to maximize children's growth. Supportive activities usually have minimal adult support, while challenging experiences offer varying levels of adult support.

Challenging activities. Experiences that provide new areas of growth to children.

Supportive activities. Repeated experiences that affirm children's past learning and enhance their self-confidence.

Vygotsky (1978) pointed out that children have two levels of performance: at the first level, children are capable of achieving some tasks and learning independently; at the second, children need assistance from others. These two levels of performance affirm children's need to have a combination of supportive and challenging experiences.

Vygotsky also suggested that learning should lead development rather than the other way around. Children require challenging activities that stretch their limits of experience, knowledge, use of resources, and level of problem-solving skills in order to expand the development of new knowledge and skills, which in turn lead to a new level of proficiency.

Let's consider an example at a physiological level of development. If a child is able to balance himself on one foot for 10 seconds, and then begins practising balancing for longer and longer periods, he will soon be able to expand the time

Children need both support and challenge to maximize their learning.

frame of a one-foot balance. As he strengthens his leg and back muscles through repeated practice, he soon adapts to the challenge and learns to stand on one foot for longer periods of time. However, if the child is not provided with this opportunity to expand his motor skills, his ability in this area will be stifled. Conversely, when a child has the opportunity to practise the skill, he enhances both his physiological development and his psychological self-confidence. Thus, children must have a continuous supply of new challenges that are developmentally appropriate and that build on their interests.

Supportive and challenging experiences are achieved in active learning environments where children have a variety of enticing materials that invite exploration. The materials are open-ended, offering a variety of loose parts so that children's curiosity is sparked, leading them to explore, invent, combine, create, and communicate with others. Large blocks of uninterrupted time are weaved into the daily routine rather than fragmenting the day into defined times for separate activities with many confusing transitions.

Practitioners observe and determine the required level of adult participation to support children's learning. Practitioners examine their roles carefully and recognize when they should be involved with the play and when they need to offer genuine caring and encouragement—in this way, they create an environment of both support and challenge.

Points to Ponder

Jim and Steve are both parents of preschoolers and they are also a couple themselves, having legally formalized their relationship under Canada's new marriage legislation. Before they got together they had been in heterosexual relationships, and now they are sharing parenting and custody of their children with their former spouses. Jim has a 4-year-old son, while Steve has twin 2-year-old daughters. Both Jim and Steve are devoted parents who work hard to maintain healthy relationships with both their children and their ex-wives. For convenience, all their children attend the same neighbourhood early learning and child care centre. As an early childhood practitioner working in this centre, what is your role in accommodating the needs of these families and where might you expect the challenges to occur?

5. Recognize Children's Multi-sensory Learning Modalities

The human species is born with at least five definite senses with which to learn and cope with the world: vision, hearing, touch, taste, and smell. Each represents a unique system of retrieving information and incorporating it into our repertoire of knowledge and experience. And each sense is a source of useful information—both pleasant and unpleasant.

Piaget (1896–1980) stated that from birth to 2, children learn about their world through sensory experiences and motor activity (Henniger, 2002). Morrison (2003) suggests that multi-sensory materials "help make children more aware of the capacity of their bodies to receive, interpret, and make use of stimuli" (p. 113). Sensory materials support children in gaining observation and visual-discrimination skills, necessary for later reading and writing.

Maria Montessori's programming approach requires children to use sensory materials, which increase children's ability to think and to problem solve. Sensory materials promote children's ability to observe, distinguish, classify, organize, and sequence, and they also encourage children to engage in an intellectual process of observation and selection, referencing knowledge obtained from previous experiences and through the senses. This process forms the basis of adaptation to our environment.

Practitioners are challenged to provide environments and experiences that nurture the more dominant visual and auditory as well as the olfactory, gustatory, and tactile senses. Actualizing a multi-sensory environment promotes

Multi-sensory activities increase the child's ability to learn.

the exploration of each experience using all of the senses. Practitioners need to continually seek out novel ways to broaden children's learning using a multi-sensory approach.

6. Respect Children's Need to Have Choices

As we've mentioned before, Glasser (1998) noted that children have both physiological and psychological needs that they are genetically driven to meet. The physiological needs include safety, nutrition, and rest, while the four psychological needs are freedom, power, love, and fun. While each individual places these needs in a personal hierarchy of importance at any given point in time, Glasser (1998) suggests that freedom is the most important because it forms the basis for meeting the other needs. Without freedom to choose, children are unable to pursue their interests, passions, or potential.

Erikson (Bredekamp, 1987) identified that children desire choice—that is, they desire to make decisions about which new tasks they explore. This fosters initiative in preschool children. And the concepts of freedom and choice are interrelated. The human struggle to attain more freedom is illustrated in many arenas, including social, political, and spiritual ones. For example, we observe teenagers seeking freedom from parental control, we watch political groups seeking freedom from state control, and we see religious individuals seeking freedom from institutional control. As well, we often witness individuals changing their career paths in search of freedom.

Freedom is generally considered desirable because it maximizes an individual's ability to make choices that will meet his needs. The less freedom children have, then, the less chance there is that their needs will be met. For example, as a society, when we want to punish someone for breaking one of our laws, we take away that person's most important rights—the freedom to choose where to be and with whom to associate and how to spend her time.

The same need for freedom applies in children's learning environments. To maximize children's learning potential, the environment provides children with choices, which encourages them to make conscious decisions about what, where, and how they will learn. And having choices facilitates children's evolution in the most efficient manner.

Gestwicki and Bertrand (1999) suggest that the amount of choice provided to children is a key quality indicator of an early childhood environment. Children require choices about which activities they are interested in, how they will structure their learning activities, as well as where and with whom they will play. When young children are afforded the opportunity to make choices, they are better able to make effective decisions later in life.

Early childhood programming requires a process-oriented approach with children—i.e., providing choices and materials that support children's interests. Such an approach increases children's involvement in their learning, their interactions with people and materials, and their ability to make choices. Bredekamp and Copple (1997) remind us, however, that the materials provided must be worthy of children's attention. When materials offer children challenges and choices and freedom to think through exploration, then experimentation, hypothesis testing, and reflection are more likely to occur.

7. Honour Children's Need for Scaffolding Learning Experiences

Nature does not destroy anything; it just changes its form by evolving or building one thing on top of another. For example, in infancy, learning to roll over is used as a foundation for learning to sit up, which becomes a foundation for crawling, which then is a basis for walking, leading to running and jumping, and so on. In the same way, all learning is a process of building one experience on top of the previous ones. Previous learning acts as a foundation for the next level of learning, meaning that children always build new knowledge based on their old knowledge, and they are constantly adding to these levels throughout their lives.

As we mentioned in Chapter 1, for many the word *scaffold* connotes an image of a platform connected with poles, planks, and ties, used in the construction industry. Scaffolds are built with a strong foundation, with layers added as required. Think of this image as you are introduced to the process of scaffolding learning experiences for children.

Scaffolding plays a significant role in how children learn. The scaffolding principle is often portrayed biologically at the synaptic level, with the brain being described as a very large and complex tree with billions of branches that are subdivided into more and more detailed layers of information. New information is most easily learned or stored when the person is able to connect the new information to one or more existing branches or twigs of information already in the system. Practitioners design learning experiences by adapting the scaffolding principle of nature in space design, in equipment and material placement, in the complexity of tasks, in the sequencing of experiences, in the timing of experiences, and so on.

Vygotsky indicated the practitioner's role is important during the scaffolding process. He suggested the need for practitioners to observe children's skills and determine the level of support children require. The scaffolding process requires practitioners to provide the right amount of support that children need to move to a higher level of learning. Bruner (1985), furthermore, suggests the scaffolding process should provide a stable structure that enables children to build new knowledge. The level or amount of assistance adults provide is gradually decreased as children acquire new knowledge, skills, and abilities necessary to perform a task independently and as they become more competent. Take, for example, a young child learning to sing a song. First, the child hears the song from the role model. Gradually,

> **Scaffolding**. A fundamental principle of nature whereby one concept is built upon a previous learning structure, thereby ensuring its stable integration into the learner's knowledge or skill base.

Building one piece of information upon another through scaffolding creates a solid foundation for additional learning.

he will sing a few words along with the role model. Over time, the child contributes more words. Then, the role model pauses at parts of the song where he sings. Then, he sings the song alone. He adds more and more words to his presentation of the song, while the adult gradually withdraws as the child exhibits the ability to complete the task independently. This example clearly illustrates how learning occurs through a scaffolding process.

The scaffolding process takes many forms, such as when adults give directions, pose questions that lead the child to work through a process, or provide cues or demonstrate potential uses of materials. Practitioners require an in-depth knowledge of when and how to scaffold learning experiences for children.

Intergenerational Relationships Influence Children's Learning

There are members of our community who, although usually not trained formally in early childhood, have learned the important nurturing practices and learning processes through their life experiences. We refer here of course to the elders in the community, our senior citizens. Seniors seem to be able to condense the essence of nurturing children and bring it to the forefront of their communications with them. For example, most seniors are probably not familiar with the term *scaffolding* but are usually well aware that children "learn when they are ready." As a result, they take this awareness to their interactions with children by projecting a gentle respectfulness. Many seniors have the capacity to draw children to them by simply accepting children for who they are and trusting that they will find their way in an appropriate manner. These seniors provide children with freedom to explore, discover, and wonder, and they convey to children their belief in them. Interactions between seniors and children can be insightful and amazing to behold.

As you observe those working and sharing time with children, notice the interaction between the adults and children. Remember your shared time with your grandparents or other seniors and what made that time special for you. These are important clues for your own work with children in your profession.

SUMMARY

Creating Supportive Environments

- Children require adults and role models to nurture them. Adults guide children in developing their knowledge and skills by creating developmentally appropriate environments that display respect for children and that ensure they are treated equitably.

Observation Informs Practice

- Early childhood practitioners become skilled observers, and these observations guide practitioners in creating environments and activities that build on each child's past learning, abilities, culture, and interests.
- Early childhood practitioners prepare, plan, select an observation method, collect data, conduct data analysis, implement data, and monitor those plans.

Being, Thinking, and Learning

- There are five levels of being, thinking, and learning that can be addressed by practitioners in their work with children: the behaviour level, the mental-strategy level, the belief level, the identity level, and the spirit level. Each level requires more in-depth exploration by the child, aided by the practitioner.

Guidelines for Practice

- There are seven guidelines for practice: respect children's innate self-esteem; honour children's unique curiosity; nurture children's need for movement; nurture children's need for challenging and supportive activities; recognize children's innate multi-sensory learning modalities; respect children's need to have choices; and honour children's need for scaffolding their learning experiences.

Intergenerational Relationships Influence Children's Learning

- Most senior citizens exhibit sophisticated nurturing and communication skills with children. These seniors provide children with freedom to discover and wonder, and their interactions with children can be very insightful and educational.

FURTHER OPPORTUNITIES FOR ENRICHMENT

Research

1. Examine the research to determine what is meant by developmentally appropriate practice. What constitutes a developmentally appropriate practice? Which areas of an early childhood service would you observe to determine if developmentally appropriate practices are being followed? Cite a minimum of four sources used to gather the information.
2. How do early childhood practitioners determine which observation method is most appropriate for the situation they wish to observe? Provide examples of typical observations that would be conducted when working with infants, toddlers, preschoolers, and school-aged children, and the most common observation methods used for data collection. Cite a minimum of three sources used to gather the information.

Group Investigation

1. Seven guidelines for practice are outlined in the chapter. In groups of four, visit an early childhood centre and discuss with a staff member how each of the seven guidelines is addressed. Share your findings with others in your learning community. Determine if there are one or more guidelines for practice that are easier to implement than others. Which are most challenging, and why?
2. Complete a survey with four different types of early childhood services to determine if they use seniors in their programs. How many have senior volunteers in their program on a daily or weekly basis? How many visit seniors in seniors' residences? How many seniors bring young children to the service? In your large learning community, determine if more seniors are involved in full-day or part-day programs. Why do you think there may be a difference in senior participation?

Making Connections

1. Creating supportive environments is essential for children. Using the seven guidelines presented, explore each of the "A Day Begins in an Early Childhood Setting" vignettes in Chapters 1, 2, and 3. Determine how Jennifer exhibits each of these guidelines in her approach to working with children.
2. You have been asked to present to parents in an early childhood service the importance of curiosity to children's learning. How would you plan your presentation so that parents would learn the information by having their curiosity triggered? Would you use the same principles as with children? Why or why not?

ADDITIONAL READING

Croall, J. (1983). *Neill of Summerhill—The Permanent Rebel*. New York: Pantheon Books.

Doxey, I. M. (1990). *Child Care and Education—Canadian Dimensions*. Scarborough, ON: Nelson Canada.

Glasser, W. (1998). *Choice Theory—A New Psychology of Personal Freedom*. New York: Harper Collins.

Labinowicz, E. (1980). *The Piaget Primer*. Don Mills, ON: Addison-Wesley Publishing Company.

Montessori, M. (1914). *Dr. Montessori's Own Handbook*. New York: Frederick Stokes.

Perry, B. (2001). Curiosity: The fuel of development. Available at teacher.scholastic.com/professional/bruceperry/curiosity.htm

WEBLINKS

www.discover.com/issues/sep-05: *Discover Magazine.*

www.froebel.com: *Friedrich Froebel.*

www.wglasser.com: *William Glasser.*

www.montessori-namta.org/NAMTA/geninfo/mmbio.html: *Maria Montessori.*

www.ncrel.org/sdrs/areas/issues/students/earlycld/ea51141a.htm: *Observation methods.*

www.piaget.org: *Jean Piaget.*

www.ncrel.org/sdrs/areas/stw_esys/5erly_ch.htm: *Professional practice.*

www.kolar.org/vygotsky: *Lev Vygotsky.*

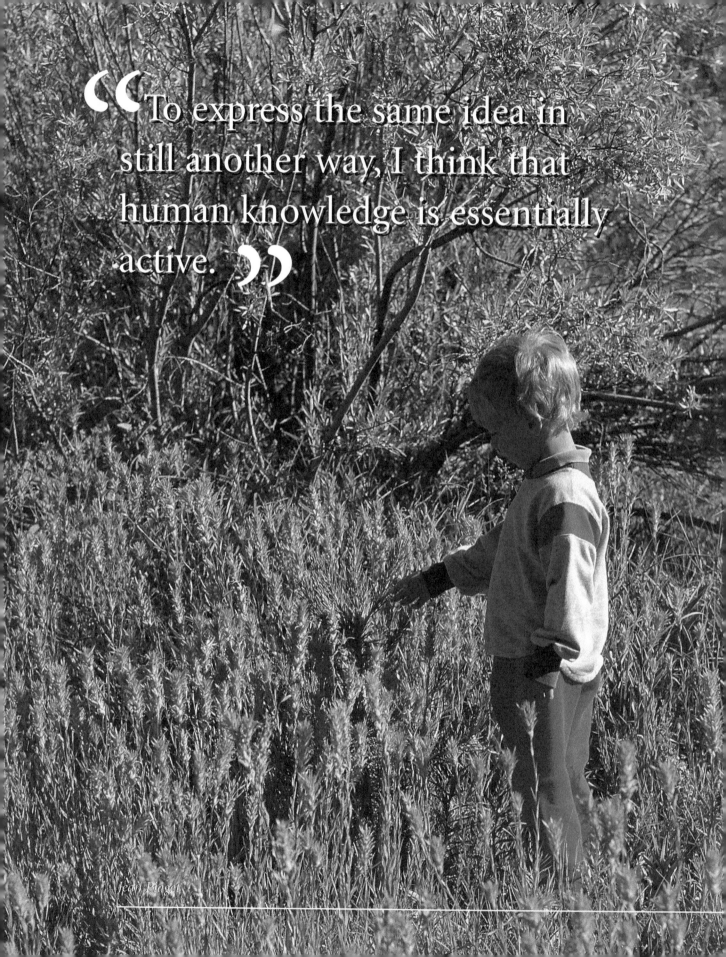

"To express the same idea in still another way, I think that human knowledge is essentially active.**"**

Jean Piaget

4

Learning Objectives

In this chapter you will:

1. Identify how and why developmentally appropriate practice guides the experiences, materials, and environment created for children.

2. Discuss why the learning process is considered multi-faceted.

3. Identify how a philosophical approach develops.

4. Discuss why early childhood practitioners examine established theories and program models.

5. Define *theory*.

6. Discuss how progressive-education, cognitive, maturational, multiple-intelligence, psychoanalytical/psychodynamic, and socio-cultural theories have influenced specific early childhood program models.

7. Describe the controversy surrounding the behaviourist theory approach in relation to developmentally appropriate practice.

8. Discuss how theories guide program models and practices.

How Theories Influence Program Models

A Day Begins in an Early Learning and Child Care Centre

Exploring Theorists and Program Models

Jennifer has three early childhood practitioner students visiting the program today. The purpose of Mandy, Sandi, and Burt's visit is to observe the children in their play and to link the program philosophy to theorists and program models studied. Jennifer enjoys meeting with student practitioners. She believes that being involved with student practitioners helps her think about how children learn and how the children's environment supports their learning. Student practitioners bring a new perspective—and this helps Jennifer think about her practices, reflect on her philosophy, and review the currency of her program.

After the students complete their observations, they pose a number of questions to Jennifer related to theories and programming models. For example, Mandy asks, "Please explain how theories such as John Dewey's have impacted your program for young children."

Jennifer responds. "Let me begin by saying that, as a team, we strive to honour the needs of the individual child first, followed by the needs of the group. Observing children in the environment and listening to them provides us with insight into potential experiences that may support their phase of development and their interests. We believe that when children feel good about themselves and the environment they are in, they are better able to communicate, co-operate, and share with others. We try to create a responsive environment that supports each child."

Jennifer then says, "We have taken an eclectic approach to our program rather than following one particular theory or program model. That is, we continuously examine theories and adopt principles and practices that align to our beliefs about how children learn. Taking an eclectic approach allows us to effectively adjust

No matter what the program model is, children require environments rich in play experiences.

programming strategies to accommodate children from various cultures and learning styles." She pauses and then says, "There are three theorists who have influenced our program design and implementation process. From your observations, let's discuss which three you think they might be and why. This discussion will help you see how theories inform practice."

Mandy, Sandi, and Burt think about this approach. Then Mandi says, "Is this one of the principles of working with children? You find out what they know, and then you guide them in ways that will help them build new information?"

Jennifer replies, "Yes. This helps the learner make connections and integrate new information with current knowledge. Well done for recognizing this process. This technique supports Dewey's philosophy that you "learn by doing."

Reggio Emilia program. A program originating in Italy that emphasizes children's relationships with families, peers, and community. The natural environment influences children's extensive use of project-based learning.

Montessori Program approach. Initially developed for children who were mentally handicapped, Maria Montessori's method requires teachers to conduct naturalistic observations and carefully prepare environments with experiences that become more complex and that are self-correcting.

Child-initiated approach. The experiences and program ideas evolve directly from children or as a result of observations the early childhood practitioners make of children during play.

Looking Ahead

In this chapter, we introduce you to how theories guide early learning and child care program models. Practitioners are constantly examining, through observation, the types of play experiences children participate in. How practitioners prepare the environment is often influenced by the theories that guide their practice. For example, in programs influenced by the **Reggio Emilia approach,** early childhood practitioners support children by participating in in-depth projects that might continue for several days or weeks. In programs using a **Montessori Program approach,** however, children's interactions with the materials are framed as work tasks, each of which has specific learning objectives for the children to achieve. Open-ended play may not be as available to children in a Montessori program as in a Reggio Emilia program.

Creating **child-initiated,** responsive play environments to meet children's needs is one of the most challenging aspects of the early childhood practitioner's responsibilities. Early childhood student practitioners require time and guidance to develop skills in observation and program design. Dialogue, observation, reflection, practice, evaluation, and refinement processes help practitioners to gain skills in planning appropriate child-initiated environments.

In the next sections, we will introduce you to a number of theorists and program models that guide and support early childhood practitioners in developing appropriate play environments for children. No matter which framework early childhood practitioners choose, they have a responsibility to devise an environment that supports the uniqueness and needs of the individual child through play experiences. Play is the central core of adapting to life and to learning.

Foundations of Early Learning and Child Care Programming

In "A Day Begins in an Early Learning and Child Care Setting," Jennifer identified that the foundation for programming is children, followed by the environment. She reminded us that theories, principles, and beliefs are continuously reviewed because they affect the approach to programming strategies. Like Jennifer, many programs use an **eclectic approach** to programming, while others follow one specific theoretical framework.

Eclectic approach. Combining aspects of different theories as a way to guide early learning and child care program design and delivery.

A Developmentally Appropriate Practice

When Jennifer indicated that children are the first focus for programming, she in essence was referring to what we call **developmentally appropriate practices (DAP).** Understanding developmentally appropriate practices is the first principle that guides our thinking about the experiences, materials, and environment created for children and with children. The National Association for the Education of Young Children (NAEYC) explains developmentally appropriate practice as understanding child development and using it as the foundation for planning experiences that are age- and skill-appropriate and that consider children's interests, abilities, and culture (Bredekamp & Copple, 1997). Developmentally appropriate practice requires early childhood practitioners to observe each child and to understand her individual phase of development. Bredekamp and Copple indicate children develop at their own pace. Each child brings his individual knowledge, personality, learning style, culture, diversity, and family values to the early childhood setting, and, as a result, early childhood practitioners must respond to the needs and interests of each child. For example, a younger child is more likely to require that dramatic play areas contain real, familiar objects, whereas a child nearing 4 years of age is able to substitute one item for another. And a 4-year-old child who has recently moved to Canada and has limited use of English for communication would require an early childhood practitioner to speak in clear, short sentences, to be in close proximity to the child, and to show the child the particular object that is being spoken about when giving instructions.

Developmentally appropriate practices. Programs designed based on child development and play.

Learning: A Multi-faceted Process

Learning is a multi-faceted process: children and adult interactions, family dynamics, the play environment, and the materials in that environment all influence play, which in turn affects learning. Play provides the venue for children to organize information, make connections with previous learning, identify relationships, and develop interconnections between current knowledge and new information.

Piaget (1962) and Vygotsky (1978) asserted that children's play experiences provide them with the foundation to actively construct knowledge and also provide them with the venue to stretch their usual levels of abilities (Hendrick & Weissman,

2006). While this view continues to guide programming principles today, providing play experiences does not guarantee that children will acquire the knowledge the adult intended. Rather, planning play experiences requires early childhood practitioners to systematically observe children during their play, ask questions of children to determine their thoughts and feelings, and collect samples of children's work to showcase their learning (McAfee & Leong, 2002). Then, practitioners can determine the types of new items that would provide intrigue, exploration, and wonderment for children. By observing and collecting data, early childhood practitioners determine the types of play materials and environmental factors that would support children's play episodes. The data also help in predicting short- and long-term play experiences that may support children's interests and their phase of development.

A Philosophical Approach

Philosophical approach. One's assumptions and understanding about how children's play, environment, and people in the environment support children's learning.

The program-planning process is guided by practitioners' beliefs or philosophy about how children learn. A **philosophical approach** is derived from a set of assumptions about how children's play supports learning and how the early childhood practitioner and the environment facilitate play and learning. A philosophical approach, as illustrated in Figure 4.1, springs from practitioners' understanding of theorists' perspectives on how children learn. For example, as you will note later in this chapter, John Dewey's progression movement influenced Waldorf programs to create environments that have a strong arts-based focus. Waldorf programs provide children with numerous opportunities to explore drama, art, and music. Other programs may focus less on art but emphasize more cognitively oriented experiences that enhance mathematical, language, and literacy skills.

Children learn through exploration. They explore their environment in many ways.

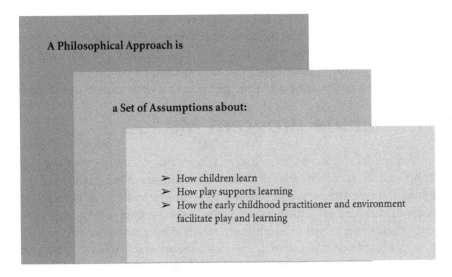

A Philosophical Approach is

a Set of Assumptions about:

➤ How children learn
➤ How play supports learning
➤ How the early childhood practitioner and environment facilitate play and learning

Figure 4.1 *Assumptions That Influence a Philosophical Approach*

The adoption of a theoretical perspective determines how the environment will be prepared and how play experiences will be planned and implemented. For example, let us say a practitioner places two large vacuum cleaner hoses in the dramatic-play centre. Suddenly, two children become interested in elephant trunks. The practitioner provides music that encourages the children to move like elephants, swaying their trunks back and forth. As the two children continue to explore elephants, the practitioner notices more children becoming intrigued with elephants. As a result, the practitioner supports the children's plan to stage an elephant parade on the bicycle path. The practitioner provides the children with clay to create elephants, wood pieces to help them make fences, blocks to lead them to construct park-like spaces for the elephants, and materials to make signs to tell others about elephants and the types of food they eat. When the children express an interest in making a large elephant for the play area, the practitioner explores with them how they could do it and supports them through the process over several weeks. One parent brings in a book about elephants, and another parent provides a poem about elephants. The interest in elephants extends into the children's play for several more weeks. Throughout the process, the practitioner and the children photograph the areas of exploration and learning. The children look at the pictures and tell the practitioner, the other children, and the parents about what they were doing when the photos were taken.

Early childhood programs that use such a project approach draw upon the theories of Jean Piaget and John Dewey and on program models such as Reggio Emilia. For example, Piaget indicated children require sequential experiences related to previous learning. In our example, the children become interested in the elephant and gain experience and knowledge; they generally expand the types of experiences they plan and the complexity of those experiences. First, the children might use replicas of elephants in their play and then wish to re-create them out of papier mâché. This sequence would support experiences moving from simple to more complex, and it illustrates how children build on their knowledge.

Children learn about their world by having opportunities to revisit experiences.

Children demonstrate Dewey's belief that they require in-depth investigation when they use resources such as books or ask questions about the types of food elephants eat or when they learn to walk with a trunk. And a long-term project process and input from parents support Reggio Emilia's beliefs that families and communities be actively involved in the projects that children are investigating.

Why Examine Program Models

A program model originates from a practitioner's understanding of the theories about how children learn and develop. Determining a programming model, organizing the environment, and developing a program plan that is responsive to the needs of children, practitioners, and families is a complex process. Regardless of the programming model used, children lead the program-plan and play-design process. As identified in Figure 4.2, early childhood practitioners consider many elements of children's development. They combine child development with their preferred program model philosophy when planning an environment for children.

Discussion about observations, what children should know, what skills they should have, how children learn and think (learning styles), strategies that facilitate learning, and ways to identify what children have learned (documentation) (McAfee & Leong, 2002) provide the clues to the future direction of program planning, which we will discuss in Chapter 7. The first step in determining a program model, however, is to examine the various theories that guide program models.

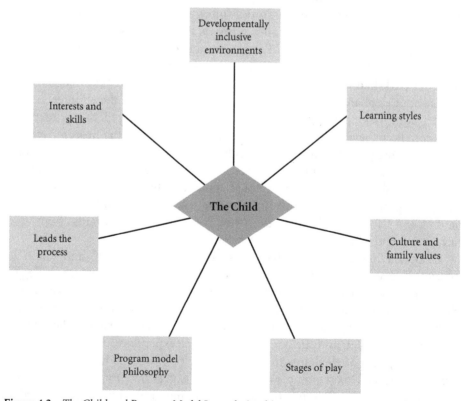

Figure 4.2 *The Child and Program Model Interrelationships*

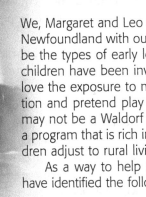

PARENTING PORTRAIT

We, Margaret and Leo Gandinice, are considering moving from Vancouver to rural Newfoundland with our 3-year-old twin daughters. One of the deciding factors will be the types of early learning and child care services available to our family. Our children have been involved in a Waldorf preschool since they turned 3, and we love the exposure to music, arts, and drama. We attribute our children's imagination and pretend play to their play experiences there. We understand that there may not be a Waldorf program in rural Newfoundland, but we are hoping to find a program that is rich in play, staffed by individuals who are willing to help our children adjust to rural living and who value some of our cultural traditions.

As a way to help us examine the early learning and child care programs, we have identified the following as essential to each facility we visit:

1. The program offers equal indoor and outdoor play experiences, where children are able to participate in outdoor experiences similar to those indoors, as well as providing active gross-motor play.
2. The program is one that offers children a rich play environment rather than one that is academically focused.
3. Teachers will accept each of our children as individuals rather than as "twins" and will accept and appreciate the children's Kenyan heritage.
4. Teachers have specialized training in early childhood studies, and the staff-to-child ratio is acceptable so that our children will receive adequate attention.
5. The environment promotes the children's creations rather than commercial products.

Our findings will help us make a decision about a new environment for our family.

Do you think that Margaret and Leo Gandinice's expectations are realistic? Can rural communities compete with urban communities in offering children and parents early learning and child care services? What skills and knowledge will early childhood practitioners in rural communities require to support the Gandinice's cultural diversity? What are the Gandinice's responsibilities to adjusting to moving from an urban community to a rural community, where most families have been established for several generations?

As you explore the theorists and program models, you will note that some theorists, and some approaches to program planning and implementation, may conflict with each other or with your beliefs. Reading about the theories and discussing them with each other helps you define your personal philosophy about how child's play and the environment facilitate learning.

Theories That Influence Program Models

Theories inform practice. A **theory** refers to a "collection of ideas, concepts, terms and statements blended to illustrate behavior" (Arce, 2000, p. 9). There are a number of theorists and theories that influence early learning and child care programs.

> **Theory.** As identified by Arce (2000), a theory is a collection of ideas, concepts, terms, and statements blended to illustrate behaviour.

Becoming familiar with the common theoretical perspectives helps you to understand how research is transferred to practice. Exploring theories also assists you in determining what you believe is best for children, how children learn, what an effective learning environment is, and what your role is in supporting children in their learning.

As a way to introduce you to the relationship of theorists to program models, Table 4.1 presents the work of six theorists who advocate a child developmental model, along with a brief overview of the program model that is most aligned to that theoretical perspective. Note how some program models draw upon a combination of theories and how some theorists have influenced the development of new program models. Think about how each theory guides program models and how program models support the way in which children's experiences are implemented. As you examine each of the theories, determine if one best matches your beliefs about how children learn, or which aspects from each theory best represent your beliefs.

Table 4.1 *Theorists and Program Model Influences*

Theorist and Perspective	Program Model	Key Influences
John Dewey Progressive Education	Waldorf	• Children learn by doing. • Activities planned according to children's needs, interests, and abilities; supports the development of the whole child.
Jean Piaget Cognitive	Creative Play High/Scope	• Children require "hands-on" experiences. • Environment set up with interest centres. • Emphasis on cognitive development.
Arnold Gesell Maturational	Montessori	• Experiences based on child's growth patterns and skills. • Continuous assessment. • Carefully prepared environment.
Howard Gardner Multiple Intelligences	Reggio Emilia	• Each person has nine different intelligences. • Emphasis on in-depth exploration of topics while collaborating with learning-community members.
Sigmund Freud **Erik Erikson** Psychoanalytical Psychodynamic	Bank Street	• All aspects of child development evident across the curriculum. • Curriculum evolves from the child. • Early life experiences positively or negatively affect future development.
Lev Vygotsky Socio-cultural Theory	Reggio Emilia	• Emphasis on the influence of community and culture, language, and play. • Child-centred project approach. • Children learn by constructing knowledge and layering ideas. • Adults stretch the knowledge base of children.

1. Progressive-Education Theory

John Dewey's (1859–1952) progressive movement began as an alternative to John B. Watson's (1878–1959) and B. F. Skinner's (1904–1990) **behaviourist theory,** which emphasizes extrinsic motivation through conditioned environments that use positive reinforcement, punishment, or ignoring the behaviour (Henniger, 2002) (see section on behaviourist theory later). Dewey believed learning and education should focus on the child and that learning experiences should integrate with daily living, preserve social values including culture, and involve interacting with peers and adults. Dewey also believed that children learn best by *doing* both physical and intellectual activities. Activities are planned, therefore, according to children's needs, interests, and abilities, and children's active involvement in the learning process is essential; children are intrinsically motivated.

Dewey's influence on how children learn is still evident in programs today. Integrated curriculum, active learning, project-based learning, child-directed learning, and group co-operative learning are credited to the progressive-education movement.

Program Models Influenced by This Theory
The Waldorf Program Approach. The **Waldorf Program approach** was developed by Rudolph Steiner (1861–1925) and influenced by the thinking of John Dewey. Steiner, like Dewey, believed that curriculum and experiences come from the children and that knowing children well is essential to planning a learning environment that supports children's whole development. Steiner suggested that an arts-based curriculum supports children's whole development, and so image, rhythm, movement, drawing, painting, poetry, and drama are core program components. Because of the arts-based experiences, attention to the environmental aesthetics is necessary. Children's appreciation of beauty and social environments promotes and strengthens interactions among children, peers, and adults. The symbolic conditions, such as stories and poetry, promote culture and influence children indirectly. When children connect with these attributes in their environment, their perceptive abilities and self-worth are enhanced. Play experiences come from children, for this is how they exhibit and build their sense of curiosity and creativity.

"Contrary to the thinking of many educators, Steiner pointed out that teachers do not provide experiences for students" (Driscoll & Nagel, 2005, p. 152). Adults provide the conditions, such as the materials, space, schedule, and options, but the children lead the program design and implementation.

2. Cognitive Developmental Theory

Jean Piaget (1896–1980) emphasized a **constructivist learning environment**. He emphasized that children require environments that allow them to be able to create their knowledge rather than receive it from teachers. Children build knowledge by having sequential experiences structured on previous experiences, and they need to repeat these experiences so that in-depth investigation and exploration

Progressive education. Coined by John Dewey, progressive education methods focus on the child. The learning experiences are integrated with daily living, they preserve social values including culture, and they are interactive with peers and adults.

Behaviourist theory. John B. Watson's theory emphasizes that children learn through behaviour-modification strategies. Learning and behaviour occur through responses and consequences.

Waldorf Program approach. This program approach emphasizes children's whole development. The program is arts-based, with a strong focus on image, rhythm, movement, drawing, painting, poetry, and drama.

Cognitive developmental theory. Jean Piaget maintained that children develop their intelligence by having interaction with their physical environment. Children take new knowledge and adapt it to their current knowledge. Piaget identified four stages of intellectual development: sensorimotor, preoperational, and concrete and formal operational.

Constructivist learning environment. Children develop knowledge from the experiences within the environment. The early childhood practitioner facilitates or guides the process of exploration, wonderment, and discovery.

leads to discovery. The adults guide or facilitate the process of discovery. Piaget identified four stages of intellectual development (Flavell, 1963); each individual goes through each stage at approximately the same age:

- **Sensorimotor intelligence** (birth to 18–24 months). Children learn about their world through sensory experiences and motor activity. The infant's sucking on her toy helps her learn through touch about things in her environment.

- **Preoperational intelligence** (18–24 months to 6–7 years). Children combine sensory experiences and motor movement with symbolic thinking. Children are egocentric during this phase, which interferes with their ability to see things from a perspective other than their own. Children find teasing is difficult to understand because they generally take things literally.

- **Concrete operational intelligence** (6–7 years to 12–13 years). Children begin to think logically and with a more critical perspective. They are now able to understand conservation—e.g., when given a ball of playdough they understand that the quantity remains constant whether the ball of playdough remains in a ball or is flattened.

- **Formal operational intelligence** (12–13 years through adulthood). During this phase, abstract and logical thinking develops, which allows children to engage in scientific investigation.

Piaget advocated children require learning environments that provide "hands-on" experiences with a variety of materials and objects to manipulate. For example, if children express an interest in the concepts of light and dark, the early childhood practitioner would offer many examples of colours that show the progression of light, lighter, and lightest, or dark, darker, and darkest. There would be options for children to explore mixing paints to achieve light and dark colours. Piaget also indicated that learning is a collaborative rather than a solitary experience, reinforcing the importance of learning communities both for children and adults. And he suggested that activities extend across the program, as this encourages children to make relationships and connections as they integrate new knowledge. For example, if children expressed an interest in crane machinery, an early childhood practitioner might place related books, paper, and writing tools in the block centre. The books provide them with a reference to the crane machinery. By examining the pictures, the children might decide to build a crane. They might need some type of string or wire to construct the crane; they might use the paper and writing tools to make signs that inform other children that they are entering a construction zone. Such play incorporates science, literacy, math, and creative arts.

Creative play. This program model encourages and supports children's play that facilitates development in six domains: personal awareness, emotional well-being, cognition, communication, socialization, and perceptual motor skills.

Program Models Influenced by This Theory

The Creative Play Curriculum. One of the newest curriculum approaches documented, the **creative play** curriculum was developed and implemented in 1985 at the University of Tennessee. This play-based, constructivist model "recognizes the importance of the development of creative individuals and the interrelatedness of developmental areas. The curriculum focuses on encouraging and supporting children's play to promote development in six domains: personal awareness, emotional well-being, cognition, communication, socialization, and perceptual motor skills" (Catron & Allen, 1999, p. 12).

The Cognitively Oriented Curriculum. Known as the **High/Scope program** model theoretical framework, developed by David Weikart, the cognitively oriented curriculum is grounded in the cognitive-development theory. This constructivist approach advocates that children learn best when they have experiences with people and objects in their environment. Similar to other programs, High/Scope stresses the development of the whole child, with an emphasis on cognitive development. Children are active learners through hands-on experiences, and they are active planners. The early childhood practitioner's primary role is to prepare an environment that provides materials and support for children in planning, experiencing, and reviewing their activities and experiences. This is described as the "plan, do, and review" process. The practitioners take an active role in asking questions that lead children to extend thinking and learning opportunities.

There are eight *key experiences* that are emphasized and that complement and guide the children's program (Hohmann & Weikart, 1995):

1. *Active listening*. Children initiate and carry out their desired tasks in the environment. Adults encourage children to use materials in a variety of ways in the environment.

2. *Language*. Oral and written language is emphasized through discussions with adults and children.

3. *Experiencing and representing*. Children are provided with opportunities to experiment and explore materials through their senses. Music, movement, art, and dramatic play are evident in the program.

4. *Classification*. Children are encouraged through small and large group dialogue to examine similarities and differences among objects.

5. *Seriation*. Children are encouraged to order objects from smallest to largest based on mathematical principles such as length, weight, and height.

6. *Number concepts*. Children are exposed to number concepts, such as "more than" and "less than."

7. *Spatial relationships*. Children explore concepts such as up/down, over/under, in/out, beside/back.

8. *Time*. Children learn about seasons, past and future events, and sequence of events.

3. Maturational Theory

G. Stanley Hall, Robert Havinghurst, and Arnold Gesell are known for their development of the **maturational theory**. Hall (1844–1924) advocated the need to observe and test large numbers of children as a way to identify the averages or types of behaviours

High/Scope approach.
A constructivist approach developed by Weikart, based on Piaget's cognitive development theory. Children construct knowledge through active learning, which broadens their cognitive and social skills.

Maturational theory.
The biological process that some theorists suggest is responsible for human development.

that are common among children at each age level. Hall's research led to the documentation of descriptive norms of children at "typical" phases of development.

Gesell (1880–1961) pursued studies on the observation of children. He recorded the changes observed as children develop, and he developed an array of assessment tools to determine the developmental patterns in childhood. He focused on 10 gradients of growth:

1. Motor characteristics: eyes, hands, and bodily activity.
2. Personal hygiene: health, eating patterns, sleeping cycles, elimination, personal hygiene, stress levels and releases.
3. Emotional expression: emotional expressions and attitudes, crying, assertive and aggressive processes.
4. Interpersonal relations: mother–child, peer-to-peer, and group play.
5. Fears and dreams: intensity of fears and dreams.
6. Self and sex: gender roles.
7. Play and pastimes: interests, arts, and culture.
8. School life: adjustment to school, interest in learning environment and curriculum.
9. Ethical understanding: sensitivity to others, response to direction and correction, ability to respond to praise and reason.
10. Philosophical outlook: beliefs and attitudes about time, space, and death (Gesell & Ilg, 1949).

Examining a child's developmental pattern continues to permeate early childhood programs today. Early childhood practitioners observe children of the same age to determine growth patterns and skills. For example, there may be two children of the same age in an early learning and child care program. One can ride a bicycle while the other child does not have sufficient balance to do so. The early childhood practitioner recognizes this through her observations and then plans a variety of balancing experiences that would support the child requiring further balance development. Gradually, the practitioner reintroduces the child to the bicycle. Programs guided by this perspective strongly advocate that children learn and develop according to their own internal maturational schedule.

Program Models Influenced by This Theory

Montessori Programs. The **Montessori programs** use the principles of the maturational theory. Through observations of children and research, Montessori identified that children pass through numerous "sensitive periods" during their developmental processes to adulthood. "She viewed these periods as genetically programmed blocks of time when young children are especially eager and able to master certain tasks" (Henniger, 2002, p. 102). For example, a toddler is interested in learning to dress herself and practises this skill daily. The adult ensures that the child has numerous opportunities to practise with materials that promote skills such as buttoning, unbuttoning, zipping and unzipping.

Montessori Program approach. Initially developed for mentally handicapped children, Maria Montessori's method requires teachers to conduct naturalistic observations and carefully prepare environments with experiences that become more complex and that are self-correcting.

During specific sensitive periods, children would interact with materials described as **work tasks**. Children are given the choice of materials that they wish to explore, and the adult demonstrates the sequential steps to be carried out when using the new material. Then, the children may use the materials, which focus on daily living, sensory, academic, or cultural and artistic experiences.

An example of a work task in a Montessori classroom is polishing shoes. On a child-sized tray, the adult organizes the buffing cloth, the polish, and the shoes. The adult demonstrates to the children what each cloth is for, how to open the polish, how to dip the cloth into the polish, how to apply the polish, how to buff the shoe and to reapply polish. Once the demonstration is complete, children may pursue the work task independently.

Montessori programs require adults to have specific training in this approach. An underpinning to this approach is that adults and children exhibit respect for one another and for their abilities and accomplishments.

Work tasks. Materials and experiences offered to children in Montessori programs that support children in learning about daily living, sensory, academic, cultural, and artistic domains.

4. Multiple Intelligences Theory

Howard Gardner (born in 1943) has devised the **multiple intelligences theory** (MI theory), using each developmental domain as the baseline. Gardner suggests that the best way to measure intelligence is by examining how individuals solve problems and create products within a naturalistic setting rather than from the results of intelligence tests.

Gardner (1999) describes nine different intelligences within each person:

1. *Linguistic intelligence.* This refers to the use of language in one's ability to read, write, and converse with others.

2. *Logical-mathematical intelligence.* This refers to one's logic and ability to use numbers, understand patterns, and complete mathematical formulas.

3. *Music intelligence.* This focuses on the ability to perform musically or to create music.

4. *Bodily-kinesthetic intelligence.* This refers to the ability to use one's body or parts of body for personal expression.

5. *Spatial intelligence.* This is the ability to create a visual image of an idea or project and then use that model to produce the item.

6. *Interpersonal intelligence.* This refers to the ability to work well with others, assume leadership roles, and communicate effectively.

7. *Intrapersonal intelligence.* This refers to having an understanding of one's own strengths and understanding which areas require further development.

8. *Naturalistic intelligence.* This intelligence is used to discriminate among living things, such as people, plants, and animals, as well other scientific issues that affect daily living.

Multiple intelligences theory. Howard Gardner's concept about the different ways people interact with the world. The nine intelligences include linguistic, logical-mathematical, musical, bodily-kinesthetic, spatial, interpersonal, intrapersonal, naturalistic, and existential.

Polishing shoes is an example of a child learning practical life skills.

9. *Existential intelligence.* This intelligence is the ability and proclivity to think about and ponder questions related to life, death, future, beliefs, and realities.

MI programming requires adults to know about children's abilities, interests, and accomplishments within each of the intelligences. Children's multiple intelligences are influenced by family, culture, and the learning community. The value placed on each of the intelligences affects the depth and level of development that children achieve.

As an example, building snowmen uses a variety of the multiple intelligences described above. First, an adult reads children a story about snowmen. After hearing the story, some children decide to make snowmen outdoors. They use sticks ands rocks to decorate the snowmen, they sing "Frosty the Snowman," and they dance around the snowmen. Throughout this process, children use aspects of the MI theory. For example, the children use their verbal skills in the discussion of how they are going to make the snowmen. They need to use spatial intelligence to think about the three-dimensional structure; they use bodily-kinesthetic skills when trying to manoeuvre the snowballs in the space available; they use logical-mathematical intelligence in judging the size of the snowballs needed. And they use musical intelligence when they sing and dance around the snowmen. The naturalistic intelligence may be triggered days later when the consistency of the snow changes and the children try to make more snowmen. Through discussion, the children will learn about how the consistency of snow is influenced by the temperature and humidity. Early childhood programs using the MI theory to guide children's learning have diverse choices of experiences that focus on each of the nine areas of intelligence. Hands-on experiences help children learn in these different formats.

Program Models Influenced by This Theory

The Reggio Emilia Program. This philosophy draws upon a number of theories for its base. Howard Gardner's theory of multiple intelligences is evident in the principle that the "environment as teacher" influences the organization of space; relationships; aesthetics; promoting choices and decisions about how to execute projects; and partnerships among children, adults, and families. As well, this theory is evident in the principle that learning options support culture, values, and children's life experiences. Further discussion on the Reggio Emilia program is outlined under Lev Vygotsky's concept of social construction of knowledge.

5. Psychoanalytical/Psychodynamic Theory

Sigmund Freud (1856–1939) described child development and behaviour from an emotional and personality perspective. He indicated that people are influenced by their early life experiences in fundamental ways that can positively or negatively affect future development. Early life experiences shape people's lives and may stay with them for their entire lives.

Erik Erikson (1902–1994) expanded Freud's work. He examined child development from a personality-development perspective, and, as Figure 4.3 illustrates,

Psychoanalytical/Psychodynamic theory. Erik Erikson's theory that children develop cognitively and socially simultaneously. There are eight psychosocial stages of development: trust versus mistrust, autonomy versus shame and doubt, initiative versus guilt, industry versus inferiority, identity versus identity confusion, intimacy versus isolation, generativity versus stagnation, integrity versus despair.

he determined eight psychosocial stages of development. Each person must resolve the identity crisis or task at each stage before she is able to effectively move to the next phase of development.

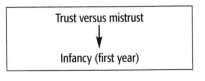

Trust versus mistrust (birth to 1 year). Infants are dependent on adults to meet their needs. When adults respond to infants' needs consistently, trust develops. When adults do not respond consistently, mistrust develops. A loving, nurturing environment is essential for building trust; otherwise, a sense of mistrust occurs.

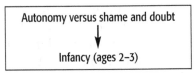

Autonomy versus shame and doubt (ages 2 to 3). Toddlers begin to test their independence by trying to carry out tasks without adult intervention. To master this, toddlers require a supportive environment that allows for the new independence to be tried and accomplished. Toddlers require approval from adults or shame and doubt develop.

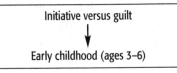

Initiative versus guilt (ages 3 to 6). Preschool children now begin to plan and implement activities and actions. Their sense of curiosity leads them to develop ideas and actualize plans. Initiative is developed in environments where exploration is encouraged and children's curiosity is appreciated. Adults ensure the environment is safe and offer security. If children are consistently unable to act upon their curiosity or if the results are negative, they will develop guilt and their sense of risk taking will be reduced.

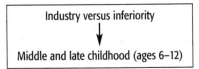

Industry versus inferiority (ages 6 to 12). During this phase, children learn the rules and expectations of society. They become productive members of society as they master skills and complete assignments. Children who gain success with their academic performance learn that industry is positive, and this is reflected in their self-concept. Those who consistently fail, however, develop feelings of inferiority.

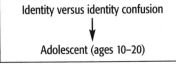

Identity versus identity confusion (ages 10 to 20). During this phase, children and adolescents are exploring who they are, what they are all about, and what direction their lives will take. They are confronted with new roles and romance. Children who are given the freedom to explore these new roles and life gain a healthy attitude about who they are. If not positively defined, identify confusion prevails.

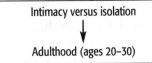

Intimacy versus isolation (ages 20 to 30). During this phase individuals form intimate relationships with others. Young adults who are able to form healthy friendships and relationships will be able to achieve intimacy. Those who do not meet this stage will feel isolated from society.

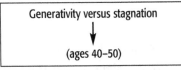

Generativity versus stagnation (ages 40 to 50). During this phase individuals begin to assist members of the younger generation in developing productive lives. Those who do not have the opportunity or do not take the opportunity to assist the next generation will experience stagnation.

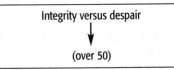

Integrity versus despair (over 50). During this phase individuals reflect on the past and on the successes or failures of their lives. For those who experience comfort and satisfaction with life, integrity is achieved. For those who think of their life as negative, gloom and despair is felt.

Figure 4.3 *Erikson's Lifespan Stages*

Being familiar with each of these stages helps to support children in resolving the crisis successfully. When a child resolves the crisis or task at each phase, she is able to see the world in a positive light, which leads to the development of a healthy personality, active participation in the environment, and socialization within the family and community (Erikson, 1968). A child who does not reach a resolution at each phase requires intervention strategies that are dependent on the child's needs.

The Program Model Influenced by This Theory

Bank Street model.
This program model, based on the work of Lucy Mitchell and Barbara Biber, emphasizes the need for children to have learning environments that support autonomy, expand knowledge, and develop self-concept and interpersonal skills.

The Bank Street Model. Originally initiated by Lucy Mitchell and developed further by Barbara Biber, the **Bank Street program model** has the underpinnings of three theoretical perspectives (Mitchell & David, 1992). Erikson's psychoanalytic theory emphasizes the child's psychological, social, and emotional development. Piaget's cognitive-developmental theory guides the intellectual component of the Bank Street curriculum. And the progressive-education theoretical perspective guides the social-learning experiences and values associated with active learning.

The Bank Street model emphasizes the need for children to have age-appropriate materials. The learning environment is designed to support the following:

- *Autonomy.* Children are encouraged to explore and manipulate the materials in the environment, based on their interests.
- *Expansion of knowledge.* Children expand their knowledge by cognitively incorporating and building on previous play experiences.
- *Development of self-concept.* The environment and the people in the environment promote respect and competence.
- *Interpersonal communication.* Children are encouraged to manage conflict and mutually support the interaction among peers and adults.

This child-initiated approach requires the program to evolve from continuously studying children rather than having a planned, prescribed curriculum. The success of this methodology is dependent on the practitioners' "knowledge and ability to recognize and skillfully respond to the individuality of each child and his or her interests" (Franklin & Biber, 1977, p. 26). The environment is arranged in learning centres. The practitioners act as role models and coaches in skill development and exploration. This model includes aspects of the constructivist principles.

6. Socio-cultural Theory

Socio-cultural theory.
Lev Vygotsky's theory suggests that children's mental, social, and language development are influenced by interactions with other children, peers, and adults.

Lev Vygotsky (1896–1934) emphasized the influence of community and culture on children's development, the role of language in developing higher-order thinking, and the importance of play for social development.

Vygotsky's theory advocates that play be the focus for both preschool and primary-grade environments. He suggested that mixed-age groups also have advantages for children. For example, when children between the ages of 4 and 6 are in the same learning environment, learning is enriched when children obtain assistance or participate in the more advanced play that evolves when children with different skill levels become partners in play.

Vygotsky identified that children learn by constructing knowledge and layering ideas through their cultural and social experiences. This requires adults to stretch the knowledge base of children, described as the zone of proximal development, as we mentioned in Chapter 3. Vygotsky (1978) described this as "the distance between the actual developmental level as determined by independent problem solving and the level of potential development as determined through problem solving under adult guidance or in collaboration with more capable peers" (p. 86). Children's play requires a higher functioning level than in other areas of daily living. Quality play-experiences require children to communicate, discuss, negotiate, and problem solve collaboratively, thereby enhancing language development and acquisition.

Program Models Influenced by This Theory

Reggio Emilia Programming Approach. This program model incorporates aspects of Lev Vygotsky's concept of social construction of knowledge. It also includes Jean Piaget's theory of cognitive development, Howard Gardner's theory of multiple intelligences, and John Dewey's perspective on progressive education (Berk & Winsler, 1995). Followers of the Reggio approach emphasize that programming needs to focus on "things about children and for children and are only learned from children" (Edwards, Gandini, & Forman, 1993, pp. 43–44). Culture, building on community resources, and parental involvement are essential. The "environment as a teacher" influences children's daily ideas and experiences, aesthetics both indoors and out, choices, and extensive use of project-based learning. The child-centred curriculum, the spirit of collaboration between adults and children in discovery and cognitive stimulation, as well as family involvement, are key tenets to this approach. The environment is prepared as a discovery-oriented place of learning (Henniger, 2002, p. 82).

The project approach to programming encourages children to engage in in-depth investigations of topics of interest to both children and practitioners. Practitioners and children work together to document children's learning through a variety of mediums, such as conversations, photographs, and artwork.

Reggio Emilia practitioners are partners with children and parents in the program design and implementation process. Observations and communication with children and parents provide data for program direction.

The Behaviourist Theory Approach

Each of the theorists presented above advocates a developmental approach to early learning and child care programming. Another theory that deserves mention is known as the behaviourist theory. John B. Watson (1878–1959) is recognized as being the leader in the development of this theory, which is based on a behaviour-modification method. Learning and behaviour occur through responses and consequences. The frequency of the preferred

When children initiate their own play, it has a level of meaning and learning that is important to them.

behaviour is increased when reinforcement is immediately provided. For example, if an early childhood practitioner is interested in increasing the frequency of a child's placing her coat in her locker, then she is rewarded the first time she does so. The rewards continue until the new behaviour is established. Then, gradually, the reinforcement is reduced. Skinner suggested that behaviours are encouraged or eliminated through conditioned environments, using positive reinforcement, punishment, or ignoring the behaviour (Kameenui & Darch, 1995). Learning theorists who use this approach indicate that it is particularly useful for children who have behaviourial challenges or disabilities (McLean, Wolery, & Bailey, 2004; Berkson, 1993).

From a developmental perspective, this theory does not have a place in early learning and child care settings because its basic premise limits developmentally appropriate practices (Henniger, 2002). However, Hendrick and Weissman (2006) suggest that our interactions with children, such as our smiles or frowns or the positive and negative attention we give to children, either encourage or discourage future behaviour, all of which is behaviourist-theory related. They caution that our behaviours with children require monitoring because "all teachers use [behaviour-modification] techniques constantly and extensively whether they realize it or not" (p. 14). Before "blindly condemning such theory, why not become aware of how often we employ such strategies on an informal basis" (p. 14).

Let's look at two examples: the first examines how a child is guided using a behaviour-modification method, while the second explores how a child is guided using a developmentally appropriate model. Think about early childhood programs that choose to allow a "time-out chair" with children. This method is a form of behaviour modification. Children are required to sit on a chair for a specific amount of time and are not allowed to have any contact with others. The thought is that by removing children from the situation they will think about their behaviour and adjust it so as not to be removed from the group. Many suggest that there are numerous ramifications for children's self-esteem, with the potential for long-lasting feelings of humiliation and shame.

Programs advocating developmentally appropriate practices, on the other hand, take a different tactic. The "time-out chair" is not used. Instead, early childhood practitioners concentrate on using positive child-guidance techniques. Using a kind but firm voice, they would indicate to the child that the behaviour is unacceptable. If the behaviour continues, through observation, the practitioner would examine the child's environment to determine trigger patterns for the behaviour. The level of stimulation the child is receiving, the child's interests, and changes to routine or family situations would be examined. Adjustments to the environment and play experiences would be made accordingly, until the child regains equilibrium in the environment.

Conversation Café

As Canada carves a national early childhood program, do we need a standardized program? Should we adapt one program model? If so, which program model would best suit Canada's multicultural society? Who decides? If there is one program model, is there a need to study other theorists who have contributed to early childhood? What is your opinion? Why?

Linking Theories to Programming

There are common themes among theorists. For example, they all tend to agree that humans develop in a gradual, sequential pattern and that individuals have their own timetable for their developmental process. They agree that no two children develop in the same way or at the same rate. They highlight play as the foundation for learning, and they indicate that play experiences should be consistent with children's interests and developmental stage, and rich in exploration and experimentation.

Theories provide the research about how children learn. Program models offer a framework to guide program planning and implementation. As new research evolves about how children learn, it is advantageous to examine that research to determine if the new information requires practitioners to adjust their thoughts and feelings about how children learn. Some early childhood practitioners will work in settings with a defined program model, such as Montessori or High/Scope. Others will seek employment in a program using an eclectic approach, where practitioners incorporate aspects of a number of theories into their program design.

A number of theorists and program models influence how play experiences are designed and implemented with children. Whichever model you follow, it is essential that it be based on child development and developmentally appropriate practice, and that it display an appreciation of diversity and high quality.

Points to Ponder

What are the advantages and the disadvantages of following a specific program model rather than taking an eclectic approach to programming?

SUMMARY

Foundations of Early Learning and Child Care Programming

- Developmentally appropriate practices guide early childhood practitioners in the experiences, materials, and environments created for children. Practitioners require an understanding of child development so that they may observe a child's phase of development and prepare an environment that supports the interests and needs of that child.
- Learning is a multi-faceted process. Adults, the environment, and play experiences provide the venue for children to learn to organize information, make connections with previous learning, and integrate current knowledge with new information.
- The program-planning process is influenced by theoretical perspectives, program models, and practitioners' philosophical approaches, which are derived from a set of assumptions about how children learn and develop.

Why Examine Program Models

- A program model originates from a practitioner's understanding of the theories of how children learn and develop.
- Children lead the program-planning and play-design process. Early childhood practitioners use their interpretation of a program model or models to observe children, determine which skills and knowledge children should have, examine how children learn and think, and determine strategies to document what children have learned.
- Understanding theories and program models helps early childhood practitioners connect theory to practice.

Theories That Influence Programming Models

- The progressive-education movement of John Dewey influenced the Waldorf program model.
- The cognitive-developmental theory of Jean Piaget influenced the Creative Play and the High/Scope program models.
- The maturational theory developed by Hall, Havinghurst, and Gesell influenced how Montessori programs are structured.
- The multiple-intelligences theory supports the Reggio Emilia program philosophy approach.
- The psychoanalytical/psychodynamic theory developed by Sigmund Freud and later expanded by Erik Erikson is reflected in the Bank Street model.
- The socio-cultural theory devised by Lev Vygotsky is evident in the Reggio Emilia program approach.

- John B. Watson developed the behaviourist theory. Some suggest that this theoretical model limits developmentally appropriate practice.

Linking Theories to Practice

- Theories inform practice. Some program models draw upon a combination of theories, while others have influenced the development of new program models. For example the creative-play curriculum model developed at the University of Tennessee, Knoxville, is based on Piaget's theory of development.
- Some early childhood programs follow a specific program model. Others use an eclectic approach, where aspects of a number of theories are incorporated into the program design.

FURTHER OPPORTUNITIES FOR ENRICHMENT

Research

1. Choose either a theorist or a program model outlined in this chapter to conduct further investigation. Are there areas of your investigation that intrigue you? Are there areas that you are still trying to explore? Are there elements that you believe require further investigation? Are there components that are now dated and don't fit within our society? Cite four sources for your research.
2. Many theorists identify that children should be the primary program-planners. Conduct further information on what *child-initiated* means. What is the role of early childhood practitioners in programs that use a child-initiated process for program design?
3. At the beginning of the chapter, we introduced you to the concept of developmentally appropriate practice. Conduct further research to determine what developmentally appropriate practice means to you and how it might impact your practice.

Group Investigation

1. Visit two early learning and child care services. Determine through observations and discussions with staff if and how a particular theorist has influenced their program model. Determine which elements of the service are directly linked to a particular theorist. How does this affect their practice? Share your responses with members of your learning community.

Making Connections

1. Why do early childhood practitioners study program models and theories? How does this knowledge affect how you work with children? Justify your answer.
2. In preparation for Margaret and Leo Gandinice's visit to your centre, what type of investigation and research would you do prior to the visit and before the children join you? If the children do come to your centre, how might their background influence their knowledge, vocabulary, and skills?
3. If you had an opportunity to work in any of the program models described, which would you be more likely to pursue? Why? What attracts you to that model? What might your role as an early childhood practitioner be in that setting?
4. You begin your placement and the early childhood practitioner indicates that next week's planned unit is "space." You are asked to plan three activities. Do you think this is appropriate? Why or why not? How would you proceed?

ADDITIONAL READING

Curtis, D. & Carter, M. (1996). *Reflecting Children's Lives. A Handbook for Planning Child-centered Curriculum*. St. Paul, MN: Redleaf.

Edwards, C., Gandini, L., & Forman, G. (1998). *The Hundred Languages of Children: The Reggio Emilia Approach—Advanced Reflections*. Greenwich, CT: Ablex.

Shipley, D. (2002). *Empowering Children: Play-based Curriculum for Lifelong Learning*. (3rd ed.). Scarborough, ON: Nelson.

WEBLINKS

www.ThomasArmstrong.com: *Fields of multiple intelligences.*

www.naeyc.org/resources/eyly/1998/05.htm: *National Association for the Education of Young Children—Guidelines for Developmentally Appropriate Practices.*

www.rlc.dcccd.edu/mathsci/anth/p101/dvlmentl/erikson.htm: *The developmental psychology of Erik Erikson.*

www.factsinaction.org/: *Facts in Action, Associated Early Care and Education.*

www.naeyc.org: *National Association for the Development of Young Children—developmentally appropriate practice in 2005.*

"You are worried about seeing him spend his early years in doing nothing. What! Is it nothing to be happy? Nothing to skip, play, and run around all day long? Never in his life will he be so busy again. "

Jean-Jacques Rousseau, *Emile, 1762*

5

The Power of Play

A Day Begins in an Early Learning and Child Care Centre

The Importance of Play

It is a usual February morning: children are engaged in various centres; some are involved with group explorations, while others are involved in creative play experiences that children initiate. Jamie is working on his own, constructing a winding roadway system with the unit blocks. He uses the car accessories as a way to travel along the road.

Jennifer has been observing Jamie construct the roadway. As Jamie starts using the cars on the highway, Jennifer approaches him and says, "This is a great three-lane highway. I like the curves, the bridges, and the hills. Where does this highway lead to?"

Jamie turns to Jennifer and says, "Moncton. Just outside Moncton." Then he says, "Hey, Jennifer, have you been fired before?" "No," responds Jennifer.

Suddenly, Jamie leaves the area and moves swiftly to the dramatic centre. He immediately picks up the telephone and dials a telephone number. He makes the sound of the telephone ringing. Stephen, a child exploring in the science and technology centre, picks up the telephone and says, "Hello." Jamie says, "Stephen, come quick."

Stephen immediately moves to the dramatic centre. Jamie points Stephen to a chair and says, "Sit at the table and have some coffee." As soon as Stephen sits down, Jamie, standing beside Stephen, says, "I got fired yesterday because I smashed the truck." Stephen says, "That is all right, Jamie. You will find another driver job." "But I have no money now," replies Jamie. "Oh," responds Stephen. Then Stephen says, "I have to go now."

Later that morning, Jamie's father arrives at the preschool and informs them that Jamie will not be returning to the preschool because his father has lost his job and the family cannot afford to pay the preschool fees.

As Jennifer reflects on the morning, she is reminded of the power of play. She realizes that play has given Jamie the venue to explore and learn about being fired.

Looking Ahead

In this chapter, we introduce you to the relationship of play to children's development and learning. We explore the process and challenges of attempting to define *play* and we outline the characteristics and stages of play. As well, we highlight the play process and ways of classifying play experiences. Then, we discuss the roles of early childhood practitioners in promoting play, including levels of play, how attitudes affect play, how observation guides practice, and the relationship of the environment to play. We conclude by outlining quality indicators for safe play spaces.

Setting the Stage

Understanding the relationship of play to child development and knowing how to develop and facilitate play opportunities that support the uniqueness of each child is a complex process. Practitioners require knowledge and skills in understanding play, observing play, and creating opportunities for play experiences that support children in having a balance of child-initiated play and practitioner-supported play. Jamie, for example, in the opening vignette, initiated his play. He used it as one of his venues to work through the stress in his family setting due to his father's loss of work. Jennifer's role as an early childhood practitioner was to provide Jamie with the environment and opportunity for play. This helped him deal with the stress that he, as part of the family, was feeling. Jamie's play reinforced to Jennifer how play supports a child's development. If Jamie had remained at the preschool centre, she might have initiated opportunities for Jamie to participate in more complex play as a way to support him in working through the stressful family event.

A well-planned environment provides children with a variety of options for their play.

Dramatic play supports children in exploring a variety of roles and their culture, while expanding their use of imagination.

In any developmentally appropriate program, children are the centre of the program. Child's play is the "central force in young children's development" (Van Hoorn et al., 2003, p. 3) and is enriched by various experience-centres in an early learning and child care setting. Throughout this book, we emphasize how play is the centre of enriching and supporting children's development and is, therefore, a key focus in this and upcoming chapters. Understanding the relationship of play to learning will assist you in planning developmentally appropriate programs for children.

Defining *Play*

Discussions about the meaning of play, the definition of play, and transferring the tenets of play to practice have long been presented in the early childhood literature. According to Van Hoorn et al. (1999), Froebel identified that children learn and develop through play. He advocated for early childhood curriculum to be play-focused and for play experiences to occur both indoors and out. But what is play?

Henniger (2002) indicates that the term *play* is difficult to define for many reasons. Play encompasses a variety of activities—from digging in the mud to building elaborate forts to making up silly stories. And each play experience engages children in different ways. Because there are no specific definitions, to help you begin to understand *play* we examine five perspectives on play from well-known early childhood theorists.

- "Play is the purest, the most spiritual, product of man at this stage and is at once the prefiguration and imitation of the total human life—of the inner, secret, natural life in man and in all things. It produces, therefore, joy, freedom, satisfaction, repose within and without, and peace with the world. The springs of all good rest within it and go out from it" (Froebel, 1889, p. 25).

- "When man plays he must intermingle with things and people in a similarly uninvolved and light fashion. He must do something which he has chosen to do without being compelled by urgent interests or impelled by strong passion. He must feel entertained and free of any fear or hope of serious consequences. He is on vacation from social and economic reality—or as is most commonly emphasized: *he does not work*" (Erikson, 1963, p. 212).

- "Play is the fundamental means by which children gather and process information, learn new skills, and practice old ones" (Spodek, 1986).

- "I believe that play is as fundamental a human disposition as loving and working" (Elkind, 2004, p. 36).

- "Through play, children learn about cultural norms and expectations, discover the workings of the world, and negotiate their way through their surroundings" (Klein, Wirth, & Linas, 2003, p. 38).

There is no one perspective that encapsulates the importance, the scope, or the complexities of play. However, by examining each perspective presented, you are able to gain insight into the breadth of opinions that exist about what play is and why children need play. These various perspectives suggest that the concept of *play* is complicated, yet it is the foundation of child development.

The Importance of Play to Development

Early childhood practitioners are constantly searching for the meaning of child's play. How practitioners interpret child's play influences and guides their practice. For example, we describe *play* as "nature's instrument to support a child's learning and development." This statement suggests that children want to play, and play fosters all aspects of development: social, emotional, cognitive, physical, and linguistic. Child's play, therefore, influences development in a profound and dramatic manner.

Understanding child's play is vital to valuing the role of an early childhood practitioner. Play is so important and intertwined in the development of children that the child's right to play is recognized in Article 31 of the United Nations Convention on the Rights of the Child. Canada ratified the Convention on the Rights of the Child on December 13, 1991.

Let's examine how play supports development. Play supports children's cognitive skills; it enhances social and emotional development; it increases children's physical development; and play increases creativity.

Cognitive-Skills Development

Representation skills.
Being able to examine an object and understand its use, and to use one object to represent another.

Play supports cognitive skills, such as language and literacy, mathematics, and the arts. Piaget, Vygotsky, and Bruner indicated that children develop their **representation skills** through play. Representation skills are essential for envisioning ideas, solving problems, and creating. For example, three children are attempting to build a fort out of cardboard and wood pieces. To do this, the children explore their knowledge about forts, internalize the information, and proceed with building. Throughout the process, as the children use their creativity they are also required to solve construction problems related to balance, symmetry, and weight. Much of the building process requires the children to use their language and social skills. As the early childhood practitioner engages in discussions with the children, he will introduce them to new words and to meanings of words related to forts as well as to the mathematical and scientific principles required for successful construction.

Social and Emotional Development

Play enhances children's social and emotional development, including self-esteem, empathy, co-operation, and respect for one another. Think of the children building the fort. They will negotiate, interact, and learn about acceptable rules, social interaction, and behaviour. In order to accomplish the construction project, the children will learn to assert their rights, accommodate the ideas of others, learn the art of compromising, and deal with anxiety, frustration, or conflict—all of which are important attributes for life. As the children participate in the process of constructing the fort, there are numerous opportunities for them to develop their feelings of worth.

Physical Development

Play provides the setting for physical development, such as balance, coordination, and muscle enhancement. Active play requires children to run, jump, roll, climb, twirl, stretch, and skip. In our previous example, as the three children built the fort, they used fine and gross motor skills. Running to fetch the large boards, carrying the large boards back to the construction site, climbing on platforms, and stretching to place each board increased the children's physical development.

Creativity Development

Play increases creativity. Singer (1973) and Singer and Singer (1980, 1985) indicate that through play children develop their imaginative thinking. As our three children constructed their fort, they were required to examine and use a variety of alternative plans. First, they tried to use a combination of cardboard and boards. Then, they replaced the cardboard with pieces of plywood. Weeks later, they brought the cardboard to their play area to be used for constructing the turrets on castles.

Child's play is often misunderstood and regarded as unimportant. Hendrick and Weissman (2006) indicate that "despite increasing evidence that play is the serious business of young children and that the opportunity to play freely is vital to their healthy development, early childhood teachers find that many administrators and parents continue to misunderstand and underestimate the importance of play in the lives of children" (p. 50). Activities and experiences that support academic skills are often more highly accepted, despite ongoing research that identifies "guided play opportunities that are based in the child's learning and interests are the most effective pedagogy for young children. Play is instrumental in setting the foundation for later academic achievement, social competence and emotional competence" (Cooke, Keating, & McColm, 2004, p. 14).

Play opportunities have been gradually downgraded and considered a privilege or a treat for children (Henniger, 2002). For example, early childhood practitioners who fall into the trap of focusing on academic skills as a way to prepare children for kindergarten may find themselves indicating to a child, "after you complete your printing you may play." In a developmentally appropriate program, children would be encouraged to print by making signs or notices conducive to their play. Rather than replacing the rich play experiences by activities that emphasize academic skills, early childhood practitioners incorporate the skills into play. For example, the three children making the fort would be encouraged to make a sign to place near the construction that read "Caution, Fort under Construction." When the focus of play is replaced with the completion of structured, academic activities, this shift contributes to custodial care at best in our Canadian early childhood programs (Coffey & McCain, 2004).

Features and Characteristics of Child's Play

Practitioners, researchers, and historians have long recognized the importance of play to children's development (Van Hoorn et al., 2003). Children require environments that are rich with play experiences and that support each developmental domain. Early childhood practitioners and children create places to play, fostered by materials and interaction among children and adults. Opportunities for spontaneous play, guided play, exploratory play, and child–practitioner partners in play are essential features within the play environment.

Three Unique Features

Many theorists who have studied play, and other theorists who have researched learning, indicate that there are unique features of child's play (Monighan-Nourot et al., 1987), as shown in Figure 5.1.

Intrinsic Motivation   When children are engaged in meaningful play, they exhibit energy, enthusiasm, and interest in exploring new ideas. The ideas and direction for play come from the child, and the satisfaction of success from the play evolves from within the child. For example, after a visit to the CN Tower, Ali becomes intrigued with towers. She decides to replicate towers in her block play. The practitioner might observe towers in her painting and might also see her use clay to construct other tall towers. Ali might work for several weeks perfecting her images of towers and learning many things about the construction and use of towers.

Active Engagement   Through child's play, children expand their use of language, their problem solving, and social interaction. Children demonstrate their attention to detail and their focus in quality play experiences. For example, as Ali

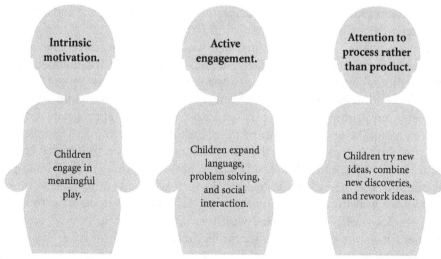

Figure 5.1   *Unique Features of Child's Play*

explores towers, the practitioner will note new words that she is expressing, such as expansive, peaks, symmetry, interior, exterior, and so on. And the practitioner might also see how she uses books and people in her environment to acquire the information necessary to get her towers to remain standing.

Attention to Process Rather than Product   Children's play is the venue for participating in the process of trying new ideas, combining new discoveries with current knowledge, and reworking ideas. Creating a visible product is secondary to the play process. Ali, for example, is more focused on learning about the science of building the towers and having them remain standing than on an actual finished product.

Points to Ponder

You have been asked to define *play* for a group of parents in an early learning and child care centre. How would you define it?

Now that you have become familiar with some perspectives on play and on how play influences children's development, we will provide an overview of the characteristics of play.

Characteristics of Play

Understanding the various perspectives on play provides a framework for appreciating the relationship of child's play to development. Henniger (2002) indicates that the foundation of play can best be understood by identifying the six common characteristics of play, which Henniger (2002) and Jalongo and Isenberg (2004) identify (see Figure 5.2).

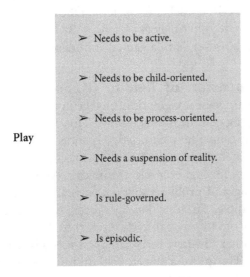

Play

➤ Needs to be active.

➤ Needs to be child-oriented.

➤ Needs to be process-oriented.

➤ Needs a suspension of reality.

➤ Is rule-governed.

➤ Is episodic.

Figure 5.2   *Characteristics of Play*

Active play leads children to develop interpersonal skills while increasing their physical development.

Play Needs to Be Active (Henniger, 2002) Children require environments that encourage them to use their bodies and materials from their environment. Children are engaged in constructing knowledge through exploration, dialogue, and interaction among peers, adults, and things (Chaille & Silvern, 1996). For example, in the case of the children building the fort, we identified how the process of building the fort supported each developmental domain. Active lifestyles, as established through rich play, are essential to the development of healthy children. Sedentary play leads to obesity and other health and development issues.

Play Needs to Be Child-Initiated (Henniger, 2002) Children require opportunities to choose materials, playmates, and type of play, rather than having adults identify the scope of the play experience. Think about Amanda, driving on the tricycle path. She decides that her tricycle requires gas. She drives it up to another child and says, "I need gas." In return, the second child obliges. He makes a noise as if gas is going into the tank, and says to Amanda, "You owe me five dollars." Other children observe this, and within minutes a gas station is created on the children's terms. They decide the location of the gas station, the services it provides, and the roles of each of the children. The children construct the play and determine the intensity of the play according to their needs and abilities.

Play Needs to Be Process-Oriented (Bruner, 1972) Children require the freedom to engage in play experiences for the pleasure of the experience rather than to have a finished product at the end of the play episode. Jamila, a 3-year-old, decides that she is going to make a school. She moves tables and chairs into rows. She puts paper and pencils on the table, and she invites other children to come to school. She takes the role of the teacher—i.e., telling the other children what to do. Gradually, children move to other play experiences. By having the opportunity to play the role of teacher, however, Jamila gained confidence without fear of failure.

Play Needs a Suspension of Reality (Henniger, 2002) Children require the freedom to use their imagination, engage in pretend, and "step outside the comfort box" by trying new ideas in new ways. This option for creativity, spontaneity, and exploration is how new knowledge is added to children's repertoires. When creativity, spontaneity, and exploration occur, children are more likely to gain knowledge necessary for higher levels of thinking. And these skills are necessary for critical thinking and problem solving, as well as language and literacy enhancement. For example, Suzanne has just been to a performance of *The Nutcracker*. Suzanne decides to play ballerina. As part of the process, Suzanne tries one move and then another. She may verbalize that she is a ballerina, and she may dress up as a ballerina. This process engages children in creative play and allows them to move from reality to fantasy.

Play Is Rule-Governed (Jalongo & Isenberg, 2004) Children determine rules, and they apply them to different settings, play episodes, and peers. They may maintain the rules or change them depending on the play scene. For example, Jamila determined the rules for the children wishing to play school with her. She clearly identified that she was the teacher.

Play Is Episodic (Jalongo & Isenberg, 2004) Children change the play and shift the goals, depending on the play scenario and on the level and sophistication of strategic thinking. For example, think of the story of the Three Bears. One day Jamie may play the role of Papa Bear, and another day be very happy playing the role of Goldilocks. The roles that children take on may change depending on which children are involved in the play experience and the resources available that trigger a particular child's interest. Children's play is unpredictable.

Children require the freedom to play and access to materials that support many types of play. The types of play and intensity of play change as children develop. In developmentally appropriate programs, practitioners observe each child's play and use the data as a guide to determine the types of experiences and potential materials children will benefit from.

Why Provide Rich Play Experiences?

Play is the single most important activity in the lives of young children (Linder 1993; Berk & Winsler, 1995; Auxter, Pyfer, & Huettig, 2001). Because of its importance to child development and to programming, student practitioners should become familiar with how play interacts with each child's development. Your understanding of play will affect how you guide children's play, how you organize the environment, the types of observation you conduct, how you plan experiences for children, and how you interact with individual children and with groups of children.

Play has many benefits for children's development. Henniger (2002) identifies that "every aspect of a child's development is enhanced through play" (p. 142). As a new early childhood student practitioner, you may not observe the relationship of play to development at first glance. However, as you begin to observe children and gain insight into the various types of play that children participate in, you will start to make connections. As a way to introduce you to how play interacts with development, we highlight seven benefits of play. Figure 5.3 summarizes why we provide play experiences for children. Table 5.1 outlines the core cognitive and social concepts children learn through play.

Children Adapt to Their Home and Community Environment through Play

The beginning elements of a child's culture are transmitted through play. The materials, toys, and accessories that adults provide influence children's learning about their families and others. For example, children living in a rural fishing

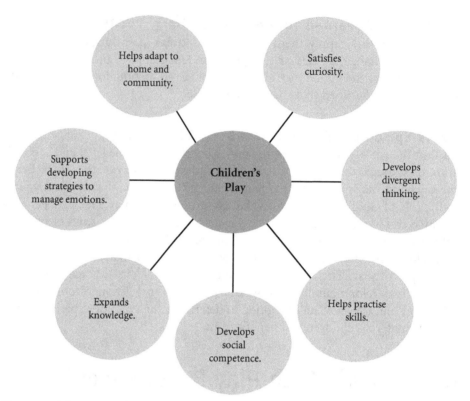

Figure 5.3 *Why We Provide Play Experiences for Children*

Table 5.1 *Concepts Children Learn through Play*

Language and literacy skills. Children practise their verbal and non-verbal communication skills by listening, taking turns, and responding. They gain an understanding of sounds used in the pronunciation of words, how words are used, and meanings of words. They begin to recognize the relationship of printed words to spoken language.

Esteem-building. Children gain a sense of accomplishment through successful play experiences; they recognize their skills and talents and those of other children. They take risks as a way to learn and gain further skills.

Contribution to learning communities. Children learn social skills, such as sharing, taking turns, negotiating, contributing to others, and compromising. They take on leadership, partnership, and teamwork through dialogue, creative thinking, decision making, co-operation, and collaboration.

Learning foundational concepts. Children gain concepts associated with their five senses—hearing, seeing, smelling, tasting, and touching. They acquire knowledge about logical-mathematical and scientific concepts, such as classification, seriation, balance, weight, numeration, time, predictions, consistency, and height.

Kinesthetics. Children become aware of their body and space. They develop their own way of expressing movement. They increase their knowledge about cultural kinesthetics, such as how different cultures greet each other. Children observe, personalize, and interpret gender movements.

village in New Brunswick learn about the culture of fishing through play with shells, nets, lobster traps, and other recycled materials.

Children Satisfy Their Curiosity

Through play, children explore and experiment as a way to understand their world, and through this process they satisfy their curiosity. For example, a little boy becomes intrigued with constructing a train in the block centre. He becomes so interested in trains that he wants to know what he would need to do to take the train outdoors and construct it in the snow. He wants to find out if he can build tunnels in the snow and weave the train within those tunnels.

Construction play contributes to children's developing scientific and mathematical principles, while increasing their imaginative play.

Children Develop Divergent Thinking (Pepler & Ross, 1981)

As children play with materials, they have the opportunity to be creative, to project possible ways to use the materials, and to think about expanded uses of the materials. This process develops abilities to problem solve, make predictions, and take risks to determine if ideas work.

Children Practise Skills

Children learn what they can do, they test ideas, they practise specific skills, and they compare their skills with their peers' (Wasserman, 1992). For example, Marciella has been watching her friend Morgan ride her bike without training wheels. Marciella wants to try as well. She tries, first with one wheel being removed; then, days later, tries with the second training wheel removed. She tumbles but continues to try until she has mastered the skill.

Children Develop Social Competence

Through social play children form human bonds, learn about themselves, and gain communication skills (Hughes, 1999). Play—with adults, peers, and by oneself—is a necessary process for social development. Participating in play in the social context provides the foundation to build social skills required for adult functioning within a family and a society.

Children Expand Knowledge

Children interact with people, materials, ideas, and images. These interactions and experiences lead children to explore new roles, new ideas, and meaning. Connecting new information with current knowledge contributes to building new knowledge. Anna, for example, likes to draw stories on sheets of paper and then have the early childhood practitioner staple them together. After observing Jennifer, the practitioner, many times, Anna decides to try to use the stapler. It takes her a few tries and some guidance from Jennifer. With this new skill, she is able to make books for her own use and for other children too.

Children Develop Strategies to Manage Emotions and Stress (Johnson, Christie, & Yawkey, 1999)

Through guided play, children are able to deal with the effects of stress. Play that encourages physical activity, interaction, dramatic episodes, and places to be alone helps children to express their emotions or to reduce their stress. Think about Jamie in the opening vignette. It was through his play that he worked through some of the stress he was feeling. Other children use play to come to terms with the birth of a new sibling or the departure of a parent or significant person in the child's life.

The Play Process

Children reach the world of adulthood by engaging in a progressive play process, where each step builds on what children have previously learned. The play process is influenced by children's age, their developmental level, and their exposure to developmentally appropriate play experiences. Children reach a plateau at each phase in the play process. When this occurs, they build on achieved skills and perfect new or modified skills. Children advance from their natural levels of play only when they are ready and only when they have had adequate experience at each phase.

Generally, during childhood, children advance through five phases in the play process and reach the sixth phase during adulthood.

Phase 1: Body Play

A child's first toy is his own body. Recall observing an infant carefully studying his own hand or foot, moving it this way or that, and noticing the effect. Piaget identified this body play as exploration. This exploration process is used to gain information (Driscoll & Nagel, 2005). Infants explore visually, they show preferences for faces and patterns, they imitate facial expressions, and they watch things that move. Children learn to control their body movements and to understand the impact these movements have on the world around them. Once children have gained information through the exploration process, play occurs when infants repeat or practise experiences and combine or reconfigure information gained from previous exploration.

Body play illustrates the beginning of play for infants.

Phase 2: Motoring Movement Play

As infants begin to creep, crawl, and advance toward toddlerhood, their interest in play expands. The constant movement in the play of older infants and toddlers encourages them to learn the fundamentals of balance and coordination. The toddler's world expands, and he is able to accomplish skills such as running, jumping, walking on tiptoe, climbing, turning around, and rolling on the ground. Children feel sheer joy in movement. Without the opportunity to explore the range of body movements and their relationship to the world, they may become severely impaired, both emotionally and physically. Movement, space, and exploration are essential to the play process.

Phase 3: Imaginative Play

Between the ages of 3 and 4, children's play evolves from movement for the sake of movement to intentional activity. What began as freedom to move, run, jump, and climb now has a purpose (Driscoll & Nagel, 2005). Children begin to work on skills such as jumping high, walking on one foot, and hopping, and pretend play emerges from children's imagination and from things that they observe

Mobility skills add new adventures to a toddler's world. The opportunities for play are expanded.

or hear in their environment. During this stage, children absorb much of the physical and emotional environment and use daily living experiences to guide their play. This phase provides insight into how children perceive their world.

Phase 4: Intentional Imaginative Play

Between the ages of 4 and 6, fantasy play increases in intensity. Children also display intentional imaginative play when they take objects and concepts and turn them into something that they need for the play situation. Children at this stage exhibit role-playing skills. They are able to make mental images of how objects and situations can be integrated into one play experience. For example, some children are playing doctor–nurse, and suddenly other children with their trikes and wagons become ambulance drivers. Two or more play episodes flow into one another. Play is no longer solely the imitation of an act observed—rather, play now has a purpose.

During this phase, children's cultural backgrounds, family life experiences, and environments influence their play. Children's developmental levels, combined with their life experiences, contribute to their interests in play, their ability to take on different roles, their level of energy used in play, their physical skills, and how they play.

Phase 5: Peer Play with Rules

Play among children ages 6 to 10 moves from being innovative, imaginative, and spontaneous to becoming more structured and governed by rules. The play tends to be physically active, team-focused, and competitive, and children use materials purely for their intended purpose.

Imaginative play expands children's vocabulary, their interactions with others, their problem-solving skills, and their creativity.

Children begin to determine strategies, negotiate rules before games, and take turns.

Phase 6: Adult Play

Adults, like children, learn through play in the context of relationships. Most adult hobbies and pastimes are vehicles for adult play, and adults exhibit their innovation and imagination in play by drawing on their competence as caring observers of human relationships. Adult play occurs in competitive venues and social events, and consists of human exchanges, observations, sharing of stories, and reflections. Adults construct new knowledge about concepts and perspectives through these interchanges. And while play takes on new forms in adulthood, it remains important to living a balanced life.

Classifying Play Experiences

How children play and what materials they play with guide child-initiated program planning. By observing children in play, early childhood practitioners have the ideal context for determining all aspects of children's development—physical, cognitive, social, emotional, kinesthetic, and interpersonal. Play is children's natural and authentic way of dealing with their environment. When practitioners observe children in their natural surroundings, practitioners gain a better perspective on children's behaviours and levels of development.

Mayfield (2001) indicates that Piaget's, Parten's, Smilansky's, and Seagoe's categorized play stages can assist practitioners in determining children's phases of play in relation to their cognitive, social, emotional, and physical-developmental norms. Each play-stage perspective outlined (see also Table 5.2) provides insight into the complex nature of child's play. Understanding these play stages provides a beginning point for your observations and helps you to understand how play experiences interface with child development. Early childhood student practitioners require time and experience in assessing the quality of play and using the data to guide program planning. We outline further the relationship between play and programming in Chapter 6.

Piaget's Stages of Play

Piaget (1970) suggested that children advance through three stages of play (see Figure 5.4), and that each play stage is interconnected to children's cognitive-development phase:

1. *Functional/sensorimotor play.* Occurs with children between the ages of birth and 2 years. During this phase, children engage in simple, repetitive functional muscle movements that occur concurrently with the sensorimotor phase of cognitive development.

2. *Symbolic/dramatic play.* Occurs with children from about 2.6 years to 7 years of age. Children use objects as props or take on roles other than being children. This play period is related to the preoperational phase of development.

PARENTING PORTRAIT

Working through the Maze

Suzanne, a mother with a 3-year-old daughter, is preparing to return to the work-force. Suzanne does not know what she should look for in choosing group care. She knows that she wants Jasmine to be able to have lots of play opportunities, especially outdoors. Suzanne and her mother discuss what Suzanne should look for, but Suzanne's mother indicates she is of little help because she was a "stay-at-home mom."

In trying to work through the maze, Suzanne consults a couple of friends who have recently chosen group care for their children.

Tanya indicates, "I would examine the level of training that the staff has. The more training staff have, the more likely the program will support the interests and needs of the children." Tanya also suggests that "centres that have students from col-lege or university Early Childhood Education programs have better child–adult ratios and better supervision. These centres seem to have solid practices."

Mary Ellen highlights to Suzanne the importance of the environment. She says, "I would look at the environment. Is it clean, is it calming, and is it aesthetically pleas-ing? Examine the types of child-related materials that are available to the children. Are the materials available so that children may get them at their leisure, or do chil-dren require the intervention of staff? Is there lots of equipment for fine-motor and gross-motor play? Can children use exploratory materials, such as sand, water, or paper, at their discretion?"

Tanya says, "I am just beginning to understand the importance of play and the environment to learning. The more parent-information sessions I attend and newsletters I read, the more I understand my role in Jordan's play. Therefore, I would want a centre that has a strong parent–child component."

Mary Ellen indicates that she needs a centre that appreciates diversity. She reminds Suzanne that she has one child with atypical developmental patterns, and therefore she examines how the staff develop a supportive, respectful environment for each child. She becomes attuned to attitudes, open partnerships, communica-tion skills, and understanding of child development and programming.

After listening to Tanya and Mary Ellen, Suzanne says, "It is a maze to me. I want the best for my child, but I don't know what the best should look like or feel like. Choosing child care is a difficult task for me because I don't know a lot about it. All I can do is continue to learn and hope my instincts are correct." Mary Ellen and Tanya agree and then offer to arrange for Suzanne to visit their children's centres.

Weeks later, Suzanne has made a decision about care and she indicates that she is grateful for Mary Ellen's and Tanya's input and mentoring.

What advice would you give Suzanne? If you were an early childhood prac-titioner in a centre that Suzanne visited, what information would you wish to emphasize about early learning and child care? Why? What questions might you ask of Suzanne?

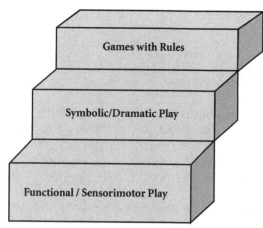

Figure 5.4 *Piaget's Stages of Play Development*

3. ***Games with rules.*** Occurs among school-aged children. Children agree on rules before beginning play, and they deal with the consequences should the rules be broken. This play period concurs with the concrete-operational phase of development.

Smilansky's Contributions to the Stages of Play

Constructive Play Stage Sarah Smilansky (1968) added to Piaget's play stages. She suggested that children between the ages of 4 and school-age participate in sophisticated social/dramatic play, and she labelled this the *constructive play* stage: role playing dominates the play, and the participants use props, creativity, and imagination with materials to construct items needed to enhance the play experience. Social interaction is necessary to carry out this stage of play.

Parten's Stages of Play

Mildred Parten (1933) studied play from the social-behaviour perspective. Her work continues to influence how researchers, theorists, educators, and practitioners examine children's play. She suggested that children's play progresses through a series of stages:

1. Solitary Play The child generally plays alone, without interaction with other children or with the materials being used by children nearby. Although Parten suggested that this play was generally observed in children up to about 2 1/2 years, more recent research identifies *solitary play* may be present in a variety of ages and is influenced by the context of the play (Monighan-Nourot et al., 1987). Hendrick and Weissman (2006) indicate that children engage in varying levels of solitary play. They also suggest that solitary play provides children with the opportunities to develop ideas, thoughts, and abilities to try play ideas on their own.

2. Parallel Play From about 2 1/2 to 3 1/2 years, children play independently or beside peers, but not with peers. The materials used may be similar, but there is no sharing of materials in the play episodes. Van Hoorn et al. (2003) suggest this type of play represents the first phase of group play. Children begin to test peer relationships and co-operative skills. Okagaki et al. (1998) indicate that children with disabilities use *parallel play* as a way to participate in play with peers, but at their own pace.

3. Associative Play Children at about 3 1/2 to 5 years of age start to play with other children. They share play materials and participate in similar activities, but lack true co-operation. Being with other children is as important as the play experience itself.

Table 5.2 *Examples of Play Stages*

Type of Play	Description	Example
Cognitive Play Functional/ sensorimotor	Simple, repetitive muscle movements, with or without materials.	Infants throwing blocks from high chair. Toddlers using a jack-in-the-box. Preschoolers repeating a pattern in block structure.
Symbolic/dramatic	Objects used in play as props, or children taking on roles other than being children.	Infants use blanket to disappear. Toddlers pretend to eat toy as a cookie. Preschoolers pretend to take on the role of a nurse.
Games with rules	Predetermined rules and consequences understood before the play begins.	Infants playing pat-a-cake. Toddlers playing simple games. Preschoolers playing simple games.
Constructive play	Role play dominates play. Creativity and imagination combined with materials to construct items based on a plan.	Preschooler use props such as chairs to create a movie theatre.
Social Play Solitary	Playing alone, without interaction with other children. Use of materials different from children nearby.	Infants playing on the floor beside other infant, but no acknowledgment. Toddler playing beside other children but showing no interest in others. Preschooler playing by self with own toys.
Parallel	Playing independently or beside peer, but not with peers. Materials used may be similar, but no sharing of materials in play episodes.	Infants and toddlers playing near other, but with little interaction. Preschoolers using shared materials, but not participating in the same play.
Associative	Playing with other children, sharing materials, and participating in similar activities. Being with other children as important as play experience itself.	Preschoolers playing with the same materials, but not necessarily with the same goals.
Co-operative	Playing with other children, and now as group. Children determine common goal and work toward attaining goal through negotiation, role assignment, and problem-solving interaction.	Older preschoolers build beach resort; each child has role in determining what will be at the resort and how to construct it.
Co-operative–competitive	Child part of a team. The team works together to achieve victory.	School-aged children become members of a team. Each child has a role and works with team members to achieve results.
Unoccupied	No engagement in play.	Infants, toddlers, and preschoolers in the environment, but engaged in non-activity.
Onlooker	Observes other children or adults in play	Infants watch sibling play nearby. Toddlers observe another child with toy. Preschoolers watch others on the new climber before deciding to try it.

4. Co-operative Play Children between the ages of 4 and 5 begin to partici-pate in this highest level of *co-operative play*. Group play occurs, initially by deter-mining a common goal that each child works toward attaining. Co-operative play becomes more advanced during primary school.

Parten also identified non-playing time and onlooker play:

Unoccupied Behaviour Parten also identified that there are times when chil-dren are not playing, which she labelled *unoccupied behaviour*. She described it to be when children appear to be wandering around the room without a specific pur-pose. Mayfield (2001) indicates that "many contemporary researchers do not con-sider this to be a category of play, but rather a non-activity" (p. 268).

Onlooker Play Parten also described children as participating in *onlooker play*, which refers to children who observe other children or adults in play but do not participate in the play. Younger children may use this as a way to learn about how particular materials may work, while older children may also use this strategy as a way to determine their interests, determine ways to participate in play episodes, or decide how to become involved in play.

Seagoe's Contributions to the Stages of Play

Co-operative–Competitive Play Seagoe (1970) added to Parten's play phases of development. She identified that children between the ages of 7 and 8 move to a *co-operative–competitive play* that involves play that is focused on team victory, such as soccer and hockey.

The transition from one stage of play to another does not mean, however, that the previous stage disappears or that children may not come back to a particular stage. For example, a 4-year-old child who has been in an early childhood setting with the same children for two years may exhibit all of the characteristics of being at the co-operative play phase. Take that same child and place him in a new setting. There, he may revert back to solitary play. He will move through the phases more quickly as he gains comfort in the environment.

Accommodating Children

Atypical Development

While all children play, those with atypical developmental patterns may play differ-ently from other children. Jalongo and Isenberg (2004) suggest that children with atypical development may explore their play environment less, and the opportuni-ties for social play may be more limited than for children with typical developmen-tal patterns. Children with atypical development may require modifications and adaptations to the play space so that they too have every opportunity to participate in play. For example, an early learning and child care setting would provide dress clothes in a dramatic centre that may be used by a child using a wheelchair.

Practitioners support all children in learning through play. Intervention, encouragement, role modelling, and extending play opportunities that will assist all children depending on their phase of development, are important to the quality of play children engage in. For example, if Maggie wishes to play in the dramatic centre but does not have the language skills to negotiate with other children, you, the practitioner, would assist her in making her needs known to the other children. You may also become a play partner with Maggie until she is established in the play with the other children.

Diversity

Children's play is influenced by their culture and diversity. For example, in cultures and families that value natural environments for their children's outdoor play, children's play evolves from using props such as sticks, rocks, tree branches, and snow. Other children who may be new to Canada and from a warmer climate, may not have developed the skills to play in the snow. Children with autism often engage in repetitive play, gradually taking the risk to try new ideas (Atlas & Lapidus, 1987). Children coming from regions where water is rationed are less likely to initially participate in water play. Early childhood practitioners observe children and listen to children during their play. Valuable insights into cultural, family, and community celebrations and traditions (Jalongo & Isenberg, 2004) are gained through observation and discussion. When appropriate to the play, exposing children to toys and materials from other cultures supports them in expanding their interest in and knowledge about diversity, increasing their social roles, and learning new problem-solving skills as they attempt to use unfamiliar materials.

The Roles of Early Childhood Practitioners in Promoting Play

Initially, you as early childhood student practitioners may think of your primary role as playing with children. As we examine the relationship of play to children's development, however, it becomes clear that early childhood practitioners and student practitioners have many roles and responsibilities in promoting play. That being said, you may wonder, "What are the roles of early childhood practitioners in children's play?"

Adults' Roles in Promoting Play

Adult have four roles in promoting play:

1. Adults exhibit a nurturing attitude toward both indoor and outdoor play each season. Adults ensure the play environment meets established criteria for safety, design, play opportunity, and child interest in the indoor and outdoor play areas. Adults promote the need for an equal balance of indoor and outdoor play and ensure that all toys and materials promote

balance, equality, and respect in the areas of gender, race, culture, and social behaviour.

Adults create the environment so that there are a variety of play options available to children, and they ensure that the toys or materials presented are appropriate in number. For example, Catron and Allen (1999) suggest that there be 50 percent more play items and experiences than the total number of children in the program. In a play space with 16 children, then, there would be at least 24 items and experiences. Children who have too many materials to choose from at one time are prevented from inventing new uses for the materials, which may inhibit creativity. When children have limited materials available to them, they become bored or anxious, resulting in an increase in negative behaviour.

2. When the environment is prepared with adequate options, intrigue, and freedom to explore, adult direction and intervention is limited, thereby increasing the quality of children's learning. Auxter, Pyfer, and Huettig (2001) and Sanders (2002) all advocate that a child's day include equal opportunities for indoor and outdoor active play through a variety of interest/exploratory centres, physical-movement sites, and places to pause. Play environments empower children to make choices (within reasonable, safe boundaries) over the play experience.

3. Adults conduct observations. Through observation, which is a continuous process, practitioners obtain information about children's strengths, interests, and areas requiring further development. Moreover, observations are used to guide and develop ideas about the types of play materials and support that may further develop the play episode. And observation helps to determine if the needs of the individual child and groups of children are being met.

4. Adults promote play, which requires practitioners to observe and conduct environmental scanning. Then they can effectively question children in ways that encourage them to bring their own experiences into play. Children's play is usually more creative and imaginative when it is triggered by their daily living experiences. Finding the appropriate balance of facilitating play, becoming involved in play, and modelling particular behaviours through play is challenging. When adults interrupt children's play, the development of their neural pathways *can* be inhibited. Neural pathways are developed as children engage in the thinking and problem-solving processes needed for the play episode. Promoting creativity and imagination in a play experience reduces violent play. Today, children's play is influenced by TV shows, movies, and toys associated with programming. The more children's play becomes creative, the less violent it will likely be, thereby increasing positive interactions and socialization skills.

Adult Levels of Participation in Play

As shown in Figure 5.5, Johnson, Christie, and Yawkey (1987) identify three levels of adult participation in children's play experiences. The first level is identified as *parallel play*, where the adult plays beside the child, not with the child. The adult may use materials similar to those of children nearby. The purpose of this play is to role model positive play behaviours, without directly using words or disrupting the play episode.

The second level of adult participation is described as *co-playing*, where the adult participates in the play episode. The child determines the adult's role while controlling the play. The adult role models positive behaviours, as well as expands the use of language and problem solving.

The third level of adult participation is referred to as *play tutoring*. The adult participates in the play episode by taking control of the play for a short period of time. Then, the adult encourages the child to expand the play into new directions.

Heidemann and Hewitt (1992) maintain that adults must examine carefully when and how they become involved in children's play. Figure 5.6 outlines their five-point scale, which depicts the least intrusive to most intrusive ways in which adults intervene in play.

Conversation Café

If play is so important, why is it being replaced with academic skills? What are the societal changes that are impacting this change? What do early childhood practitioners need to do to bring play back to children's lives? How will this be accomplished?

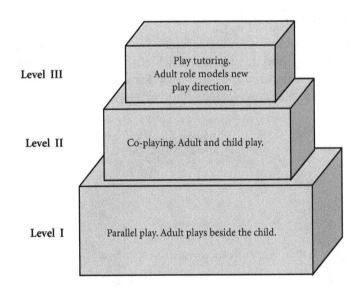

Figure 5.5 *Adult Levels of Participation*

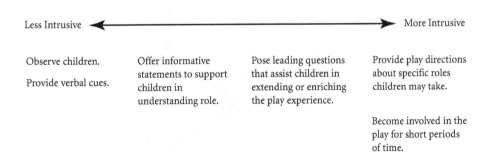

Figure 5.6 *Adults' Involvement in Children's Play*

Quality Indicators for Safe Play Spaces

Children require safe play spaces for optimal development. In fact, the design of play spaces influences the level and ease with which children explore, wonder, and discover. Safe play environments are enhanced when early childhood practitioners consider the following quality indicators, as illustrated in Figure 5.7.

Developmentally Appropriate Materials and Equipment

Children are developmentally different and require materials and equipment that support their particular skill level and interests. Equipment appropriate for an 8-year-old may be too big for a 3-year-old. For example, a trampoline is inappropriate for a 3-year-old. Most childhood injuries occur when children play on equipment designed for older children, or where materials have not been regularly maintained.

Fall Surfacing Zones

The leading and most serious injuries to children in play areas are caused by children falling on inappropriate surfaces. Shock-absorbing surfaces help cushion falls and prevent serious injury. The *Canadian Standards Act* (CSA) guidelines for indoor and outdoor play areas include standards for safety surfacing and fall zones.

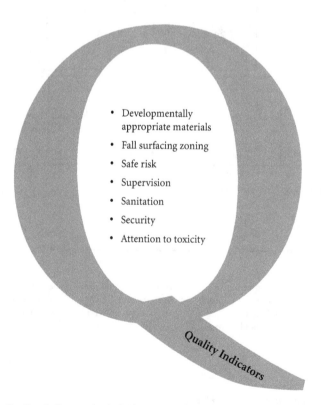

- Developmentally appropriate materials
- Fall surfacing zoning
- Safe risk
- Supervision
- Sanitation
- Security
- Attention to toxicity

Quality Indicators

Figure 5.7 *Quality Indicators for Safe Play Spaces*

Safe Risk

Children require safe play environments that offer both challenges and safe risks. Play environments that are too safe are not only boring, but children will find ways to take risks and engage in challenges, often in ways that are hazardous. A quality play environment is both safe and challenging. Children have a developmental need to climb. If challenging and appropriate climbing options are not available to children, they will attempt to climb on rocks, benches, and other less safe items, simply to meet their climbing needs.

Supervision

The play area and the equipment are designed to complement the amount of available adult supervision. Activities and experiences that are safe when supervised can be hazardous if left unsupervised.

Sanitation

Wherever children gather, viruses, bacteria, and conditions such as head lice spread from child to child and to early childhood practitioners. All play areas, both inside and out, require a design that promotes easy cleaning and sanitation. Water fountains are available at children's height, and children are guided on their appropriate use. Children are taught how to blow their noses, how to dispose of tissues, and how to effectively wash their hands.

Security

In today's world, parents are fearful that their children may be kidnapped or abused by a stranger. To support safety and security, children's indoor and outdoor play areas are enclosed and designed so that practitioners have appropriate visibility at all times.

Toxicity

Modern society uses toxic substances in homes and in early childhood centres. Exposure to environmental pollution—including cleaning supplies, paint, lawn and garden treatments, and pressure-treated wood in children's play structures—can affect young children's playing and learning. Practitioners eliminate toxic products used within the environment. If toxins have been used in the outdoor environment, practitioners take precautions with children.

SUMMARY

Defining *Play*

- Play is difficult to define. There is no one perspective that encapsulates the importance of play. Common to all, however, is that "children learn and develop through play."

The Importance of Play

- Play supports children's cognitive skills, such as language, literacy, mathematics, and the arts. As well, play enhances social and emotional development, such as self-esteem, empathy, co-operation, and respect for others. And play increases children's physical development, including balance, coordination, and muscle development. Finally, play increases creativity.

Characteristics of Play

- Play needs to be active, child-initiated, process-oriented, and have a suspension of reality. Play is rule-governed and episodic.

Why Provide Rich Play Experiences

- Rich play experiences provide children with opportunities to adapt to their home and community, satisfy their curiosity, develop divergent thinking, practise skills, develop social competence, expand knowledge, and develop strategies to manage emotions and stress.

The Play Process

- Children advance through five steps in the play process: body play, moving play, imaginative play, intentional imagination play, and peer play with rules. And as adults, they enter the sixth phase, identified as adult play.

Classifying Play Experiences

- Piaget suggested children advance through three stages of play: functional/sensorimotor play, symbolic/dramatic play, and games with rules.
- Smilansky indicates, in addition to Piaget's stages, that children advance through a constructive play stage.
- Parten outlines four stages of play: solitary, parallel, associative, and co-operative. She also identifies that children exhibit unoccupied behaviour as well as onlooker play.

- Seagoe indicates that the final phase of play is co-operative–competitive play. She says this is evident when children begin to focus on a team victory rather than on an individual's performance and success.

Children with Atypical Development

- Children with atypical development play, but they may require modifications and adaptations to their play space and play experiences.

Play and Children's Diversity

- Children's play is influenced by their culture and diversity. When appropriate, children may be exposed to toys and materials from other cultures.

The Role of the Early Childhood Practitioner in Promoting Play

- The early childhood practitioner has four roles in promoting play: exhibit a nurturing attitude toward both indoor and outdoor play, prepare an environment with a variety of play options, participate in continuous observation, and promote play.
- There are three levels of adult participation in children's play experiences: parallel play, co-playing, and play tutoring.

Quality Indicators for Safe Play Spaces

- Safe play spaces have appropriate materials and equipment; fall surfacing zones; safety considerations; appropriate levels of supervision, sanitation, and security; opportunities for safe risk; and attention to toxicity.

FURTHER OPPORTUNITIES FOR ENRICHMENT

Research

1. This chapter highlights how important it is for children to have opportunities to engage in play episodes that allow for choice, exploration, freedom, discovery, and wonder in both indoor and outdoor environments. Research traditional, creative, and adventure playgrounds and determine how each supports or inhibits children's play. Justify your positions.
2. The type of play experiences designed for typical 3-year-old would differ from those designed for 4-year-olds. How would they differ? Why?

Group Investigation

1. Part of the process of understanding play and the stages of play is to observe and categorize the types of play children are involved in. Rubin, Maioni, and Hornung (1976) combined the cognitive play classifications identified by Smilansky with Parten's socialization categorizations. Using the classification form below, read each of the statements and determine where you would place each type of play on the rubric. Discuss your responses with others. Compare the results. Discuss the differences and justify your answers.
   a. Jamila and Jama are both playing with blocks in the block centre. There is no dialogue between the two children.
   b. Marti, Martine, Mandy, and Melissa are playing hopscotch in the front garden.
   c. Uwe is looking at a book from the book tree, under the tree.
   d. Kenyo is leaning up against the fence.
   e. Jaylene and Dillon are using the jack-in-the-box.
   f. Marc, Tanner, and Wally have determined how and where they are going to build a fort in the snow.

	Functional	Constructive	Dramatic	Games with Rules
Solitary				
Parallel				
Associative				
Co-operative				
Unoccupied				
Onlooker				

Source: Adapted from the research of Rubin, Maioni, & Hornung (1976)

2. Using the same type of classification-rubric form above, observe three children in three different play episodes. Record the type of play episode on the rubric. Compare your results with other members of your learning community. Discuss differences and try to determine which observations led to the placement of the play episode.

Making Connections

1. Observe a group of children involved in play. Using Table 5.1 in this chapter as a guideline, identify the concepts children are learning through their play. Provide specific examples of the type of play and the concepts being learned. If you had a 3-year-old child with limited speech, how might a dramatic-play centre support that child in enhancing speech? Provide examples of items you would consider placing in the dramatic centre. Which role would you play? Why?

ADDITIONAL READING

Canadian Child Care Federation (2002). *Outdoor Play in Early Childhood Education and Care Programs.* Ottawa, ON: Canadian Child Care Federation.

Johnson, J. E., Christie, J. F., & Yawkey, T. D. (1999). *Play and Early Childhood Development* (2nd ed.). New York: Longman.

Shipley, C.D. (1993). *Empowering Children: Play-Based Curriculum for Lifelong Learning.* Scarborough, ON: Nelson Canada.

WEBLINKS

www.cayc.ca: *Canadian Association for Young Children.*
www.csa.ca: *Canadian Standards Association.*
www.cpra.ca/e/index.htm: *Canadian Parks/Recreation Association.*
www.ccie.com/wf/index.php: *World Forum on Early Care and Education.*

"Our greatest gift to children is to provide them with a stimulating play environment."

Barbara Crossley, 2005

6

Creating a Responsive Environment

A Day Begins in an Early Learning and Child Care Centre

How Environments Impact the Feeling Tone

Jennifer walks to the early childhood centre one morning. She admires the beauty of the outdoors created from the snowfall overnight and the continuing snowfall this morning. She notices that the snowflakes are large, fluffy, and falling slowly and that they are staying on her eyelashes. As Jennifer approaches the centre, she marvels at how the snow is collecting on the evergreen trees that define the centre's property line. The clean, freshly fallen snow changes the appearance of the short deciduous bushes in the front garden—they take on new life.

When Jennifer enters the centre, she observes four children sitting on the soft yellow cushions covering the window bench. The children appear to be watching the arrival of parents and children. Jennifer enjoys the children's chatter and the warm, cozy feeling she experiences within the environment. She notices how light from the sconces on the window edges picks up the paint colours of the wall and gives the room a soft brightness contrasting with the grey, overcast natural light. Jennifer thinks to herself, "It is a wonderful winter's day."

As she approaches the children at the window seat, Hillary says, "Mommy brushed snow from the car. She couldn't find the brush, so do you know what she used?"

Jennifer replies, "I think your mommy used a broom."

Hillary says, "No-o-o-o."

"I give up."

With laugher in her voice, Hillary says, "She used her hands, and her hands got all cold. She couldn't find her mittens so she took my mittens."

Aidan pipes up with, "My daddy just turned the windshield wipers on."

Three other children join Hillary and Aidan at the window. From the reading area, they pull soft, overstuffed, pale-yellow-and-mint-green child-sized chairs over to the window seat. Jennifer enjoys listening to their voices and their giggles.

Suddenly, three children come running up to Jennifer, asking all at once, "Can we play in the snow?" Jennifer replies, "Of course you may. It is a wonderful winter's day. Let's get ready."

Looking Ahead

In this chapter, we introduce how responsive environments support children in developing a feeling of comfort, and we show how comfort influences children's play and development.

In Chapter 2, we identified the five elements of early learning and child care, and in other chapters we introduced you to the *what* and *who* of early learning and child care. In this chapter we introduce you to the *where*—children's environments.

This chapter will help you begin to understand that when environments are designed in ways that offer children materials and experiences and provide them with a feeling of comfort, the environments become another way to spark children's curiosity and lead to learning. The environment is as important as the people in the environment. In essence, this chapter will assist you in connecting how children's physical life spaces and the objects and people within those life spaces impact how children's minds and bodies develop.

In "A Day Begins in an Early Learning and Child Care Centre," Jennifer recognized that environments that have soft, movable furniture—such as the yellow-and-mint-green child-sized chairs—support children's interactions and build a sense of community. She encouraged children and adults to create cozy areas, such as in the front window, and she acknowledged that when children gather in a comfortable environment, language is enhanced and new ideas are developed, which was confirmed when the children determined their interest in playing in the snow.

As you begin to observe and work in various early childhood settings, you will notice an array of environments—some responsive to the needs of children and others not. Some will have a wide variety of materials and equipment and a sense of order and will make you feel alert and alive, while others will contribute to your feeling tired and having limited energy. Some settings will have a calming effect; others will overstimulate you. Early childhood practitioners continuously examine and evaluate the play environment to determine its affect on children. The **feeling tone** in the environment influences how children and adults respond to the people and things in it and determines the depth of play they engage in.

Why Early Childhood Practitioners Plan Responsive Environments

In the past five years, governments and the general public have increasingly recognized the importance of children's early learning and child care experience during

Responsive environments support children's play and curiosity.

Feeling tone. Refers to the way an individual takes in experiences and physical sensations and processes sounds, smells, and tastes, and how these are filtered as pleasant, unpleasant, or neutral experiences.

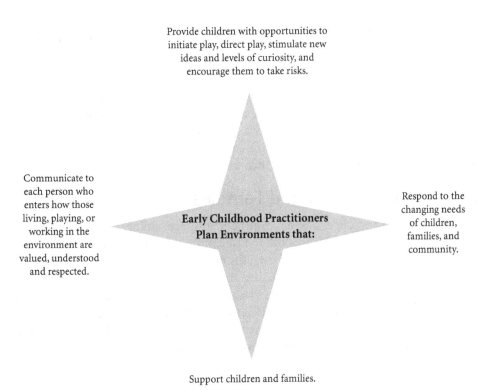

Figure 6.1 *Why Practitioners Plan Supportive Environments*

the first six years of life on their "development, future success at school, and on their overall health and well-being" (Beach et al., 2004, p. 2). Children's play environments and the delivery of children's programs are the two primary venues through which support is given to children's development.

To maximize children's developmental potential, early childhood practitioners are attentive to the environment children spend the day in. Early learning and child care program practitioners have as one of their program outcomes the need to create environments similar to comfortable, supportive home environments. Figure 6.1 illustrates the four reasons early childhood practitioners plan responsive environments for young children.

To Provide Children with Play Opportunities and Encourage Taking Safe Risks

Early learning and child care practitioners plan environments that provide children with opportunities to initiate play and direct the play, that stimulate new ideas and levels of curiosity, and that encourage children to take safe risks. In programs with infants, for example, practitioners ensure that there is adequate, cozy, protected floor space and materials that encourage infants to begin to roll, creep, crawl, and stand. The toddler environment is expanded to include more space for walking, running, jumping, and balancing. Practitioners provide increased choice of materials in a protected space that is suitable for filling, dumping, and pouring. The preschool environment provides a variety of interest centres, materials, and space allocations to accommodate children's changing needs.

To Communicate Value, Understanding, and Respect

The early learning and child care environment communicates value, understanding, and respect to each person who enters the environment. For example, the environment provides a comfort feeling upon entry through the sounds of soft music playing, the aromas of baking, and the ambience of natural lighting, combined with the beauty of the indoor and outdoor aesthetics. The people, the physical space, and the materials in any environment contribute to the feeling of comfort and security. If the environment is not correct, a feeling of insecurity develops.

To Support Children and Families

An early learning and child care environment supports children and families. For example, the range of experiences offered to children complements their developmental processes. Early childhood practitioners examine the current phase of development of each child. Then, using the typical patterns of developmental norms that children progress through, practitioners are able to predict the types of experiences that will support each child's development in three months, six months, and nine months. This information helps practitioners to develop long-term program outcomes needed to support the projected upcoming developmental needs of children enrolled in the program.

To Respond to the Changing Needs of Children, Families, and Community

Families with young children today differ from our families and from our parents' families. Families require programs and staff that offer some flexibility and specialized services to meet their needs. As a result, early learning and child care centres respond to the demographics of the families using their facilities. Centres may hire staff, for example, who speak the language of the parents and who have an understanding of the traditions, cultures, and values associated with the family dynamics. All of this builds effective working relationships with parents and communicates to parents that each child and family is important to the centre and that the staff are there to support them. Centres devise policies, procedures, and practices that support children, and they consider how each practice affects the family unit. For example, if a family is unable to actively participate in the program in ways that other families do, that family is made to feel that their child is as important as those children who have parents actively engaged in the program.

As some families leave a centre and new families enter, the staff may need to make changes to services to accommodate those new families. Think about a centre whose clientele has generally served white, anglophone families. Suddenly, a local manufacturing company is purchased by an international company. To establish the new manufacturing company, the parent company transfers many families of different nationalities to the region. This influx of people with cultural differences brings changes to the types of child care needed, the ways in which family and child care relationships are established, the roles of parents within the centre, and the programs needed to support families, children, and staff in this new community. Or think about a centre that incorporates community events into children's realm of experiences. For example, practitioners might introduce children to the concept of a community celebration, such as Art in the Park. This introduction might spark children's interest; they might initiate replicating an Art in the Park display, either at their early learning and child care centre or as part of the community celebration. Practitioners might then provide children with additional resources, such as samples of artwork. Perhaps community artists could offer children exposure to various techniques and materials. Each of these examples requires staff to respond to the changing needs of families and community.

How Children Adapt to Environments

Child growth and development theory provides early childhood practitioners with insight into the necessity of exposing children to supportive early childhood environments. For example, the primary developmental task of the growth and developmental process of infants/children after birth is to adapt to the world outside the mother's uterus. Adaptation to an environment is necessary for survival, security, and cognitive development. *Adaptation* refers to an organism's ability to modify its environments or to find ways to fit with the environment (Vasta, Miller, & Ellis, 2004). Piaget asserted that adaptation to an environment requires "changing the environment to meet one's needs and changing oneself to meet the demands of environment" (Van Hoorn et al., 1999, p. 24).

Infants' survival is made possible by the design of the human brain. Like all mammals, humans have a section of the brain, known as the *reptilian brain*, that is responsible for survival of the species and is the oldest and most primitive part of the brain. It controls the body functions required for sustaining life: breathing, body temperature, heartbeat, swallowing, visual tracking, and the startle response. These are automatic responses, not left to the risk of learning; rather, they are present at birth to ensure survival. Through the process of evolution, the human brain has developed into four sections: reptilian, somatic, mammalian, and neo-cortex. This development has given humans the ability to experience emotion, to reason, to deal in abstractions, to communicate verbally, and to be goal-oriented. To integrate the function of each section of the brain, infants and young children innately adapt to the environment outside the uterus. This adaptation and integration process takes place through play and the interaction within the environment.

Each child's ability to adapt to a new environment varies depending on the comfort level and security of the home setting and extended settings and on the child's developmental level. For example, John Bowlby (1969, 1989) believes that infants are biologically equipped with and exhibit certain characteristics that promote an emotional bond between infants and caregivers, which promotes survival. "The baby cries, clings, coos, and smiles. Later, the infant crawls, walks, and follows the mother. The infant's goal is to keep the primary caregiver nearby" (Santrock, 2002, p. 187). More recently, Bjorklund and Pellegrini (2002) suggest children have an intuitive need to engage in an adaptation process to their environment. For example, when children are given the freedom to participate in rough-and-tumble play, they are gaining an understanding of social signalling. They begin to experience and recognize the give-and-take in a relationship, they gain a sense of interpersonal communication, and they start to distinguish the

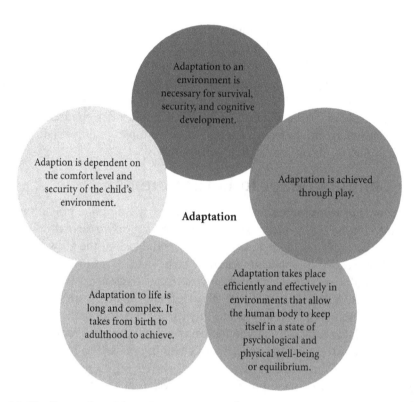

Figure 6.2 *Key Factors about Adaptation*

"good" feelings acquired from others, feelings that provide them with discomfort—from all of which prepare children for adaptive challenges of later social behaviour expectations across different phases of development.

As illustrated in Figure 6.2, the human process of adaptation to life is long and complex and takes from birth to adulthood to achieve. This adaptation and learning process takes place efficiently and effectively in environments that allow the human body to keep itself in a state of psychological and physical well-being or equilibrium. Adaptation in humans is achieved the same way as in all mammals—through an innate ability to play. The play process is most effective in environments where individuals feel comfortable and do not need to expend their energy to decrease stress levels.

How Responsive Early Childhood Environments Support the Adaptation Process

Responsive learning environment. Includes people, ideas, objects, and places that support children by creating a stress-free, psychologically and physiologically comfortable place to play.

Early childhood environments are described in terms of how the people, objects, and physical space respond to the needs of the child and are identified as responsive environments. Jalongo and Isenberg (2004) suggest children's environments refer to "all the influences that affect children and adults in early childhood settings" (p.148). We examine environments in terms of a **responsive environment**.

Examining the elements that make up responsive environments is not new. Froebel emphasized the importance of play both indoors and out, and he determined a need for unity and balance within the environment (Dudek, 2000). As well, Waldorf determined that children's environments require attention to colour, furniture, natural lighting, and natural objects within both the indoor and outdoor play space. Harmonizing the play space with the natural beauty of the environment supports children in their exploration of learning new things, new ideas, and new knowledge. Advocates of the Emilia Reggio program perspective suggest environments convey many messages to children, parents, and visitors. Attention to the physical space and the overall environment is essential in Emilia

Practitioners play an important role in creating a responsive environment and in nurturing children within that environment.

Reggio programs because it "fosters encounters, communication, and relationship" (Morrison, 2003, p.118). The arrangements of physical space and the people within the space contribute to creating a responsive environment.

Children require an environment that provides social and emotional security (Mayfield, 2001). In addition, children need social and emotional security before they will participate in "cognitive adventures" (Szanton, 1998, p.67). Children entering early learning and child care programs learn to adapt or modify their behaviours to the particular climate, program expectations, food sources, and program structure. When children feel comfortable and secure, they increase their success in adapting to their environment, which then helps in developing skills necessary to become productive members of a family, a community, and society.

Characteristics of Responsive Environments

Creating a responsive environment is one of the most important roles of the early childhood practitioner, because it is the environmental surroundings that directly affect how children behave, develop, and learn (Jalongo & Isenberg, 2004). There is no established set of criteria for responsive environments within the early childhood literature; however, based on research, observations, and practice, the following points, also illustrated in Figure 6.3, help us to understand the benefits of responsive environments.

Responds to the needs and developmental unfolding of growing children.

Is created when early childhood practitioners are attentive to the physical space, architectural features, and type and placement of materials.

Ensures play opportunities combine some organizational structures and some freedom.

Makes provisions for individual differences.

Exposes children to natural light.

Positively influences children's behaviour.

Promotes experience-based learning with a flexible schedule.

Shows happy/active children.

Is beautiful, comfortable, and exciting.

Is stress-free.

Figure 6.3 *Characteristics of a Responsive Environment*

Responds to Children's Needs and Development

A responsive environment is responsive to the needs and developmental unfolding of the growing child. It is designed to positively affect children's play and learning, because children are happier, more socially and cognitively competent, exhibit longer concentration, use more language skills, and engage in more co-operative play in environments that are appropriately designed (Trawick-Smith, 1992). The environment impacts children's growth and development and later academic performance (Berner, 1992, 1995; Boss, 2001a).

Is Stress-Free

A responsive environment is stress-free. Canadian children, like their adult family members and caregivers, are experiencing more life stress than they did in years past. Stress occurs when there is an imbalance between environmental demands and human resources (Evans & Cohen, 1987). When children feel a sense of acceptance, comfort, and esteem, they are able to engage in the adaptive process more easily. For example, when children have a sense of security and there is a change in staffing, they adjust more easily to the new staff. The play-space design and the feeling tone created by the adults within the play space challenge children's adaptive coping resources (Evans & McCoy, 1998).

In early learning and child care environments that restrict the timing of children's moving from one experience centre to another or that do not provide children with personal or quiet space, feelings of insecurity and discomfort increase. Children then feel environmental stress. Privacy nooks offset some of the stress from high levels of stimulation, crowding, noise, or feelings of distress.

Exposes Children to Natural Light

Indoor/outdoor play spaces are designed to expose children to natural light. Exposure to daylight is associated with higher levels of student performance (Hathaway, 1995; Plympton, Conway, & Epstein, 2000; Reicher, 2000). Some studies suggest that children's language, social, emotional, and physical development progress more rapidly in outdoor play spaces than in indoor play spaces, due to increased freedom to play, access to natural light, and an increase in body movement.

Shows Happy, Active Children

A responsive environment shows evidence of a noise level of happy, active children. The humming sound of children playing in an active environment increases healthy interaction among children and adults. In fact, noise levels in children's environments affect their learning (Boss, 2001a; Chan, 1979, 1980; Tanner & Langford, 2003). Environments where children yell and scream, or where early childhood practitioners use loud voices to manage children, negatively affect the "feeling tone" of the environment. And this type of noise impedes children's abilities to concentrate and learn (Jalongo & Isenberg, 2004).

Positively Influences Children's Behaviour

A responsive environment positively influences children's behaviour. Aggressive and negative behaviours decrease when children feel good about the environment they are placed in. The more comfortable children feel in the environment, the more likely they are to exhibit prosocial behaviours (Dudek, 2000). When children feel physically and psychologically safe, there is less need for the fight-or-flight response.

The organization of the indoor and outdoor physical space affects children's behaviours regardless of the experiences offered. Because current research links children's behaviour, learning, and development to their environment, there is an increased need for early childhood practitioners to examine and create environments where children and adults feel comfortable, secure, and free from fear and chaos (Berner, 1992, 1995; Boss, 2001b). Quality programming ensures that children have equal access to indoor and outdoor play space.

Includes Organization and Freedom in Play

A responsive environment ensures that play opportunities combine some organizational structure and some freedom. The organizational structure is in place to support children's need for order and predictability (Bredekamp & Copple, 1997; Hendrick, 2001). For example, children feel comfortable when they become familiar with the program routine; e.g., they know that outdoor play occurs after group time and before lunch.

Promotes Experience-Based Learning with a Flexible Schedule

A responsive environment promotes experience-based learning with a flexible schedule. The freedom to choose experience-centres and to engage in play for long or short periods supports children in their creativity and gives them the opportunity for expansive play and stress-free learning. For example, if children become absorbed in making a large block structure, the early childhood practitioner allows them to continue their construction rather than disrupting them because it is time to prepare to return indoors.

Responsive environments provide many play options. Block building offers many play options and is therefore an important option for children.

Provides for Individual Differences

Another characteristic of a responsive environment is that it makes provisions for individual differences for stimulation and rest, for noise and quiet, and for interactions and privacy. Practitioners are attentive to reducing the crowding and hurrying of children. They examine the environmental factors and adjust them accordingly in an effort to create a calming, relaxed environment where children feel the comfort of a homelike setting. For example, if the noise level begins to escalate to a level that is beginning to reduce children's engagement in their play, the early childhood practitioner will rotate from one play space to another speaking with children softly and becoming involved in their discussions, while touching children gently. This often brings calmness back to the play area. The practitioner may also bring out an interesting item for children to explore, or start an activity or experience that will attract some children away from their previous play station. If those strategies have limited success, the practitioner may need to specifically ask the children how they can collectively reduce the noise level.

Is Beautiful, Comfortable, and Exciting

A responsive environment is beautiful, comfortable, and exciting. Dewey, at the turn of the 20th century, emphasized four things that were important to children: "conversation; . . . inquiry; . . . making things . . . and artistic expression" (Dewey, 1990/1956, p. 47). He claimed that children learn through play and through the imaginary worlds of "making-believe" (p.44). According to Uline (1997), in the 1930s Dewey explored the relationship of the physical space to play and learning. Dewey expressed the need for children to have "large grounds, gardens, and greenhouse." He described "open-air" interiors, the importance of having a variety of workspaces, and the feeling of a "well-furnished home" (Upitis, 2005, p.8). For example, natural wood tables and chairs would be preferred over the popular coloured-plastic furniture: For not only do wood products last longer, but natural wood reduces unnecessary colour stimulation within play space.

The physical space and the placement of the materials impact the quality, depth, and opportunities for play expansion.

Is Attentive to Physical Space

A responsive environment is created when early childhood practitioners are attentive to the physical space, the architectural features, the type and placement of materials in the environment, and the flow of the play options. For example, early childhood practitioners place experience-centres in groupings using a wet/dry and noisy/quiet arrangement. This supports children in diversifying their play and provides a natural flow from one area to another.

Planning the Physical Space of Responsive Environments

Children require their physical space to be safe and comfortable for play. They also require environments that support them in engaging in experiences that promote the development of new skills, the exploration of materials and community events, and the satisfaction of their curiosity. Children benefit from environments that encourage relationship building between people, objects, and ideas, and that have a strong aesthetic appeal for children and adults (Borgia, 1991; Tarr, 2001). Children are either motivated or stifled by the design and presentation of the environment. The quality of the interactions between children and adults is influenced by the possibilities of engagement that the environment affords (Lackney, 2000).

Early childhood practitioners continuously examine the design patterns and physical set-up of the play space to determine the positive and negative attributes of the environment. The placement of materials and equipment in early childhood environments requires careful consideration, because merely placing materials in designated experience-centres does not constitute a responsive environment. Practitioners make adjustments as needed to ensure children experience a comfortable play space.

The presentation of the play space communicates the value that early childhood practitioners place on children; the practitioners' philosophy about how children's play contributes to learning; and the behavioural expectations within the setting (Gandini, 1998; Rinaldi, 1998). The physical play space's appearance provides insight into the types of experiences children are exposed to, the children's role in guiding the program, and the expected behavioural standards for children.

Design Features of Responsive Environments

The early childhood practitioner's role is significant in creating a responsive environment. For example, a practitioner who has access to and appreciates green space is more likely to encourage children to explore, wonder at, and appreciate the natural learning opportunities that are abundant outdoors. She will encourage children to examine worms, frogs, plants, water, ice, and other elements of the natural landscape. She will engage and support children in playing outdoors during the four seasons and in a variety of weather conditions. Design features impact children's experiences and can also influence the early childhood practitioner's roles and daily assignments, as well as the interpersonal relationships among practitioners. Figure 6.4 illustrates the nine design features of a responsive play space environment.

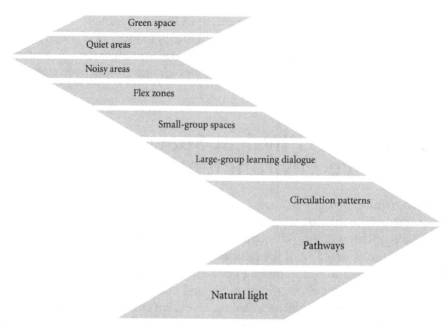

Figure 6.4 *Design Features of Responsive Environments*

Green Space Green space includes trees, grass, gardens, and places to play. It has social and psychological benefits to both children and early childhood practitioners, providing visual relief from indoor stimuli. It increases children's movement and gross motor development, which in turn reduces tension. The more green space available, the higher the level of air quality. Ideally, children should have the opportunity to play on the green space while outdoors and have it visually accessible while indoors. Viewing nature, whether in the form of gardens, natural hills, or natural or humanly created landscape, is a source of comfort and a trigger for creativity and curiosity.

Quiet Areas A responsive play environment provides quiet areas for children to pause, have quiet, and relax, read, listen to music, or contemplate areas of interest to them. These areas are found both indoors and out. Cozy spaces allow children to see and hear others, and are located in unobtrusive areas.

Noisy Areas Noisy areas support the sociability of play. Children develop plans, have informal contacts with other children, and engage in the social networks needed to execute their play. A large amount of space is available in this area, because of the exuberant play that occurs.

Flex Zones Flex zones refer to areas indoors and outdoors that are designated as multipurpose areas. Children may use the space for dramatic play one day and use the same space as a wet area for science discovery on another day. A large percentage of the furniture and equipment, therefore, is movable. Stationary furniture, such as a stage, allows for the flexibility of children's play.

Flex play zones allow children to use the same space in different ways and for different types of play.

Small-Group Places Places located both indoors and out that encourage small groups of children to gather for play, conversations, focused experiential projects, or group planning. For example, a small group of children may become interested in examining towers. The children may use the small-group places to share their books about different towers or discuss how they are going to construct the tower. Small-group places are also beneficial for children new to the centre, because they provide children with a sense of belonging and security, which are key factors for children in adapting to environments outside their family setting.

Large-Group Learning Dialogue A special open space is important to allow children and early childhood practitioners to come together for short periods to participate in group dialogue or activities that support children in using their bodies, participating in music, or testing new skills. The area is located where children have access to natural light as well as a view of the outdoor green areas.

Circulation Patterns Circulation patterns are established so that children may move from one experience-centre to another with ease. Wide passages provide children with freedom of movement. Children may choose to pause, observe, or determine where to play next. Indoor circulation patterns are designed so that natural light is unrestricted and so that, where possible, children can observe the green space. Moreover, circulation patterns allow children to move easily, and limit crowding. For example, a child wishing to move from the art centre to the block centre may do so without needing to walk through other experience-centres, such as the dramatic area.

Pathways Pathways are used to separate the various experience-centres and areas for play. Early childhood practitioners create a variety of pathways that allow children to know their boundaries, yet provide them with the freedom of movement necessary to explore the various parts of the play environment.

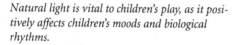

Natural light is vital to children's play, as it positively affects children's moods and biological rhythms.

Natural Light Children benefit from natural light during their outdoor playtime and when indoor play areas are placed near windows. Research indicates that natural light affects children's moods and biological rhythms, and impacts their growth, physical development (Lackney, 2000), and later academic skills.

Core and Secondary Attributes of Play Space

The sciences of physiological and educational psychology have given early childhood practitioners the rationale for responsive-environment design principles. The interior and exterior room-design principles provide an appropriate framework for developing positive physical play and space for children.

Children and adults flourish in play space that feels comfortable, much like our homes. Responsive environments have five core attributes: unity, rhythm, harmony, balance, and spatial partitioning. Secondary attributes include variety, focus points, light and colour considerations, and air quality. We outline each attribute below.

Unity Each area of the early childhood environment is planned with objects and colours that relate to each other in some way. Through repetition of colour, pattern, line, and shape, unity is established. "Unity with nature is a central theme for Froebel" (Upitis, 2005, p. 6). He identifies this as essential in play environments for children. Children learn best in natural play spaces. For example, all of the tables, chairs, and shelving units within the environment are of natural wood, rather than coloured plastic. The room colours, although varying in shades, are of complementary hues.

Variety The colours, shapes, patterns, themes, and objects are varied. The combination of variety and unity brings harmony to each play area. For example, in the art centre, materials may be presented in different types of baskets. In the manipulative area, the materials may be presented in different-shaped boxes. These subtle differences combine principles of variety and unity.

Focus Each part of the early childhood environment has a focus, and experience-centres and focal points are well defined. The practitioner examines the environment's natural conditions and uses them to guide the areas to be emphasized. Keeping the floors, walls, and ceilings neutral helps to emphasize the environment's natural elements. As well, focal points facilitate social interaction (Evans & McCoy, 1998). For example, placing a curiosity table near the entrance provides children with intrigue as they enter the environment; placing a cuckoo clock in the dramatic centre heightens children's level of curiosity and brings focus to the area.

Rhythm Rhythm is continuity. Rhythm is achieved by using repetition of shapes, colours, and textures, while progression is mastered with attention to transition or sequence. Colours, textures, and shapes flow from one play space to another and from indoor to outdoor and vice versa. Elements of one play space may be emphasized in one way in one area and emerge in a different way in another. For example, indoors, the literacy centre is a quiet area where reading material is displayed on shelves. There are soft, cozy chairs available for small groups of children. Outdoors, practitioners locate the literacy centre under trees or in a protected area. They place small baskets in the area, filled with books and magazines for the children to explore. They provide waterproof blankets and benches. There are clear connections, however, between the indoor and outdoor play spaces. For example, children may use science materials both indoors and outdoors. Functional covered areas and transitional experiences are in place to accommodate a flow between the indoor and outdoor play spaces.

Harmony Harmony is achieved by placing materials and experiences together that naturally flow together or combine comfortably because they are closely related in principles, problem-solving requirements, and expansion of learning options. For example, practitioners place sand and water close to each other because when children combine the two materials together, the change to the sand is intriguing and the options for expanded play become more complex.

Spatial Partitioning Spatial partitioning requires an examination of both stationary and movable experience-centres. Spatial-partitioning groups have clearly defined criteria. Well-defined play spaces encourage exploratory play and greater peer interaction, and they facilitate positive child behaviour. For example, the block area is partitioned with Plexiglas walls so that the area is easily supervised yet provides children with a defined space for their building. This partitioning creates flow and reduces the possibility of stress caused by block structures accidentally being destroyed. The environment is open-concept and composed of a variety of experience-centres, with loose parts that support children in their wonder, exploration, and discoveries.

Light and Colour Responsive environments balance the colours in each room with nature. Early childhood practitioners consider the intensity and availability of light in each area throughout the day and in the changing seasons. Practitioners choose colours that create a soothing, calming environment. They provide access to natural daylight by using the outdoor play space as an equal extension of the indoor play space. Indoor space uses windows, skylights, and full-spectrum lighting to provide as much access to natural lighting as possible. Table 6.1 explains the impact colours have on children.

Balance A dynamic space creates balance by providing contrast between its elements: thick with thin, hard with soft, horizontal with vertical, open with enclosed, and large with small. By juxtaposing different shapes within the overall space, action, or lack of action, occurs. For example, it is preferable for larger spaces to flow from the centre of the room and for smaller spaces to flow from the periphery, because smaller areas are more likely to attract the children and provide them with a sense of security. Think of a large table with a bouquet of flowers in the middle. Your eye naturally focuses on the bouquet of flowers rather than on the surrounding table surface. Large spaces are used more often for larger group experiences, while the smaller space becomes more intimate for children. Children are better able to control their sense of equilibrium in appropriately designed smaller spaces than in large open spaces because they feel secure.

Air Quality The quality of the air affects comfort, health, and mental alertness. Increased levels of fresh-air intake through ventilation systems or operable windows reduce a polluted indoor air environment (Lackney, 2000).

Table 6.1 *Preferred Colours for Early Learning and Child Care Environments*

Colour affects many aspects of our lives, including the way we think and learn (Hathaway, 1995). Early childhood practitioners focus on both visual ergonomics and aesthetics to create a warm, inviting, positive, and productive play space. Children require rooms that look pleasant and feel spacious. Colours such as blue and green appear to give rooms a feeling of space and openness. Warmer colours, such as yellow, make rooms seem smaller.

Yellow. Increases awareness, stimulates interest and curiosity. It supports the development of imagination, spirituality, and inspiration.

Green. Relaxes the nervous system and thought processing. Along with access to the natural environment, it has a calming effect on children.

Blue. Is the most mentally relaxing of all colours. Hues of blue are often used to create calm environments for children, especially for those whose activity level is in the high range.

Red. Creates energy. It can evoke a fight-or-flight response. It increases blood pressure and heartbeat, increasing anxiety. Red is not a colour recommended for young children's environments.

White. Symbolizes coolness and sterility. It is not recommended for early learning and child care environments, unless used in small amounts for accenting particular areas.

Warm, calming colours are used for children under the age of 6, while cooler colours are used more as children get older.

Traditional Physical-Space Considerations

Some of the traditional physical-space considerations early childhood practitioners make include the following:

- Safety and accessibility of exits guide physical-space arrangements.
- Indoor and outdoor spaces are given equal consideration. An outdoor area adjacent to the indoor area encourages children to move freely between experiences and environments.
- Provisions are made for environmental conditions, such the ozone ratings in the hot summer temperatures in southern Ontario and the cold temperatures in the northern parts of Canada. As well, spraying of agricultural areas or green space is considered.
- A combination of defined and open space supports children in exploring and trying out new play opportunities, while also increasing interaction among children. Practitioners divide the space in such a way that children feel secure (Caples, 1996, p.15).
- The placement of the experience-centres and the pathways between each experience-centre allow children to observe each potential activity. A bypass route allows children to move to experience centres without disrupting other children engaged in an experience.
- The geometry of the play space allows the practitioners to have visual access to the total space in the area.
- Practitioners group experience-centres according to dry, wet, noisy, and quiet categories, and the materials are arranged so children may make choices (see Figure 6.5).
- Practitioners group materials into well-defined experience-centres as a way to support children in making choices and becoming involved in play that leads them from simple to more complex discoveries.
- Indoor and outdoor storage units display stored materials clearly and attractively. Other storage within the environment allows unused material to be removed from the play space so that children are not confronted with clutter.

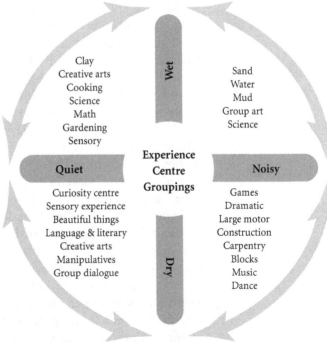

Figure 6.5 *Experience-Centre Groupings*

Environmental Aesthetics in Responsive Environments

Early learning and child care environments are usually defined in the context of safety and aesthetic pleasingness (Tarr, 2001). As a result, early childhood practitioners examine aesthetic environments in terms of decorations on walls and design elements, such as furnishings, storage, lighting, and temperature. However, current research suggests early childhood practitioners move beyond these two components and include environmental aesthetics as an essential component of a responsive environment.

Environmental aesthetics is one of the newer areas of study developed in the latter half of the twentieth century. It focuses on "the ways in which humans experience the world through their senses" (Carlson, 2002, p. 1), and incorporates the environmental perceptions and aesthetic preferences of individuals in environments, cultures, and seasons. As a result, attention to the "aesthetic appreciation of human-influenced and human-constructed as well as natural environment" (Carlson, 2002) is necessary.

Malaguzzi (1991) recommends that early childhood practitioners focus on the play-space aesthetics because they have a major influence on children's comfort, security, and the development of self-esteem. Children learn more easily in environments where they feel comfortable and experience a sense of order. Malaguzzi (1991) also says the aesthetic dimension of play spaces is essential "because of its power to organize, promote pleasant relationship between people of different ages, create a handsome environment, promote choices and activity and its potential for sparking all kinds of social, affective, and cognitive learning" (p.6). As well, the Reggio Emilia approach stresses the "environment as a third teacher" (Gandini, 1998, p.177). Early childhood practitioners inspired by this program approach look critically at their environments, including classroom aesthetics and purpose of displays (see Table 6.2). They ensure displays are attractively presented and have meaning for the group of children. When children are no longer interested in the displays, the displays are removed.

Aesthetically appropriate play spaces support children in developing a positive self-image, increasing sensory and perceptual activity, developing language, solving problems, and forming concepts. Children make a series of interconnected discoveries about the physical, cultural, and social elements of their world, and they are better able to create and discover new information in aesthetically appropriate environments than in those that do not emphasize aesthetics.

Isahi, Ungerleider, Martin, Schouten, & Haxby (1999) help us to understand the effects of our environments on development and learning. They indicate that the way children's brains deal with visual images plays a significant role in their learning. They suggest that the circuitry in the brain's visual system responds to each visual stimulus the brain is exposed to. The greater the number of visual stimuli the brain must process, the greater the amount of oxygen the brain requires to process images through the circuits. Cluttered environments require energy for the brain to suppress images not necessary for the task at hand,

Environmental aesthetics. Focuses on how individuals experience their world through their senses, by incorporating their environmental perceptions and their aesthetic preferences in environments, cultures, and seasons (Carlson, 2002).

Table 6.2 *Taking Inventory of a Responsive Environment*

1. What feeling tone does the play space convey to the children, staff, parents, or guests?

2. What realistic level of maintenance must be considered?

3. Does the colour scheme support the intended feeling tone?

4. Is the layout of play space conducive to traffic flow and ergonomics?

5. Do patterns, materials, colour combinations, and furniture overpower the play space, creating a feeling of visual clutter?

6. What natural elements and textures are currently available? What new ones would enhance the synergy in the play space?

7. What elements of the play space provide most comfort to the children? Why? What elements provide least comfort to the children? Why?

8. How are the indoor/outdoor play spaces used to complement the feeling tone?

9. Are the centres of experiences or focal points visible and appropriate to the interests of the children?

10. Are the natural-light elements used to complement the play space?

increasing children's activity levels and often negatively impacting their behaviour. Less visual chaos and clutter reduce overactivity and promotes a more calming, caring environment.

How Environments Affect Children's Behaviour

As Table 6.3 illustrates, environments that are not aesthetically appropriate create anxiety, while clutter and the use of commercial products contribute to environment anxiety. And while adults learn to protect themselves by screening out details of the environment that make them uncomfortable, children have an immature nervous system, reducing their ability to screen out the environmental chaos. Think of the "messy desk." Most adults are able to let the clutter build to a particular level; then our discomfort begins to interfere with our ability to be productive and feel comfortable. As a result, we make adjustments to the environment—we clean the desk. Young children do not possess the ability to screen out environmental clutter. When children experience anxiety, it affects their processing mechanisms, coding processes, and memory functions, making play and learning more difficult.

Cluttered environments also contribute to children's becoming overwhelmed, which reduces their attention span and ability to complete tasks or be productive. Clutter also interferes with children's use of imagery. Imagery is the foundation for many academic skills, such as listening, speaking, reading, and writing, memorizing facts, solving math problems, and understanding scientific processes. One of the most appropriate ways to assist children in developing skills in imagery is by preparing an aesthetically interesting and varied play environment.

Commercial products used in early learning and child care centres do not necessarily reflect children's real interests. For example, cartoon figures are often used in early learning and child care environments (Tarr, 2004). These materials suggest that children need to be entertained rather than recognizing their need for an environment that is responsive to their curiosity (Dahlberg, Moss & Pence 1999; Rinaldi, 2001; Tarr, 2003). Negative imagery, such as cartoons, has the potential to influence children to value and accept stereotyped images as part of the environment (Rosario & Collazo, 1981), which influences their perceptions of male and female roles in home and societal settings. Responsive environments, on the other hand, provide children with diverse examples of the roles of people in society, with an emphasis on equality.

Points to Ponder

Is there a place for cartoon-like characters to be displayed as part of the decor in early childhood environments? Why or why not?

Table 6.3 *How Environmental Conditions Impact Children's Behaviour*

Response to Environmental Conditions	Impact on Children
Anxiety	• Changes children's processing mechanisms, coding processes, and memory function. • Causes distraction. • Reduces time on task. • Impedes intensity of play experience. • Reduces ability to be creative.
Feeling overwhelmed	• Reduces attention span. • Causes inability to complete tasks or be productive. • Interferes with child's use of imagery. • Causes distraction. • Increases negative behaviour, such as biting, hitting, kicking.
Psychological discomfort	• Reduces verbal interactions, language acquisition, and vocabulary expansion. • Reduces social interaction. • Reduces tolerance for cultural, gender, family, or atypical-development differences.

The environment influences how children and adults play and respond to others. "Children and adults tell us how the room should be by their behaviour" (Greenman, 1988, p.136). The physical-environment presentation is as much a part of the program as the experiences and materials that are used to trigger children's exploration. For example, children who have high activity levels may have trouble adjusting to environments that require them to spend large portions of time indoors confined to small experience-centres. Children who have low thresholds for distraction may not adapt well to noisy play spaces. In fact, children adapt to environments in their own way.

The verbal and non-verbal communication and interaction among children and the practitioner is influenced by the psychological comfort within an environment. Interactions are richer, language acquisition stronger, and children more verbal in calm, aesthetically pleasing environments. When children are too crowded or uncomfortable, inappropriate social interactions occur (Henniger, 2002). Children are more prone to exhibit hitting, biting, and kicking if they feel anxious or overwhelmed.

Children's respect for cultural differences and for differences due to gender, family unit, or atypical development is influenced by environmental conditions. The early learning environment is designed to weave in many materials, toys, and experiences that expose children to diversity. For example, if a centre has a child who comes from a country where camels are part of the environment, other children would be exposed to camels through displays, books, and discussions. Or, for a child confined to a wheelchair, displays and materials would be organized so that she too can manipulate her environment with as much ease as other children can.

How Environments Affect Children's Creativity

Commercial products increase visual clutter and impede children's potential to respond to the world's rich and diverse heritage of art forms (Feeney & Moravcik, 1987; Tarr, 2001), negatively impacting children's creativity and, as a result, their outlet for reducing stress. Responsive environments offer opportunities for children to reflect on ideas, values, beauty, and attitudes representative of diverse cultural backgrounds. Locally appropriate and developmentally appropriate materials are evident within the environment, and display materials and objects vary. Children are encouraged to explore them through various senses, such as sight or touch.

Aesthetically interesting environments also promote creative thinking. Children's originality comes from their uniqueness of perception and not, as many think, from an innate talent. Children will invent things in play when they make new connections between new and old perceptions. Inventiveness and creative thinking evolve when children develop the ability to look and see, to listen and hear, and to imitate. Children require an environment that promotes new play experiences and provides the excitement of fresh perception; for, like adults, children respond to the space they find themselves in.

Conversation Café

Research indicates that children's environments affect behaviour. What environmental conditions should be examined to see if the environment might be negatively affecting a child's behaviour? Which conditions are more likely to have a negative impact on a child's behaviour? Why?

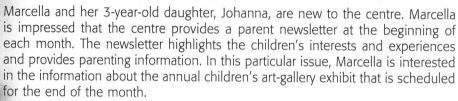

PARENTING PORTRAIT

Marcella and her 3-year-old daughter, Johanna, are new to the centre. Marcella is impressed that the centre provides a parent newsletter at the beginning of each month. The newsletter highlights the children's interests and experiences and provides parenting information. In this particular issue, Marcella is interested in the information about the annual children's art-gallery exhibit that is scheduled for the end of the month.

Three days before the exhibit, Johanna expresses great enthusiasm and excitement about the upcoming exhibit. She says, "Mommy, Mommy, when you come to see it, it will be so beautiful." Marcella does not understand why Johanna is so excited. She asks Johanna, "Why will it be so beautiful?" Johanna replies, "'Cuz of my picture."

On the day of the event, Marcella is indeed struck by the beauty of the children's creations. There are watercolour paintings, block exhibits, and sand sculptures. The watercolour work is mounted and framed in a variety of ways; the simplest drawing and creations become enhanced. The block structures have interesting patterns, some with symmetry, others without. And the sandbox has pathways and accessories leading to identifiable and unidentifiable sculptures. Children and parents move from one exhibit to another, sometimes observing, other times stopping to think about new ideas or to speak with children nearby. The combination of being outdoors and the gleeful sounds of children make it a peaceful place to be.

As Marcella approaches Johanna's exhibit, Marcella feels tears on her cheek. She is struck by the vibrancy of the colours Johanna has chosen. Johanna says, "Look Mommy, see the bird and my kitties."

Suddenly Marcella realizes that she has thrown many of Johanna's pictures in the recycling, not even looking at them. She recognizes for the first time that Johanna's artwork is important. She thinks it might be interesting to incorporate Johanna's creations into the family living environment. She looks forward to discussing this with Johanna and being able to choose pieces together.

> What knowledge has Marcella gained about Johanna since attending the children's art gallery? What did she realize about the impact that outdoor environments have on children and adults? How did this experience help to further connect Marcella and Johanna to the early learning and child care setting?

Creating Psychological Comfort in the Responsive Environment

In responsive environments, early childhood practitioners work toward addressing the psychosocial needs of the children and staff. This is accomplished by creating a play and workplace atmosphere that provides physical and emotional comfort.

The atmosphere or climate in any responsive environment is created by the interaction of the individuals working and playing within the physical space. Some of the factors that directly influence an early learning and child care climate include the following:

- The centre's administrative practices, such as staffing procedures and access to professional development.
- The value placed on the staff and children.
- The value the early childhood practitioners place on children.
- The strategy used to promote prosocial behaviours among the children.

An atmosphere or climate that is comfortable for children and practitioners is one in which the individual feels comfortable and happy and free from psychosocial or physical stress. Although mild stress can be a motivator for adaptation, anything beyond mild stress interferes with children's abilities to cope. And any event or situation that interferes with children's perceived ability to cope is considered psychological discomfort or stress. When children experience fear or are unable to see a course of action or a solution to the challenge, they become emotionally, cognitively, or physically overwhelmed. Common stress-producing events include abuses of power, betrayals of trust, entrapment, helplessness, pain, confusion, or loss.

Children experience psychological comfort when they feel support and understanding from practitioners. And such support should take the form of simply encouraging children to work through an area being explored and encouraging them to try to do things for themselves. Providing children with instant solutions is *not* support. But working within children's understanding of the situation and offering limited information to help them find solutions to challenges *is* support. Children feel comfort when respect is given to them.

Practitioners create a responsive environment by paying attention and giving consideration to children's wishes. And practitioners exhibit respect for children by paying attention to children's need for privacy, their need to be alone, and their need to offer an opinion, and by appreciating what children bring to the program. Courteousness and receptiveness to children's families also indicate respect. Laughing *with* children, not *at* them, is essential in developing a comfortable environment.

When children show signs of stress, the early childhood practitioner interacts with them to attempt to understand and reduce the psychosocial impacts arising from the stressor and the resulting distress. Then the practitioner manages the behavioural changes that result from the stress. The practitioner observes the environment to assess the impact of the climate at the time of the children's stress-response, in order to determine what factors may have influenced the change in the environmental comfort level. For example, you notice that for the past three days, Marty, a 3-year-old in your centre, has begun pushing children, especially when she plays in the dramatic centre that is set up as a pet store. You examine the environment to determine if there may be something in the environment that is triggering this aggressive behaviour. You continue to observe Marty over the next few days and note that when in the dramatic centre she plays the role of a dog, and it is in that role that she becomes aggressive with the other children. You enter the dramatic centre with Marty to engage in some play about dogs. You also determine that it would be advantageous to speak with Marty's mother to see if there have been incidents with a dog that may be triggering this behaviour. Over several more days, you discover that Marty was bitten by a dog as a toddler and continues to fear dogs. You recognize that it is healthy for Marty to use the dramatic centre to work through some of her fears, but that it is also important to protect the other children. Your role becomes supporting Marty and the other children through a variety of positive experiences involving pets, especially dogs.

Environments that provide feelings of comfort and security contribute to children's exploring, discovering, wondering, creating, inventing, and interacting with others in a positive, caring manner. The feeling tone we experience in our daily environments affects who we are, how we communicate with others, how we act, how we learn, and how we develop.

SUMMARY

Why Plan Responsive Environments

- To maximize children's developmental potential, early childhood practitioners plan environments that support, value, and respect children and families. They provide children with opportunities for play, and they respond to the changing needs of children, families, and community.

How Children Adapt to Environments

- Children require play environments that provide them with comfort and security and that are developmentally appropriate.

How Responsive Environments Support Children's Adaptation Process

- Adaptation to an environment is necessary for children's survival, security, and cognitive development. The adaptation to life is long and complex. When children are in play environments that allow them to feel psychological and physical comfort, they develop the skills to become productive members of families, communities, and society.

Characteristics of Responsive Environments

- Responsive environments support the needs, differences, and developmental unfolding of growing children. Such environments are stress-free. They provide indoor and outdoor play space, they show evidence of happy, active children, and they positively influence children with a balance of organizational structure and freedom. They are beautiful and show evidence that practitioners have paid attention to the physical space, the architectural features, and the placement of materials in the environment.

Planning the Physical Space of Responsive Environments

- Practitioners consider design features, such as green space, quiet and noisy areas, flex zones, small and large group places, circulation, pathways, and natural light. They also examine the core and secondary attributes of the environment, including unity, variety, focus, rhythm, spatial partitioning, harmony, light and colour, and balance. Safety, environmental conditions, defined and open spaces, and the placement and storage of materials are also examined.

Environmental Aesthetics in Responsive Environments

- Aesthetically appropriate environments support children in the development of their self-image and contribute to language development, problem solving, and concept-formation abilities.
- Environments that are not aesthetically appropriate contribute to children's anxiety, stress, and negative behaviour, which interfere with children's processing mechanisms, coding processes, and memory functions, in turn affecting play and learning. Following the core and secondary attributes in designing play spaces supports practitioners in creating responsive environments.

How Environments Affect Children's Behaviour

- Children's behaviour is affected by environmental aesthetics. Anxiety and a feeling of being overwhelmed are common among children in cluttered or overstimulating environments. Play skills, communication skills, and respect for the environment also influence respect for culture and diversity, positively or negatively.

How Environments Affect Children's Curiosity

- Children's creativity is negatively influenced by visual clutter. Aesthetically interesting environments promote creative thinking.

Creating Psychological Comfort in a Responsive Environment

- Children experience psychological comfort when they feel support and understanding from practitioners. Practitioners, in turn, create responsive environments by respecting children, appreciating their characteristics and the diversity they bring to the environment, and creating environments that meet the children's needs.

FURTHER OPPORTUNITIES FOR ENRICHMENT

Research

1. Research why early childhood practitioners are becoming more concerned about natural light and green space for children. How do these two elements support children's development? What are the negative impacts on children's development when these two elements are absent from early learning and child care environments?

2. The information presented identifies the importance of children's having equal access to indoor and outdoor play space. Conduct further research to examine the benefits of outdoor play to children. Examine how outdoor play supports the development of the whole child, and determine how to provide equal access to indoor and outdoor programming throughout Canada's four seasons.

Group Investigation

1. Using the guidelines in Figure 6.4 (the nine design features of a responsive environment), observe an early learning and child care centre's indoor and outdoor space to determine the locations of each of the design features. Are there features that are more evident indoors than outdoors or vice versa? Are there features that are not evident to you? How might you change the environment to make the design feature more prominent?

2. Visit an early learning and child care centre. Using the wet/dry, quiet/noisy guidelines in Figure 6.5, examine the placement of the experience-centres both indoors and out. Then, using the core and secondary attributes for room design outlined in this chapter, determine which of the attributes are evident in the centre displays. Would you recommend relocating some of the experience-centres? If so, why? Which attributes might require further attention? Devise a new environmental plan for the play space, and include the rationale for each of the changes you recommend.

Making Connections

1. Displays for children require attention to detail. Visit an early learning and child care facility. Observe children at play and determine a particular area that they express interest in. Then, devise a bulletin board or a table-top display that would model the principles of effective displays for children. How would you communicate to parents the significance of the display?

2. In "A Day Begins in an Early Learning and Child Care Centre," Jennifer discusses the feeling tone of the early learning and child care environment. Review what was significant about that environment. Then, think about working and learning environments for you. Identify what type of environment is most appropriate for you and what type is least appropriate. Describe what happens to you when you are in the "right environment" and the "wrong environment."

What signs might children exhibit when they are in the right environment and the wrong environment? How might you adjust the environment?
3. Based on the descriptors of design features of responsive environments, colour, and the experience-centre groupings, devise an environment suitable for infants, one for toddlers, and one for preschoolers for both the indoor and outdoor environments. What are the similarities and differences in design that must be considered for each age group and for both the indoor and outdoor play spaces?

ADDITIONAL READING

Curtis, D., & Carter, M. (2003). *Designs for Living and Learning: Transforming Early Childhood Environments*. St. Paul, MN: Redleaf. Available from NAEYC.

Greenman, J. (1987). *Caring Spaces/Learning Places: Children's Environments That Work*. Bellevue, WA: Exchange Press.

Greenman, J. (1998). *Places for Childhood: Making Quality Happen in the Real World*. Bellevue, WA: Exchange Press.

Harms, T., Clifford, R., & Cryer, D. (1998). *Early Childhood Environment Rating Scale*. Rev. Ed. New York: Teachers' College Press.

WEBLINKS

www.colourmatters.com/khouw.html: *Colours.*
www.coe.uga.edu/sdpl/researchabstracts/visual.html:*Lighting and colours.*
www.brighthorizons.com/Site/pages/ResourceRoomEnvironment.aspx: *Environmental designs.*
www.umaine.edu/cci/ec/growingideas: *Inclusive environmental designs.*
www.nectas.unc.edu/inclusion: *Natural environments and inclusion.*

> "The foundation blocks for a healthy, learned, productive population must be laid within the critical early years (0-6) so that our people can achieve their maximum competence and coping skills."

The Honourable Margaret Norrie McCain

7

Planning Experiences in the Responsive Environment

A Day Begins in an Early Learning and Child Care Centre

Bringing Children and Community Together

It is the second week of November on Deer Island, N.B. Jennifer and the children are getting dressed in their warm, windproof clothing. They are going to walk to the Leonardville wharf for lunch. It is lobster season in the Bay of Fundy, and the children will join their parents, grandparents, and the community fishermen for lobster chowder.

Upon arriving at the wharf, the children slip into their personal flotation devices (PFDs), most having little or no difficulty with the fasteners. These children have been coming to the wharf since they were babies, and they appear comfortable on the wharf. The children quickly rush to help the fishermen select, from a lobster crate, the lobsters that the fishermen will cook for chowder. The fishermen encourage each child to test the shells for hardness. Then, the children pass the hard-shelled lobster to the fishermen, who will place the lobsters into a boiling pot of ocean water. This is the first step in chowder making.

While the lobster cooks, some children help the fishermen prepare the lobster traps for the boats. These children fill the bait bags and pass them to the fishermen, who tie them and place them in the traps. The children and fishermen speak easily with one other, both generations comfortable in the activities, despite the cool –3° Celsius temperature and the fact that they fill the bait bags with bare hands. The fishermen and children discuss the best kind of bait. One child speaks of his lobster bait choice "as red fish" while another says "my daddy uses herring." The fishermen listen intently to the children, enjoying the "innocence and life" the children add to the fishermen's day.

Once the bait bags are complete, these children move about the wharf, joining the other children playing with the buoys, climbing up and over the lobster traps, and draping herring nets and blankets to make shelters away from the cold wind. Jennifer is intrigued by the way the children play together. She notices that James speaks more with the other children and the fishermen here then when he is at the early childhood centre. She notes that Jennie has excellent spatial relationships as the children build structures using lobster traps.

A fisherman calls to the children to tell them it is time to prepare the ingredients for the lobster chowder. Some children remain playing, while others help the fishermen by preparing the onions, celery, carrots, and potatoes as the few strips of smoked bacon cook to crisp in the bottom of the chowder pot. When the chowder is ready, this small fishing community sit together on the wharf to enjoy the hot lunch.

As Jennifer listens to the chatter among the fishermen and the children, she is reminded of the importance of intergenerational relationships and how locally appropriate experiences support programming at the centre. This is how children's interests are expanded and how they learn about community, culture, and society.

Jennifer is excited to see how the children will extend their play back at the centre, because two of the fishermen are bringing lobster traps and nets to the centre for the outdoor dramatic centre. She is going to place them near the wooden boat.

Experience-centres support children's need to explore, wonder, and experiment with materials and ideas.

Looking Ahead

In this chapter, we will introduce the roles of children and practitioners in program planning, the types of experience-centres found in quality early learning and child care settings, why program planning is important, and which processes we use for program planning. You will note that this chapter builds on earlier information presented in Chapters 4, 5, and 6.

Planning experiences in a responsive environment requires early childhood practitioners to have a thorough understanding of child development, child's play, strategies for facilitating play, and techniques for creating responsive environments to support each child. You will note by examining previous chapters that understanding all of these processes will help you begin to connect information on how children learn, the importance of play, the role of practitioners, and how environments influence play and learning with the program-planning process. Each of the previous chapters provides foundation information about children's needs that will help practitioners and children to engage in planning responsive environments.

Developmentally Appropriate Practice

Children's programming is designed to support all levels of children's development as well as their interests. Practitioners prepare environments that are responsive to the physical, social, emotional, and cognitive abilities of each child. The experiences naturally draw children to explore and discover play opportunities and participate in creative adventures or imaginative play. The experiences also contribute to building interpersonal relationships with peers, other children, and adults. As illustrated in Figure 7.1, developmentally appropriate programs are characterized by three common principles:

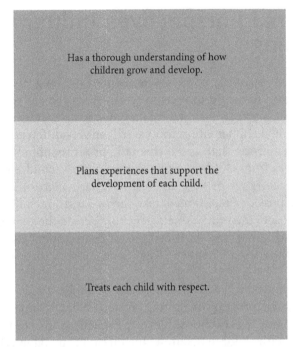

Has a thorough understanding of how
children grow and develop.

The Practitioner

Plans experiences that support the
development of each child.

Treats each child with respect.

Figure 7.1   Practitioners' Roles in Developmentally Appropriate Environments

1. Practitioners have a thorough understanding of how children grow and develop, and they use this information to guide the types of experiences they provide for individual children and for groups of children.

2. Practitioners plan experiences that support the development of each child, rather than planning for groups of children.

3. Practitioners treat each child with respect. Each child is accepted and advocated for with materials and experiences that vary in complexity and materials, and that make experiences culturally relevant for children.

Practitioners use child development as their guideline for practice. This knowledge influences the experiences they offer to children, how they offer those experiences, and how the play experiences build on previous learning and expand further learning and development. Developmentally appropriate programs support children in gathering information, exploring, and experiencing the topics of their choice at their own pace and at their level of understanding. Early childhood practitioners plan some potential play experiences, and children plan others. But the child determines the play option that he wishes to engage in.

Examine the vignette "Bringing Children and Community Together." Note Jennifer's approach with the children. She role modelled many developmentally appropriate practices. For example, she supported children in having choices: some filled the bait bags, while others played with the buoys and the lobster traps. She observed each of the children to determine their level of play and to note specific developmental attributes that became evident in the outdoor setting. She used this field trip as a way to offer the children new experiences in the days to come by adding lobster traps and nets to the outdoor dramatic centre.

Personal Perspectives Influence Program Planning

Emergent program. Describes the experiences that are offered to children as a result of children's exploring ideas and interests that are cognitively challenging and meaningful to them.

Thematic program. Program experiences available to children are organized around an idea or topic originating from either the children or the early childhood practitioner.

The program planning process is influenced by the goals and philosophy of the early learning and child care centre and that of the early childhood practitioner. For example, if you are in a setting that follows an **emergent program** process, the planning and documentation process will be very different from that of colleagues working in a centre that uses a **thematic program** approach. The emergent program evolves from children. Practitioners observe children's interests as a way to determine the range of their interest in a particular topic or whether they have ideas for a project. Practitioners take their cues from children. In a thematic program approach, the practitioners generally decide the themes that they will present to the children, and each experience centre offers children play experiences related to the theme. The theme may be as short as three days or extended over a few weeks.

Practitioners' values and beliefs about children, play, and learning influence their preferred program-planning process. What is important is that whatever approach practitioners choose, developmentally appropriate practices must guide their work with children. Examine the questions in Table 7.1. These will help you think about your perspectives on children's choices, parents' roles, and the types of experiences you feel are best for children.

Table 7.1   *Questions Practitioners Ask as Part of the Program-Planning Process*

The program-planning process leads early childhood practitioners to ask questions and reflect upon elements such as these:

1. How does the play space support play, exploration, wonderment, and learning?

2. What are the appropriate materials needed to support the children's interests and developmental levels?

3. What strategies support children in exploration, discovery, and wonderment?

4. What is the role of the local community in children's learning?

5. How are community resources incorporated into the children's experiences?

6. How are family contributions utilized?

7. What is the role of each child in making choices about his play experiences?

8. Should groups of children be required to play in areas for specific periods?

9. How will you use the indoor and outdoor spaces for experiences?

Why We Design Early Childhood Programs and Not Curriculum

Early learning and child care programs are play-focused. Play enables children to progress along the developmental sequence, from the sensorimotor intelligence present during infancy to preoperational thought in the preschool years to the concrete-operational thinking of a school-aged child (Piaget, 1971).

Early childhood practitioners document planned activities, available experience-centres, community-awareness elements, parent involvement, field trips, and special-interest centres (Crossley & Dietze, 1996) that will be available to children. Through dialogue, early childhood practitioners and children create a dynamic, changing, and exciting play environment. The documentation of these experiences is called a **program plan**.

Program plan. A suggested plan of action that guides practitioners in planning potential experiences that will trigger children's curiosity.

The program plan is the centre's formal plan, which reflects its mission statement and its intended expectations for children. The program plan links the centre's practices with the centre's philosophy and beliefs about how children learn, how they develop, and what materials, projects/topics, and community events the children will be encouraged to explore.

The presentation and organization of play experiences in early learning and child care centres varies from program to program and from region to region. Some of this variation stems from the interpretation of the meaning of the terms **curriculum** and **program.** The Canadian early childhood sector uses the two terms interchangeably (Crowther, 2003), even though they differ in meaning and in the way that learning opportunities are approached and delivered.

Curriculum. A prescribed set of learning outcomes presented to a group of children.

Program. A term used to describe the process for documenting the ideas or experiences that occur in early learning and child care programs before children enter the school system.

The term *curriculum* has its origin in the educational sector and primarily targets cognitive learning. Children at approximately 4 years old begin to enter programs administered by provincial departments of education, such as junior and senior kindergarten. These programs have a prescribed curriculum. For example, in New Brunswick, by the conclusion of kindergarten, children are required to be able to print upper- and lower-case letters, recognize 15 sight words, reproduce names, identify familiar words, and have phonological awareness. According to Beane (1995), a prescribed curriculum implies that a teacher presents pieces of information to a student. The traditional curriculum presents segregated pieces of knowledge that impose order on what information is learned. There is some controversy as to whether this methodology impedes the development of critical-thinking skills, personal and collaborative skills, and problem-solving abilities, all of which are central to thinking and learning (Jones et al., 1987; Tinzmann et al., 1990). Curriculum in educational settings may be viewed as more prescriptive than programming designed for early learning and child care settings.

The term *program,* on the other hand, refers to a plan or sequence of experiences that practitioners present to children to support identified goals. Early learning and child care programs are play-focused, and children initiate many of their experiences. Consequently, developmentally appropriate early childhood programs devise and deliver programs rather than prepare curricula. This approach to learning supports children's developmental adaptation to living in a family, community, and society. Because early learning and child care programs advocate that children's play is the way in which they learn, practitioners provide children with play options rather than prescribed curricula. Therefore, in Canada we use the term *program* to describe the process for documenting the ideas or experiences that occur in early learning and child care programs.

Why Program Planning Focuses on Developing Meaningful Children's Experiences

Through play, children adapt to their physical, cultural, and social worlds and negotiate their environment (Klein, Wirth, & Linas, 2003). Children's experiences are influenced by a variety of social, cultural, and physical factors, all of which interact and contribute to children's personalities and growth and development process (Lackney, 2000).

The effective delivery of the children's program encourages practitioners to explore ways to present experiences that will be meaningful and exciting to children. When practitioners follow developmentally appropriate practices, they develop an inclusive play environment and experiences for all children.

Theories of learning and development have evolved as a result of considerable research in the sciences of developmental psychology, neurology, and evolutionary biology. The process of program-planning, direction, and implementation comes from these sciences. As a result, practitioners organize information into child-meaningful and child-understandable units to prevent isolated or non-related learning. The more meaningful the information and the attention paid to the continuity and sequence of the experiences presented, the more effective is children's learning. All elements of the program should be related to one another, so that a systematic body of ideas and experiences can be expanded continuously into larger and more meaningful patterns. For example, think about children learning about ice. First, they need to have experience with water in liquid form. They need information on temperatures, and they need to acquire experience with combining water and varying temperatures before they can truly understand the process of how water turns to ice.

Holt (1969) reminds us that the child "wants to make sense of things, find out how things work, gain competence and control over himself and his environment, do what he can see other people doing" (p. 184).

How Children's Interests Influence a Program

Children's interests stem from their life experiences from birth to their current time in life; the number and variety of life experiences depend on the richness of their environments. Children aged 4 and younger have few life experiences with resultant knowledge from which personal interests evolve. Because of their limited life experiences, however, designing a children's program that evolves entirely from children's identified interests reduces children's options for learning. Children require environments that support their need to satisfy their curiosity. Environments that introduce children to items, ideas, and materials that are fascinating and new to the child (Hendrick & Weissman, 2006) are most beneficial in expanding curiosity.

Early childhood practitioners are role models: they create environments that trigger children's wonderment and interest. Time for exploration and learning supports children in satisfying their curiosity. For example, Hunter just returned from visiting his grandparents in St. Thomas, Ontario. While there, just after a snowstorm, he, his parents, and his grandparents made a large snow bear. Hunter showed children pictures of the bear and told them how he used water to make the snow right, and how his daddy showed him how to use the palm of his hand to pack the snow around the feet. He told the children how, just before he went to bed, he and his grandpa would take the water hose and spray the bear. This exchange of information triggered the other children's interest. As a result, three weeks later Jennifer and the children made a snow bear.

The available experience-centres influence program planning. Practitioners observe children's play in experience-centres to determine their interests, material requirements, and play options, and to determine how their development is supported through play.

Points to Ponder

Are there specific experience-centres that remain constant? If so, which ones and why? Do some support more focused play than others do? If so, which ones?

Early Learning Experience-Centres

Arce (2000) describes the *program* as all the related experiences that affect children. The program focuses on the developmental characteristics and interests of young children—the learners. The various experiences the practitioner plans or that evolve spontaneously from the children become the core guide for programming with young children (Arce, 2000, p. 4).

The terms *experience-centres* and *interest-centres* are often used interchangeably. We use the term *experience-centre* because *experience* implies action and activity, whereas *interest* connotes passivity; also, interest-centres may not require children to engage in any physical activity.

Early childhood practitioners often organize information in the topic/interest format in the form of experience-centres that are well defined and available in both the indoor and outdoor play spaces. Some of the experience-centres remain constant, although the materials are rotated. Specialized experience-centres are available for a short term, depending on when children's interest wanes. And each experience-centre encourages a different type of play (Pellegrini, 1985; Rubin, 1977; Pellegrini & Perlmutter, 1988). For example, a dramatic centre generally encourages interactive play. A manipulative centre may attract more isolated play, while an art experience may influence parallel play. Practitioners examine the developmental needs of each child and plan play opportunities within the experience-centres to support the specific developmental needs of a particular child or of a group of children.

Characteristics of Experience-Centres

Experience-centres are designed to support a flexible program that matches the interests of the children. The presentation of the experience-centres and the materials placed within them influence how children's curiosity is triggered and the depth of the play that children engage in. In general, experience-centres display seven characteristics:

Offer Balance Experience-centres offer a balance of experiences and activities, some planned and some unplanned, some indoors and others outdoors. Some of the experiences are active and some quiet. Daily-living skills, community resources, and community uniqueness are incorporated into topics/interests.

Provide Opportunities Experience-centres provide children with opportunities for active learning, freedom of choice, decision making, communication, problem solving, and exploration of ideas and interests. Materials within the experience-centres contribute to children's manipulation of materials and ideas, exploring, experimenting, questioning, communicating, and creating new knowledge, either individually or with another child or adult.

Build on Knowledge and Spark Exploration Experience-centres build on children's knowledge about local or global culture and should spark children's sense of exploration and originality (Isbell, 1995; Isbell & Exelby, 2001; Jalongo & Isenberg, 2004). The materials practitioners place and rotate within experience-centres integrate potential learning options that reflect children's identified interests or that are part of a project's investigation component.

Encourage Experiential Learning Practitioners design experience-centres that encourage children to engage in experiential learning and to use all of their senses. For example, developing a flower shop in the dramatic centre offers children the opportunity to use cognitive skills, such as mathematics, when they play at selling flowers. Children combine their fine motor skills with their sense of aesthetics and kinesthetics as they arrange flowers in vases and pots. And they use their sense of touch to determine where to hold the flower and the stem in the flower-arranging process.

Allow for Creative Expression Experience-centres allow children the greatest opportunity for creative expression through hands-on experience with the materials. In the above example, providing children with fresh flowers to use in the dramatic centre after they have experience with artificial flowers increases the richness of the experience because they become familiar with the scent of the flowers and they gain an understanding of how the stems of natural flowers differ from those of artificial ones. Wooden blocks provide a more natural sensory experience to children than plastic blocks. Wooden blocks generally offer a more open material for children; this, in turn, expands their potential for creative expression.

Provide Props to Expand Thinking Skills Practitioners supply experience-centres with props intended to expand children's thinking skills, including reasoning, verbal, and writing skills, as well as problem solving and critical analysis. Children's thinking skills develop when they engage in a play experience that offers them new challenges and that requires them to think about processes in a new way. Practitioners encourage children to use information or knowledge they have and incorporate it with new information gained from exploration. Discovery thinking should then occur. For example, when Molly plays in the block area, she takes the information she has about creating structures that have walls and bridges and then combines that information to create city blocks by making enclosures and patterns. Molly needs a solid knowledge base, followed by success in constructing walls and bridges, before she is able to move to the next phase of block building.

Experience-centres that include enticing materials with loose parts or open-ended attributes encourage children to "explore, invent, combine, create, and communicate" (Gestwicki & Bertrand, 1999, p. 93). These processes develop thinking skills.

Provide Child-Initiated Play Opportunities Experience-centres provide child-initiated and child-directed play opportunities. The materials and the arrangement of those materials support children in becoming self-sufficient in their exploration, wonderment, and discovery.

Common Experience-Centres

As identified in Chapter 6, experience-centres are most effective when set up using the "wet/dry, noisy/quiet" arrangement. The number and type of experience-centres available may vary in early learning and child care centres, depending on space availability. Some early childhood environments may have all of the centres we describe below and illustrate in Figure 7.2; others rotate the experience-centres available. The descriptors are intended as an introduction only. You will gain more in-depth knowledge as you visit and work in early learning and child care centres.

Dramatic Experiences The primary objective of the dramatic centre is for children to use their imagination. Dramatic centres include props, costumes, and equipment appropriate to children's age range. Props are changed or added to daily and include an interesting variety to spark children's interest in exploring a particular idea, theme, or role. Through dramatic play (including movement to music, exploration, pantomime games, and story dramatization), children explore, develop, express, and communicate ideas, concepts, and feelings.

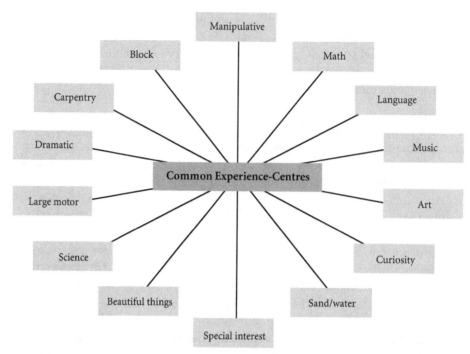

Figure 7.2 *Common Experience-Centres*

Block Experiences Blocks are multi-purpose, open-ended materials. The block centre encourages children to be productive and creative as they release energy. An appropriately arranged block centre offers children an infinite variety of expressive opportunities, from patterning to physics to engineering principles required for bridge- and structure-building. Block experiences support children in practising sorting, grouping, comparing, arranging, making decisions, co-operating and role playing—all of which form the foundation for mathematical and scientific skills.

Practitioners enhance dramatic play when they offer interesting props and initially engage in play with children.

Math Experiences Early math experiences focus on concepts such as same/different and more than/less than, sets, units, and combinations. Practitioners present these math concepts informally in day-to-day play experiences. They highlight mathematical principles during activities such as art, cooking, games, dramatic play, block building, and language experiences. For example, children acquire an understanding of shapes, colour, and order through block play, and then this knowledge is incorporated into essential mathematical logic concepts. Through cooking activities, practitioners present measurement and how quantities are related, and children identify the significance of order.

Science Experiences Science experiences introduce children to skills in observing, exploring, measuring, comparing, classifying, predicting, and discovering. Science experiences also increase children's language skills and general knowledge and improve their small muscle development and eye–hand coordination. In addition, through science children learn about the environment and the life cycles of humans, animals, and plants. Some of the most successful science experiences will be unplanned, resulting from the events of the day. For example, an early childhood practitioner and children may discuss what happens to water when it is put outside on a cold day. A child who is intrigued by this conversation may decide to put hot water in containers outdoors on a cold day. The child will probably observe the changes that occur as the water freezes—from steam to ice on the surface to solid ice. When the child expresses this interest, the practitioner may offer the child some other interesting options of water/ice play, such as making ice cubes and placing those ice cubes in the water table.

Block play forms the foundation for mathematical and scientific skills, as well as social interactions.

Sand/Water Experiences Sand/water experiences support children's science and mathematical concepts. Sand and water are naturally soothing sensory substances and therefore provide a venue for both learning and relaxation. Sifting and scooping activities improve physical dexterity, while sinking and floating, and wet and dry concepts enhance cognitive and social skills. Interesting props added to these centres ultimately magnify children's opportunities to explore. Frequently changing props and mixtures in the tables as well as combining sand and water together lead to further exploration and discovery.

Art Experiences Through art, children develop thinking and planning skills and ways to develop their own ideas. The primary objective of art experiences is to promote children's creativity, develop their sensory awareness, and expand their imagination. Art experiences provide children with the pleasure of working with and manipulating materials, and fulfill their need for movement, self-expression, and achievement. Moreover, art experiences are open-ended, free-flowing, and support exploration by combining a variety of mediums, such as paint, paper, glue, string, foil, and fabric.

People tend to include crafts as art. The creative possibilities inherent in craft production are limited by the craft itself and therefore are not recommended as part of the art program. Art experiences should focus on processes rather than product. For example, one child may choose to use paint rollers, paint brushes, sticks, or special fabric to create a piece of art at the easel. Another child may use a tennis ball and marbles to create a piece of art by placing paper in a box and rolling the ball and marbles and paint in the box.

There are many ways that children develop creativity. Having a variety of art mediums contributes to children's trying new ways of reproducing their ideas.

Language Experiences Early learning and child care programs provide children with appropriate role models and opportunities to experience communication skills and language processes. Acquiring vocabulary, learning to express thoughts, and speaking with confidence evolve as a result of a comfortable environment and planned language experiences. The language component is integrated throughout the program and during group discussion times. Early childhood practitioners converse with children, parents, and colleagues and, in so doing, model the use and versatility of language. Children increase their language skills by participating in dialogue in a group and by responding to open-ended questions. Children do the bulk of their thinking through language; children see relationships, make classifications, draw inferences, hazard guesses, predict outcomes, formulate conclusions, make generalizations, and solve problems all through the process of language and literacy. Reading to children, introducing children to nursery rhymes and poetry, using finger plays and a word board all support children in language acquisition.

Music Experiences Music increases children's perception, use of imagination, language skills, and self-expression. The music component is active and encourages children to explore with sound and rhythm. The other goals include enjoying singing, moving to music, and responding to rhythm. Music experiences contribute to children's developing listening skills, memory strategies, and the ability to follow directions. Children use their brain's dual hemispheric activity when engaged in musical activities: the brain's left hemisphere plays a role in the recall of melody and rhythm; the right hemisphere is involved in the reproduction of melody. Children use both hemispheres when they experiment with their own rhythms, melodies, and words. This physiological process is invaluable to brain development.

Large-Motor Equipment and Experiences Large-motor experiences are essential for young children because through this type of play they learn to control their physical movements and understand their kinesthetic space. Children require constant access to experiences that will allow them to climb, balance, and coordinate movements. Large spaces, time, and opportunities to walk, run, roll, jump, and climb on different ground surfaces and equipment are essential. The equipment and experiences provided also support the perceptual motor skills, such as agility, strength, endurance, sequencing, and rhythm (Wortham, 1998).

Wooden climbing structures, especially those that allow children to add and remove parts to the design, promote large-motor development. The most appropriate climbing structures have a series of wood platforms that may be rearranged periodically at different levels to support children's various developmental levels. Steps, ramps, ladders, slides, and poles help children learn to navigate their movements in ways that increase large-motor development.

Balancing apparatuses also support perceptual development. Stationary and moving experiences (Catron & Allen, 1999) that support children's balance are essential. Geometric stepping stones, different-level balance beams, and logs encourage children to participate in play that incorporates balance opportunities.

Special Interest Experiences Special interest centres or experiences reflect children's or practitioners' expressed interests. Practitioners maintain the special interest centre until children no longer are attracted to the area. These centres have no boundaries. For example, one day children may find a variety of clocks to explore—an alarm clock, a wind-up clock, or a cuckoo clock. The next day, the practitioner may put the clock's internal mechanisms on the table.

Manipulative Experiences The manipulative experiences are open-ended play materials that, through their design, increase children's complex organization of motor movement, perceptual development, language development, symbols, and mathematical concepts. Practitioners present manipulative materials to children in a sequential format, moving from simple to more complex problem solving, decision making, and reflective thinking. Manipulative materials support children in gaining concepts such as patterning, sorting, classification, graphing, and number/symbolization. Practitioners place manipulative materials both in an experience-centre and near the block centre. Beads, blocks, cylinders, rods, and spools are common manipulative materials.

Special-interest centres are intended to spark children's sense of curiosity.

Carpentry Centre The carpentry centre requires space away from other activities so that children have room to measure wood and have access to a sturdy workbench. This experience-centre, much like the art area, provides children with a venue to express their creativity and to enhance their math and language skills. For example, when a child determines he wishes to make a shelf, he will be exposed to new words such as *C-clamp*, *level*, *vise*, *saw*, etc. He will use a measuring tape to determine the length and width of the boards needed for his creation, and he will decide on a strategy for connecting his boards.

Practitioners who choose to offer this centre to children must ensure that there is good-quality, smooth wood available for the children to use. The hammers must be solid and the saws should be crosscut ones. This is one centre that requires good equipment and more supervision than the others because of the equipment the children are using.

The Curiosity Centre This centre supports children's need to satisfy their curiosity and also helps to expand children's interest and knowledge in new directions. This centre contains a group of articles that have some connection with each other and that reflect interests expressed by the children. The curiosity items are changed each day. Often, new material that will become part of the program will first appear on the curiosity table.

Beautiful Things Centre Young children are not always allowed access to the beautiful things in their home environments. One of the program objectives is to expose children to items of beauty, because that is how children develop an appreciation for form, pattern, structure, and line. Children are easily guided in examining and caring for fragile items. Some examples of beautiful things would be china teacups, paintings, fresh bouquets, and sculptures.

Group-Dialogue Experiences

Group-dialogue experiences are intended for children over 2 years of age and are most suitable for small groups of children. The primary aim of the group-dialogue experience is to support children in gaining skills in group functions. These skills include listening to others, offering ideas, taking turns, and sharing thoughts. Group experiences provide children with a sense of belonging, a sense of being a contributing member of a group, developing self-confidence in expressing ideas, and feeling comfortable in thinking and speaking spontaneously. These group times are often called "circle time." They have differing durations that reflect the group's developmental ages. The important part of group time is that the practitioner announces to the children that she will be hosting a group gathering for those children who wish to attend. Some children may choose to come initially and stay for the duration of the group time, while other children may join in after they have finished working on a particular project. Still others may not join the group, but, instead, observe from afar. Effective group-dialogue experiences support children in being active and help them to satisfy curiosity and build their feelings of self-esteem.

Group-dialogue experiences may occur more than once a day. For example, as shown in Figure 7.3, Crossley and Dietze (1996) suggest up to three group experiences, all of which are small-group and optional.

Welcome Group The welcome group is the first gathering of the day and is approximately five to seven minutes in duration. The practitioner welcomes children who choose to come to the gathering. Then, the practitioner and children discuss the experience-centres, the special activities, and projects available for that day. The children are encouraged to give input into the program or to identify a specific interest they would like to explore.

Discussion Experience The discussion experience is the second gathering of the day. This eight- to twelve-minute gathering introduces children to specific information related to a specific topic or child's interest. The practitioner welcomes the children, sings a song—usually one that requires action—has a quiet/soothing activity—such as a finger play, story/quiet group-game, or other type of presentation—followed by a transition activity. The transition activity is always active—it requires children to take turns, and it contains an element of fun. The practitioner observes which elements of the topic/experience children find interesting. This is also a time when children have input into the program design.

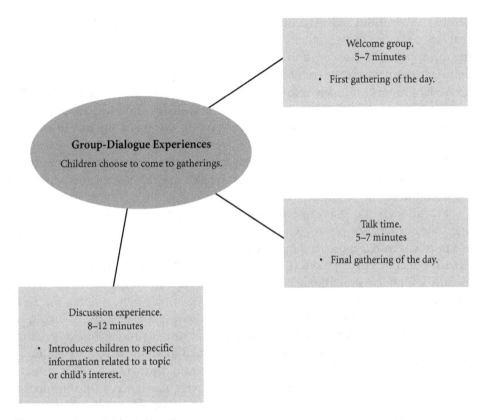

Figure 7.3   *Group-Dialogue Experiences*

Talk Time   Talk time is the final gathering of the day. This five- to seven-minute gathering provides children and the practitioner with an opportunity to discuss the experiences that the children engaged in during the day and the types of experiences the children wish to carry out in upcoming days. As a way to trigger curiosity, the practitioner may also describe an attribute of a particular experience that may be available when the children return the next day. This encourages children to think about and anticipate future activities.

Building a Program-Planning Framework

The experience-centres and the group-dialogue experiences provide the framework from which early childhood practitioners offer the play venue for children. Both the play options within experience-centres and the group-dialogue experiences require planning.

Experience-centres help children learn best about things that interest them or make sense to them. For example, Andrew is interested in how colours are formed and how he can make different shades by mixing various colours. He is learning about this through his experimentation. He spends long periods of time at the easel working with different colours and consistencies of paint. His interest is expanding, because in the last few days, Jennifer has observed him using different-width brushes and various paper textures. Andrew's process illustrates how experiences that are connected to each other and to an idea or concept offer more efficient learning, as opposed to isolated learning, as when topics are presented without prior knowledge, experience, or connections. When the experience is meaningful to children, they connect the new information with previously learned knowledge. This process requires children to organize the new knowledge and integrate it into their memory banks. Andrew processes information and material efficiently in environments that permit him freedom of choice, are active and non–teacher-directed, and where experiences are organized with a logical, consistent, recognizable flow from a simple to more complex structure. Children are able to guide this process when given the freedom.

Practitioners use many approaches to organize responsive environments into interesting experience-centres (Crossley & Dietze, 1996). For example, using "hooks" as a process-centred approach provides an opportunity for active learning in the four domains of child development (Crossley & Dietze, 1996). A **hooking strategy** refers to early childhood practitioners' placing interesting and varied materials into the play space. These materials offer children a choice of play opportunities for exploration, and time to make physical and cognitive connections with the materials.

The materials and potential experience build on Vygotsky's zone of proximal development in a scaffolding process. This helps children move to a higher level of thinking, exploring, and experimenting. "The scaffold provides a stable structure that enables a child to try out new knowledge with assistance, with the supports gradually decreased as the child becomes more capable" (Driscoll & Nagel, 2005, p. 75). Through observation, direction, cues, modelling, demonstrations, or discussions, practitioners acquire insight into the next phase of learning or scaffolding that will support children's learning and development. The dialogue between practitioners and children is important in the scaffolding process (John-Steiner & Mahn, 1996). Because preschool children have "unsystematic, disorganized, and spontaneous concepts" (Santrock, 2002, p. 217), the interaction between adults and children guides children in developing their thought processes to become more systematic and logical.

Children's experiences develop from their expressed interests. Therefore, the early childhood program is fluid, always evolving, and always flexible. An experience or project remains part of the program as long as one or more children retain interest in exploring the topic and materials. This is known as a responsive environment.

Why Program Planning Is Important

A program plan is a suggested plan of action that guides practitioners in planning potential experiences that will trigger children's curiosity. Planning experiences that support children's interests and learning is one of the most essential aspects of successful early childhood programs (Jalongo & Isenberg, 2004).

Planning requires early childhood practitioners to do the following:

- Be effective observers, set goals, select materials, and develop opportunities for children to engage in experiences that support their areas of interest and their skills (Morrison, 2003).

Hooking strategy.
Refers to the process of placing interesting and varied materials into the play space. These materials offer children a choice of play opportunities for exploration, as well as time to make physical and cognitive connections with those materials.

Conversation Café

Is there value in early childhood practitioners' deciding what is important for children to learn during a teachable moment rather than allowing children to take the lead in what their interests are and what they want to learn?

- Think, create, and arrange experiences according to children's developmental and individual needs and interests.
- Develop an organized framework that outlines the experiences and content that children will be exposed to.

Considerations in a Program-Planning Framework

As illustrated in Figure 7.4, the early learning and child care program-planning framework involves a planning process that addresses the following:

1. Identifies a Program Philosophy The program philosophy describes what the centre's early childhood practitioners believe about children, the role of play, and how children develop and learn. The program philosophy outlines the strategies and methods used to support children and practitioners in gaining new knowledge and skills. The environmental dimension describes where the play takes place, while the human-relations dimension outlines the value adults place on the uniqueness that each child brings to the play space. The program philosophy is intended to guide practitioners in how they design and deliver the children's program.

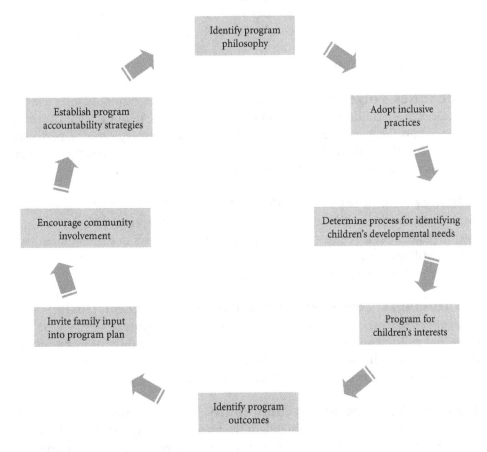

Figure 7.4 *Program-Planning Framework*

2. Adopts Inclusive Practice The children's play environment and program meet the needs of the individual children and families regardless of gender, disability, social and cultural background, ethnic group, or linguistic background.

3. Determines Process for Identifying Children's Developmental Needs Determining developmental needs begins during the first encounter with a child and family and continues as long as the child is enrolled in the program. Practitioners observe, collect, organize, and examine data continuously to determine each child's phase of development and his response to play experiences. Discussions about the observations are shared with parents and other practitioners at regular intervals as a way to acquire further insight into the interests and needs of each child.

4. Programs for Children's Interests The information gathered about children's interests and their developmental levels guides the types of play experiences offered (Morrison, 2003). An interest is identified through observation during a child's normal pattern of play and through the daily interactions with others and the environment. Practitioners may observe peer groups, pose open-ended questions to the child, and have conversations with the child's peers as a way to continuously be aware of a child's interests. Information exchanges with a child's family or comments from observations made by other practitioners also help to identify potential interests. The combination of child development and knowing the strengths, abilities, and learning styles of each child guides the program plan and implementation (Catron & Allen, 1999).

5. Identifies Program Outcomes The centre's program outcomes are the expectations for children's early childhood experiences. The long-term outcome describes how the play experiences support each child's language, motor, personal/social, and intellectual growth, as well as help her to discover relationships between her physical, cultural, and social worlds (Morrison, 2003).

6. Invites Family Input into Program Plan and Delivery Families are responsible for their children's development and for choosing the type of early learning and child care centre that best suits their children's needs. Families provide practitioners with information about their children's culture, interests, and ways they are able to support and participate in the daily program.

7. Encourages Community Involvement in Program Design and Implementation Communities may contribute to supporting family development and cultural awareness. Practitioners use resources within a community to expand children's interests or hook children into exploring new areas of interest and subsequent experience centres (Gestwicki & Bertrand, 1999).

8. Establishes Program Accountability Programs implement evidence-based assessment processes that highlight the program's effectiveness on children's development and learning. This data is available to government, funding sources, parents, and community.

Program-Planning Approaches

Now that you have explored the reasons why program planning occurs, you are ready to begin to think about how programs are planned. Program planning is influenced by practitioners' beliefs about how children learn and by the early learning and child care program model being used. Programs such as the creative-play model, High/Scope, Montessori, and Reggio Emilia have specific planning processes; other programs use an eclectic approach, combining one or more planning approaches (Arce, 2000). We present three general planning approaches.

Authentic Curriculum/Emergent Programming Authentic curriculum/emergent programming refers to indoor/outdoor play experiences that support and encourage children's interests and their need to be active.

Authentic Curriculum/ Emergent Programming. Programming that evolves in response to children's expressed interests, needs, or abilities.

The experiences unfold as children or practitioners express an interest in an identified area. Sobel (1994) identifies authentic curriculum as "the process of movement from the inside out, taking curriculum impulses from the inside of the child and bringing them out into the light of day, into the classroom" (p. 35). A topic, event, or object often comes up in children's discussions and is usually accompanied by interest, enthusiasm, and excitement or questioning.

When practitioners observe children's interest, they plan experiences for exploring the topic, event, or object. Such exploration can last minutes, days, or weeks. Emergent curriculum "evolves through continuous dialogue and documentation, frames learning as children devise and engage in projects" (Essa et al., 1998, p. 90). As children interact with other children and adults, and with materials and ideas, the curriculum for those children becomes evident (Crowther, 2003).

This approach is not and cannot be planned days or weeks in advance. Rather, it unfolds as children interact with their environment. For example, if there has been a rain overnight, as a child walks to the centre the following morning he may become intrigued by worms in the yard. The early childhood practitioner supports this child's interest in the worms as long as the interest is evident. Documentation of the play process that occurs during or after the event becomes the program documentation.

Project-Based Programming This approach is considered an integrated program method and is a form of emergent curriculum (Driscoll & Nagel, 2005). Children between the ages of 4 and 8 (Driscoll & Nagel, 2005) explore projects that are suggested either by them or by a practitioner. Often, the play and learning are made relevant by establishing connections to experiences outside of the early learning and child care centre. The developmental value of projects is the ability to work with others, to problem solve, to take initiative, and to make decisions about various aspects of the project's development and implementation. Some projects may be short in duration, while others may extend for long periods.

Initially, the practitioner and the children work together to explore the various options that the project may take. A webbing or mapping process, as illustrated in Table 7.2, may be used by the practitioner to record the children's ideas and the ways in which the children wish to pursue their project. The

Penguins	
Children's Questions	**Child-initiated Ideas**
• Where do they live?	• Use flippers to walk like a penguin.
• What do they eat?	• Make a penguin.
• How do they walk?	• Make an ice house for penguins.
• How do they feel?	• Have a penguin race with flippers.
• What do they do when the snow and ice melt?	• Make penguin out of ice.
Practitioner-initiated Ideas	
• Invite a chef to visit and make an ice sculpture with children.	
• Provide children with thermometers to check daily temperature.	
• Take children ice fishing.	
• Make a skating rink.	
• Introduce children to the care of goldfish.	

Table 7.2 *Mapping Process*

practitioner works with the children to visit and revisit their ideas as they progress with their project.

Children and practitioners may also create a documentation board. This documentation board includes photographs and descriptions of the exploration process the children engaged in as they examined the topical issue.

Thematic Approach In this approach, practitioners plan the experiences around specific topics or ideas. Topics are explored in depth for a specified period of time, with each of the experience-centres having a focus related to the theme or topic. One of the advantages of the thematic approach for young children is that it allows them to connect information from the various experience-centres. The more the children acquire information about the theme, the easier it is for them to see how the new information relates to the topic. As in other planning processes, practitioners and children may generate the theme ideas. Thematic planning needs balance, however, for if each experience-centre is theme-related, the environment tends to become saturated with the topic, which reduces play and learning options for children who may not be intrigued by the presented theme. Examples of thematic topics include polar bears, penguins, gingerbread, wheels, and eggs.

Documenting the Program Plan

The program plan is a tool or guideline practitioners use to outline the development, organization, and documentation of an integrated, child-centred, active-learning play environment. This plan is created based on input from practitioners, children, parents, and community members.

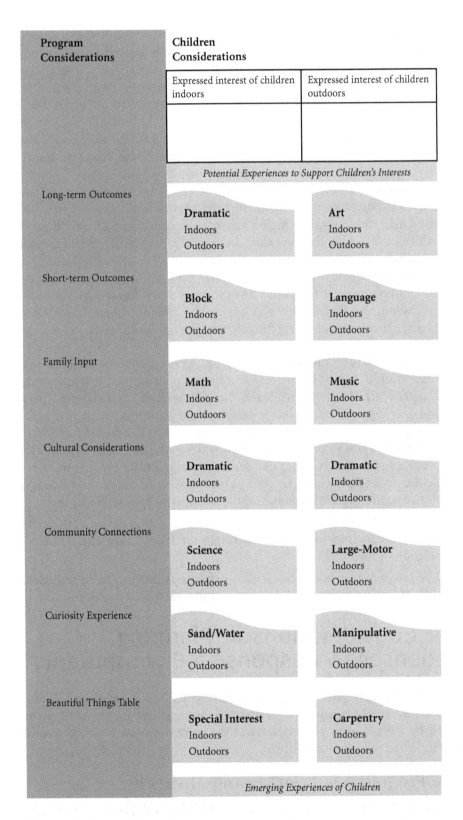

Figure 7. 5 *Program Planner Form*

Early childhood practitioners plan for both long-term and short-term experiences. Long-term planning is very general: it articulates the broad expected learning outcomes, concepts, and developmental milestones that children in each age range should develop (Jalongo & Isenberg, 2004). The long-term plan is a flexible pathway that changes as the needs of children change or as new information about children becomes available.

Short-term planning refers to the potential experiences that may be offered daily or longer. Short-term plans reflect children's interests, group experiences, and locally appropriate experiences, such as we illustrated in the vignette "Bringing Children and Community Together." Some planned experiences generally have specific outcomes intended to support specific children, and they are sequenced to help children gain simple to more complex skills. Short-term planning provides insight into the types of observations necessary, environmental changes required, and strategies for transition times.

There are many ways to document the program plan. There is no one right way, because we all bring different perspectives to the process (see Figure 7.5). However, based on the research of Bredekamp and Copple (1997) and Hildebrand (1994), the following assumptions are made about the program-planning documentation process.

1. The program plan outlines the types of experiences that the program will offer to children (see Figure 7.5) and may also identify the strategies that will facilitate children's exploring the play options. The program plan shows evidence of how children's interests are incorporated into the plan, how experiences specific to the needs of a child are addressed, and how the program will accommodate unplanned, spontaneous experiences. The program plan also outlines community awareness, family involvement, field trips, and projects. The plan shows evidence of the program-design principles/elements of sequence and continuity, scope, and balance.

2. The program plan provides the map and the direction for organizing the responsive environment, and it identifies the types of materials and the rotation of materials.

3. The program plan is flexible. It allows children's interests to be recorded, and it identifies experiences to support individual or group needs.

Other Considerations in Planning Experiences in Responsive Environments

Early childhood practitioners recognize that responsive environments require attention to a variety of considerations. Each of the considerations below may be influenced by the program philosophy and the community in which the early learning and child care service is located.

Ensure Programs Support Family Diversity

Family diversity is part of our Canadian society. Children will play and learn with other children from a variety of cultures, countries, languages, and lifestyles. Early

PARENTING PORTRAIT

Our daughter began at a combined child care and kindergarten program when she was 4 years of age. We moved to the area because of this program model. The program integrates child care and kindergarten into one setting, which allows our daughter to go to the one environment for the day. The interesting part about this program model is that Rima's early childhood practitioner and her kindergarten teacher work together to implement the day-long program. This seamless model is so important to me and to my family because it provides Rima with continuity. Before, Rima started at a before-school program, then was bused to kindergarten. After kindergarten, she was bused back to the child care for after-school care. As a parent, I do not need to worry about finding space in a child care centre that has transportation to and from kindergarten. I feel much more relaxed at work because I know that I have dropped my child off, and she was safe when I did so. I am no longer worried about Rima missing the bus to the child care centre. I also don't have the same worries of Rima adjusting to supply teachers because there is always at least one adult present who is familiar to Rima. One of the interesting observations that we have made since Rima started this program is that she has not wet the bed, she does not cry as frequently when I drop her off in the mornings, and she seems to be more content. She also now discusses the children she has played with during the day.

Should child care and kindergarten be integrated? What are the advantages of this model? What are the disadvantages? Explain your answer.

childhood practitioners support and encourage family diversity by practising **inclusive practices** and **multicultural programming.**

Inclusive Practice Inclusive practice refers to programming that considers and respects the dignity and diversity of children, families, and communities. Her Excellency the Right Honourable Adrienne Clarkson says, "The essence of inclusiveness is that we are part of a society in which language, colour, education, sex and money need not, should not divide us, but can make us more aware and sensitive to difference" (Her Excellency the Right Honourable Adrienne Clarkson, October 7, 1999).

Current early childhood play environments are intended to promote equal and equitable access for every child (Driscoll & Nagel, 2005) and to demonstrate acceptance and appreciation of personal diversity. Practitioners design play environments and experiences so that every child, regardless of skills, abilities, background, or needs, experiences acceptance and has opportunities to participate in each aspect of the early childhood program (Arce, 2000). Practitioners determine strategies to accommodate every child regardless of individual challenges or developmental diversity. Inclusive programming flows from developmentally appropriate practices, whereby practitioners continually examine and adjust the types of experiences and sequence of experiences in the play environments.

Inclusive practice. Practices within the early learning and child care program that address and accommodate the individual needs of each child, regardless of developmental phase or diversity.

Multicultural programming. Early learning and child care experiences that support staff and children to learn about and be accepting of and responsive to the cultures and traditions of all children and families within the setting.

Inclusive practice is evident in environments where early childhood practitioners present a range of play experiences that support the development of the "whole child" and provide opportunities for the integrated development of children's abilities. When "efforts to accommodate individual children occur in a learning environment that encourages successful participation of all children" (Winter, 1999, p. 165), practitioners respect, understand, and appreciate each child as an individual.

Early childhood practitioners observe and reflect on how each of the play experiences supports children in one or more of the aspects of their emotional, social, cognitive, linguistic, and physical development. Inclusive play programming is one of the best ways to contribute to children's growth in broad competencies such as problem solving, communications skills, decision making, and social interaction (Driscoll & Nagel, 2005).

As illustrated in Figure 7.6, inclusive practice accommodates the developmental needs of each child; all children are considered equal, with no one child having needs more special than those of another. When program planning is developed based on the interests and needs of each child and when the family is considered a partner in play, inclusive practice is more likely to be present.

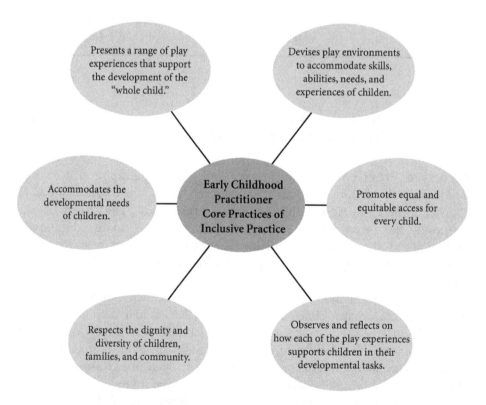

Figure 7.6 *Core Principles of Inclusive Practice*

Multicultural Programming Multicultural programming in a Canadian context focuses on establishing a play space that supports children in developing cultural sensitivity and an appreciation of diversity. Children are accepted and respected for who they are. Practitioners value diversity and recognize that cultural distinctiveness is a component of children's, co-workers', parents', and community-partners' sense of worth and identity. Moreover, values and beliefs that celebrate diversity among our families and community are role modelled. The materials, methods, and experiences that practitioners present help children develop cultural sensitivity (Vold, 2003). For example, the Canadian Child Care Federation (1994) indicates that cultural diversity is achieved in environments where practitioners "foster a knowledge and appreciation of a variety of cultures through respectful introduction of art, music, foods, clothing, literature and customs" (p. 5). Such an introduction supports children in developing tolerance and skills to get along with people who are different from themselves (Driscoll & Nagel, 2005).

In some early learning and child care environments, multicultural programming is cultivated because of the various cultures children represent. Diversity and culture are a natural part of the play environment. However, multicultural programming becomes more challenging in regions of Canada where cultural diversity is underrepresented. Practitioners seek ways to present cultural diversity in meaningful ways to children, and they should integrate diversity across the program. For example, Madoka's family comes from Japan, where women and children use hand-held fans. Madoka has been collecting beautiful fans for a long time, and last week she set up a special-interest table with her fans. This display led children to explore one aspect of Madoka's culture that was relevant and of interest to them. This approach was more meaningful to the children than had the practitioners decided to set up a display about Japan.

Before effective programming can occur, early childhood practitioners who may not have experience living in a multicultural community would benefit from thinking about their beliefs about, understanding of, and perspectives on various cultures. Gaining an understanding of the similarities and differences between cultures helps each of us to recognize biases or discomforts. Resolution of these biases and discomforts is necessary to provide positive role modelling to all children, families, and co-workers.

Families are an important resource in multicultural programming. They provide information about customs, celebrations, art, literature, and food that are part of their culture. Multicultural programming is most effective when it is implemented authentically. For example, if there are children of Chinese heritage, practitioners may set up special experience-centres as Chinese New Year approaches. Setting up such experience-centres is less effective when there are no children of Chinese heritage in the centre. Children need the "hooks" to lead them to explore and become intrigued by new learning opportunities.

Other Program-Planning Terms

There are many terms used in the early childhood programming literature that describe other important components of program planning. Here we present an overview of six terms for your review.

Spontaneous experiences. Are included in the program as a result of children's expressing an interest in a particular object, place, subject, or activity. For example, say a child becomes intrigued by a butterfly in the garden. The practitioner introduces the child to books on butterflies. Later that day, the child uses tissue paper in the art centre to create butterflies.

Teachable moments. Refers to a teaching and learning opportunity that is unplanned and that evolves in response to a child's or group of children's expressing an interest in a particular topic. Teachable moments are opportunities for children's learning that appear without planning. Pacifici and Garrison (2004) suggest teachable moments occur when children and practitioners genuinely share an interest in better understanding something or some situation and there is an interest to explore together the object or situation of mutual concern. For example, the early childhood practitioner who observes a child interested in butterflies may expand learning by exploring with the child colours, types of butterflies, motion, or flowers that attract butterflies.

Locally appropriate curriculum. Refers to experiences that are planned or that may be spontaneous from a child and that are influenced by the people, culture, or events taking place in the community. For example, taking the children to the wharf as described in the vignette at the beginning of this chapter demonstrates locally appropriate curriculum.

Family partnerships. Refers to early childhood practitioners' and families' continuity and consistency in communicating information and experiences that support children in developing a strong and secure foundation during their early years. Early childhood practitioners encourage family–centre partnerships by establishing relationships that demonstrate mutual respect and that encourage shared program decision-making. In today's world, the early childhood sector is moving from viewing families as needing guidance from early childhood practitioners to viewing families as political advocates and decision makers in the programming offered to their children.

Family-centred practice. Early learning and child care program practitioners recognize the family as the major decision-maker in children's lives. Practitioners appreciate families for the diversity and for the uniqueness that they bring to the learning community. Family-centred practices keep families informed about children's development in a respectful and supportive way, and families are encouraged to provide input into centre decisions, particularly with regard to goal-setting for their children.

Community involvement in program design and implementation. Early learning and child care programs are delivered in the communities where children live. Each family is a member of this community. As children's exposure to people and environments expands to include others beyond the family unit, it is the children's community that offers experiences to support their growth and development. Community members or community organizations partner with early learning and child care centres to provide services and experiences that support young children's development.

SUMMARY

Developmentally Appropriate Practice

- Children's programming reflects children's level of development and interests.
- Child-development principles and the developmental level of each child, within a respectful environment, influence practitioners' practice.

Personal Perspectives Influence Program Planning

- The program-planning process is influenced by the goals and philosophy of the early learning and child care centre and practitioners.

Why We Design Early Childhood Programs

- Early learning and child care programs are play-focused.
- The term *curriculum* has its origin in the educational sector, suggesting a prescribed set of activities or knowledge. The term *program* refers to a plan of intended procedures or course of action. The latter complements play environments.

Early Learning and Child Care Program-Planning Process

- Early learning and child care programs have meaningful children's experiences. They ensure that children's interests influence the program and experiences, that there are a variety of experience-centres, and that there is a program plan and that supports the program philosophy and planning approach.

Experience-Centres

- There are seven core characteristics of experience-centres.
- The most common experience-centres include dramatic, block, math, science, sand/water, art, language, music, manipulative, and large-motor centres. Other centres include special-interest, carpentry, curiosity, and beautiful-things centres.
- Group experiences include the welcome group, discussion experiences, and talk time.

Program Planning

- Program planning guides practitioners in planning potential experiences that trigger or build on children's curiosity and interests.
- Program planning requires early childhood practitioners to be effective observers, set goals, select materials, create experiences that support the needs and interests of children, and develop an organized framework for planning and implementing experiences.

Program-Planning Framework

- The program-planning framework requires identifying a program philosophy, inclusive practice, a process for determining children's developmental needs, programming for children's interests, program outcomes, family input, community involvement, and program accountability.

Program-Planning Approaches

- There are three general planning approaches: authentic curriculum/emergent programming, project-based programming, and thematic programming.
- Early childhood practitioners incorporate family diversity, inclusive practice, and multicultural programming into planning experiences for a responsive environment.

Documenting the Program Plan

- Early childhood practitioners plan both long-term and short-term experiences.
- The program plan outlines the types of experiences that they will offer to children. It provides the map and direction for organizing the responsive environment, and it allows for children's interests to be recorded.

Other Considerations

- Early childhood practitioners create play environments that promote equal access for every child. Respect for diversity of children, families, and community is evident.
- Cultural diversity is achieved with practitioners who gain knowledge and appreciation of a variety of cultures.

FURTHER OPPORTUNITIES FOR ENRICHMENT

Research

1. Examine research on inclusive practice. What knowledge, skills, and attitudes are required by early childhood practitioners to implement inclusive settings? What areas do you think you require further development in, based on the research conducted?
2. You were introduced to a variety of experience-centres. Choose four and research more specifically how each supports children's development. Include potential materials and experiences that may increase children's level of curiosity.

Group Investigation

1. Visit two early learning and child care programs. Examine the following:
   - The types of experience-centres that are available both indoors and out.
   - The program-planning approach used.
   - How the community becomes involved in the program.
   - How staff record the program plan.
2. Your group has been asked to present a recommendation on a program-planning model to a board of directors. What program-planning approach would you choose? Why? How would you support practitioners not familiar with the model in gaining comfort and skills with the model? What are the advantages of the model to children?

Making Connections

1. Maggie is 3 years of age. She has recently become interested in watering the plants. When you observed this, you placed magazines and books about plants and flowers around the centre. You notice that Maggie gravitates to them. Based on that identified interest, which three experience-centres could you set up to support Maggie's interest? What would you include in them and why? How would you record this on a program planner?

2. In "A Day Begins in an Early Learning and Child Care Centre," Jennifer highlights the importance of intergenerational relationships. How may practitioners build that concept into programs that are in large urban areas or rural areas? Why is that important for children and adults? How does it support children's growth and development?

3. Examine the "Parenting Portrait." How does this consistent program model potentially affect children? How does it impact on family? In your response, think about later learning, behaviour, family learning and development, and quality learning environments. How do you envision this model affecting the teaching and learning needs of kindergarten teachers and early childhood practitioners? Should there be different educational requirements for kindergarten teachers and practitioners? Why or why not? Explain your answer.

ADDITIONAL READING

Arce, E. (2000). *Curriculum for Young Children*. Albany, NY: Delmar.

Catron, C. & Allen, J. (1999). *Early Childhood Curriculum*. Upper Saddle River, NJ: Merrill.

Crowther, I. (2003). *Creating Effective Learning Environments*. Toronto, ON: Nelson.

Dodge, D. & Colker, L. (1992). *The Creative Curriculum*. (3rd ed.). Washington, DC: Teaching Strategies Inc.

Hope Irwin, S. (1996). "Strategies for serving all families through family resource programs." Available at **www.cfc-efc.ca/docs/cafrp/00000126.htm**.

Peterson, E. (1996). *A practical guide to early childhood planning, methods, and materials*. Needham Heights, MA: Allyn and Bacon.

Schweinhart, L. J., Weikart, D. P., & Larner, M. B. (1986). "Consequences of the three preschool curriculum models through age 15." *Early Childhood Research Quarterly, 1:* 15–45.

WEBLINKS

www.highscope.org/Research/curriccomp.htm: *"Different effects from different preschool models."*

www.rochester.edu/Warner/preschoolcurriculum/index.html: *"Preschool curriculum for the 21st century."*

www.specialinkcanada.org/about.html: *Specialink—The National Centre for Child Care Inclusion.*

www.toronto.ca/firstduty: *Toronto First Duty Project.*

journal.naeyc.org/btj/200507/03geist.pdf: *"Yeah buts—that keep teachers from embracing an active curriculum."*

"Our natural space is inviting. Gardens are a little overgrown, vegetables enthusiastically producing, and everywhere there are little bugs to find and worms to hold, birds to hear and squirrels to chase. We learn here about the world, about each other and about ourselves."

Sally Kotsopoulos, 2005

8

Standards of Quality

A Day Begins in an Early Learning and Child Care Centre

A Giant Is Playing Here

The sun is warm after yesterday's rain. The children are playing outdoors. Some children have their high green, blue, or yellow rainboots on, while others are wearing their waterproof ankle boots. Most children have taken off their raincoats as they play on this autumn morning with the leaves in glorious colour.

Jacques approaches the water stand to pour himself a glass of water. As he drinks, his eyes scan the ground around the stand. The ground under the evergreen trees is soft from the rain. Jacques notices large footprints in the ground cover. He crouches down and appears to be intrigued by something on the ground. He suddenly says in a loud voice, "Who made these footprints?"

Several of the children gather around. "I'm not sure," Jennifer replies.

Another child places her foot in the footprint. "This is s-o-o-o big!" she exclaims.

Jacques says, "I think a giant made it."

A discussion ensues in an attempt to determine just what a giant is. Suddenly, the children come to a consensus. They indicate that a giant is big and has big feet. The children ask Jennifer, "How will we know if the footprint belongs to a giant?"

Jennifer is interested in how the children appear to be intrigued by the thought of a giant. She sees a children's project in the making. Jennifer replies to the children, "I believe we will need to explore this further. Do any of you have any ideas about how we could determine if this footprint belongs to a giant?"

As the children express their ideas, Jennifer prints them on the outdoor blackboard. As in previous projects, Jennifer uses the blackboard as a way to capture the children's ideas. She will bring the children back to these ideas later. The children gradually disperse to go look for more giant steps. As they do, Jennifer thinks about how this experience and this potential project support the documented outcomes for the program. She recognizes the importance of this child-initiated play and relates it to the benchmarks identified for dramatic play and language enhancement. Jennifer determines her need to review the dramatic play and language quality indicators, which will help her in expanding the children's play experiences.

Jennifer and her team are working toward strengthening the dramatic play and language enhancement as a result of their last formal assessment and evaluation process. Jennifer reflects on the excitement the children expressed about the "giant footsteps." If the children continue to express an interest, it will be the perfect project to use to expand dramatic play and language-programming innovation. This possibility reinforces to Jennifer why she chose this career.

Looking Ahead

In this chapter, we will introduce the process of examining early learning and child care environments to determine their quality, effectiveness, and areas requiring further development. Learning about standards of quality, as outlined in Chapter 2, supports the *how* of early learning and child care; as you may recall, the *how* is knowing about the scope of children's needs and devising early childhood practices and services. Children require quality experiences that support their development phase as well as their culture, needs, and interests. Early childhood practitioners are continuously examining the quality of early learning and child care programs being offered, and they devise strategies to improve their program and practices. High-quality programs are achieved by practitioners working toward implementing programs for children that exhibit the characteristics of **best practice.**

Best practice. Refers to evidence-based outcomes that describe an ideal early learning and child care practice.

Designing play environments that meet the developmental needs and interests of each child is probably the most challenging and important role of an early childhood practitioner. Assessing the quality of the experiences and the overall program—and knowing how to make the necessary changes—is probably the second most important attribute.

As provincial and federal governments increase their financial contributions to early learning and child care, assessment of the quality of services being provided will become standard practice. Accountability to the stakeholders sets the stage for program reform in the early learning and child care sector.

There are a number of program considerations that interact with standards of quality. This chapter introduces you to the concept of standards of quality, and how continuous assessment supports the development and implementation of quality programming.

Children's exploration, wonderment, and learning are enhanced when children become intrigued with new experiences.

Defining *Quality*

In the opening vignette, "A Giant Is Playing Here," Jennifer observes the children, determines their fascination with the giant, and builds upon their interest. She facilitates dialogue with the children as a way to support them in exploring the giant's footprints. At the same time, Jennifer uses cues from the children to guide her in identifying the types of changes that would strengthen the play in the dramatic centre. Her actions illustrate her attention and commitment to developing high-quality care and experiences for the children.

One of the primary purposes of early learning and child care centres is to create environments that positively support children's growth and development. No two programs are the same, nor is the way in which *quality* is defined. Program philosophy, children's needs, family expectations, program location, socioeconomic conditions, and community perspectives all affect how *quality* is defined. And funding availability, policy supports, staff development, family–centre relationships, and child–practitioner interactions contribute to how individuals characterize program quality.

High-quality early learning and child care experiences produce long-lasting benefits to children, families, and communities (Friendly, 2004; McCain & Romonow, 2005), and, in fact, the quality of early learning and child care will determine the quality of our future in Canada (Friendly, 2004; McCain & Romonow, 2005). Consequently, the quality of early learning and child care is becoming as much a priority as accessibility to programs. However, Crowther (2005) says the concept of *quality* is difficult to define because families, children, practitioners, and other professionals may each have a different perspective on what constitutes *quality*. For example, one family may measure quality by the amount of exposure children have to the arts, while another family may measure quality by the communication among centre staff, children, and family.

The Canadian government, in its *Multilateral Framework on Early Learning and Child Care* (2003) provides a broad definition of *quality*. Early learning and child care "should be of high quality to support optimal child development. Examples of initiatives that support high quality early learning and child care could include enhancements to training and support, child/caregiver ratios and group size, compensation, recruitment and retention, physical environment, health and safety and learning environment" (p. 3).

According to the findings of the Canadian Child Care Federation and Child Care Advocacy Association of Canada's *Perceptions of Quality Child Care* (2003) report, the public divides the quality elements of child care into two groups: 1) "those elements describing quality of care provided to the child; and 2) those elements describing the quality of the system of child care" (p. 8).

The Canadian Child Care Federation, in its *National Statement on Quality Child Care* (1994), describes quality child care as being "provided by trained caregivers who are child-centred and supportive of families in Canada, their values, and needs. It is developmentally and culturally appropriate for each child in its service" (p. 8). Quality is ensured by "building, maintaining, and adopting national principles, which reflect regional and cultural variables" (p. 8).

The Organisation for Economic Co-operation and Development, in its *Starting Strong: Education and Care* report (2001), states: "definitions of quality differ considerably among stakeholder groups and across the countries. Although national quality guidelines are necessary they need to be broad enough to allow individual settings to respond to the developmental needs and learning capacities of children" (p. 2).

Early childhood practitioners' past experiences, values, and beliefs about how children learn, grow, and develop influence how they define *quality*. Defining *quality* is, therefore, a fluid process: perspectives change and evolve as practitioners gain more exposure to children and increase their interactions with children, families, and other early childhood practitioners, and as new research becomes available.

Indicators of Quality

Quality indicators.
Predetermined outcome-measures used to determine the level of quality to be achieved or that has been achieved.

Many factors affect quality, so practitioners use **quality indicators** to guide discussions on quality. Quality indicators are predetermined outcome-measures used to determine the level of quality to be achieved or that has been achieved. These indicators are not objective tests or hard numerical targets; rather, they are indicators that focus on the program outcomes. For example, a quality indicator would be identified if program experiences were child-initiated. The following serves as a framework for understanding quality indicators:

1. **Personal suitability and educational preparation of early childhood practitioners.** The Canadian Child Care Federation indicates the need for early childhood practitioners to have experience and formal post-secondary studies in early childhood education. Practitioners participate in continuous learning that supports their areas of interest, specialization, or identified needs. They mentor new practitioners entering the sector.

2. **Early learning and child care environments.** Early learning and child care programs "respond to children's needs by offering continuous opportunities for learning and nurturance. The goals of the services are determined by the needs of children and the shared philosophies of parents and care providers . . . All practices that take place are based on sound child development theories and practices" (Canadian Child Care Federation, 1994, p. 4).

3. **Group size and ratios.** Small group-sizes support the quality of the interaction among children, peers, and adults, and they provide more opportunities for each child to have one-on-one dialogue with practitioners (Canadian Child Care Federation, 1994).

4. **Adult interactions.** The early childhood practitioner develops and nurtures an "open, friendly and informative relationship with each child's family and encourages their involvement" (Canadian Child Care Federation, 1994, p. 7). Practitioners foster mutual respect, trust, and co-operation among colleagues, peers, families, and community partners.

5. **Health and nutrition**. Effective health and nutrition principles and practices are role modelled on a daily basis. "A child develops lifelong eating habits as a result of early eating experiences" (Crowther, 2005, p. 168).

6. **Safety.** Practitioners examine indoor and outdoor play space and programming strategies to ensure that safety practices are adhered to, while allowing and encouraging children to take safe risks.

7. **Partnerships**. Early learning and child care staff form partnerships among parents, colleagues, all levels of government, training institutions, and provincial, territorial, and national organizations related to early learning and child care (Canadian Child Care Federation, 1994).

8. **Respect for cultural values and diversity**. Early learning and child care settings incorporate family and community cultural attributes into the program.

9. **Assessment and evaluation**. Early learning and child care programs establish a process for evaluating and assessing all aspects of their program delivery. Action plans are developed, implemented, and evaluated at frequent intervals as a way to monitor the intended change in practice.

10. **Family support**. Early childhood practitioners respect and support the needs and attributes of families.

Figure 8.1 provides examples of quality indicators that complement the preceding framework.

Lero and Brophy (2005) suggest that "general underfunding of child care programs and low staff wages have an impact on so many factors with respect to quality" (p. viii). They outline six core factors that negatively impact quality:

- Poor staff morale, low wages, and high rates of staff turnover.
- Supervisors being required to provide child care "on the floor" and complete the extensive administrative responsibilities.
- Limited access to supply staff for programs.
- Limited financial resources for materials, curriculum resources, and support for staff's participation in professional development.
- Limited access to a range of staff-development opportunities.
- Stress and workload.

These findings are consistent with other studies. Friendly (2004) identifies that the amount of public financing devoted to ECEC programs overall is severely inadequate" (p. 48). She directly links the financial component to the uneven quality of early learning and child care programs across Canada.

Currently, our national and provincial/territorial governments (excluding Quebec) are developing agreements to support the development or enrichment of early learning and child care programs and services. Part of the strategy is focused on improving families' access to affordable, quality early learning and child care programs. This will mean that early childhood practitioners will be required to identify quality indicators and benchmarks that will be used for the assessment and evaluation of their program services.

Figure 8.1 *Indicators of Quality*

Examples of Indicators of Quality

Suitability and Training of Early Childhood Practitioners
- Continuous learning.
- Formal post-secondary education.
- Share knowledge with colleagues.
- Have a professional code of ethics.

Child Development and Learning Environments
- Are developmentally appropriate.
- Encourage children to engage in social interactions, make choices, have a balance of indoor and outdoor active play.
- Have a variety of places, people, and experiences.

Group Size and Ratios
- Encourage small group-sizes.
- Plan experiences that support small groups of children.
- Establish experience-centres that accommodate small numbers of children.

Adult Interactions
- Encourage open communication among children, colleagues, peers, families.
- Use effective communication strategies.
- Recognize different cultural styles of communication.
- Maintain positive learning-community environment.

Health and Nutrition
- Provide current information on health and nutrition practices.
- Model active-living strategies and establish health practices.
- Use natural light as a primary source of light.

Safety
- Encourage children to take safe risks.
- Establish emergency procedures.
- Examine environment for potential safety hazards.

Partnerships
- Foster parent and practitioner partnerships.
- Provide support and mentoring for new early childhood practitioners.
- Encourage interactions among a variety of professionals and families.

Cultural Diversity
- Acknowledge cultural differences.
- Encourage family and community participation in program.
- Expose children to visual arts and customs of families within the centre.

Assessment and Evaluation
- Encourage input from children, families, and community.
- Establish a formal and informal assessment and evaluation process.

Family
- Develop partnerships with families.
- Encourage involvement of families.
- Celebrate family diversity.

How Quality Is Determined: The Assessment and Evaluation Process

To determine the level of quality that early learning and child care programs offer children and their families, continuous assessment and evaluation processes are necessary. Early learning and child care programs may be assessed in a variety of ways—there is no standard model.

Meeting licensing standards and applicable regulations is only a small part of the journey in an assessment and evaluation process. Practitioners distinguish between the standards and regulations that they cannot change, usually set by external agencies, and those things that are more directly within the control of the administration and staff of any early learning and child care centre.

The assessment and evaluation of quality programming for young children require a variety of tools, as well as objective and subjective methods of data collection. The method chosen influences the data collection, and the quality indicators examined determine the effectiveness of that component of the program. Each program component becomes a piece of the assessment puzzle. Examining each program component helps to identify the areas requiring further development.

The purpose of assessing the quality levels is to determine the value and appropriateness of the programming and experiences offered to children and families using the service. Practitioners have distinct roles and responsibilities within the assessment and evaluation process. These distinct roles contribute to all elements and perspectives of the program being examined. This holistic approach maximizes the opportunities for the continuous improvement of practices that support quality benchmarks.

Program assessment and evaluation have three primary objectives, as outlined in Table 8.1.

Table 8.1 *The Purpose of an Assessment and Evaluation Process*

- Document program effectiveness.
- Provide information for program improvement.
- Align program practices with program standards and benchmarks leading to best practice.

A significant component of assessing the quality of a program focuses on children's developmental needs and children's responses to experiences offered to support those needs. The assessment and evaluation process uses a team approach, with input from early childhood practitioners, the children, program administrators, families, and boards of directors. This assessment team gathers information about children's strengths, needs, progress, and interests. The team also examines a measure of the practitiners' actions or practices to determine how and how well the program outcomes have been achieved. Then, the team evaluates the data collected and uses the information to make recommendations about continuous improvements to programming.

Assessment. The act of observing, gathering or collecting, and recording information relevant to desired program outcomes. Assessment is also the process of judging and documenting the value and worth of the elements of the children's program for the purpose of making recommendations and decisions about current and future program delivery.

Evaluation. The process of forming or making judgments from the information gathered and making recommendations based on the results during and after an assessment process or event.

While assessment and evaluation are different processes, each plays a key role in determining the standards of quality. Think of **assessment** as the act of observing, gathering or collecting, and recording information relevant to desired program outcomes, and as the process of judging and documenting the value and worth of the elements of the children's program for the purpose of making recommendations and decisions about current and future program delivery. Think of **evaluation**, on the other hand, as the process of forming or making judgments from the information gathered and making recommendations based on the results during and after an assessment process or event. The evaluation segment requires early childhood practitioners to document effectiveness and discuss results. They also present options for improvement in identified areas. See Figure 8.2 for an example of an assessment and evaluation process.

The Roles of Administrators and Practitioners in the Assessment and Evaluation Process

Administrators Administrators have the overall responsibility for ensuring that children and families have a high-quality program (Lero & Brophy, 2005). Administrators devise total-quality-management strategies to maintain or increase the quality of programming experiences offered to children. The program assessment and evaluation process assists administration/leaders in:

- Determining trends in child learning, appropriate developmental outcomes, and program-participation strategies.
- Evaluating the effectiveness of the program, early childhood practices, and service delivery.
- Determining the level of funding and resources needed to provide an early learning environment that is safe, healthy, and stimulating.
- Identifying the ongoing professional-development needs of staff.
- Facilitating policy development.
- Being accountable to all stakeholders—children, staff, families, boards of directors, and the community at large.

Assessment

- Observing, gathering, and collecting information.
- Recording information.
- Judging the value and worth of program elements.
- Documenting the value and worth of program elements.

Evaluation

- Forming judgments from the information gathered.
- Making recommendations based on results after assessment.
- Documenting effectiveness and discussing results.
- Presenting options for improvement.

Figure 8.2 *Assessment and Evaluation Process*

Early Childhood Practitioners Early childhood practitioners use the assessment and evaluation process to guide them in the design and delivery of the children's program. Early childhood practitioners:

- Determine individual children's needs/interests and developmental milestones.
- Plan experiences and activities for individuals and groups of young children based on their expressed interest or on practitioners' observations.
- Use data to effectively communicate with families about their children's development.
- Use data to examine the developmental levels of children and determine specialized services and interventions that may be needed to support particular aspects of a child's growth and development.
- Identify areas of the program or practices that require further development or evaluation.
- Are accountable to all stakeholders—children, staff, families, boards of directors, and the community at large.

The Process of Assessing and Evaluating Quality

Practitioners and administrators must not confuse provincial or territorial licensing standards/regulations for early learning and child care environments with quality measures. Some administrators and early childhood practitioners may focus almost exclusively on meeting licensing standards and regulations and think that they are meeting measures of quality. However, such standards are "minimum standards" that centres must achieve to be able to offer services to the public. They primarily establish minimum levels for environmental conditions and programming requirements necessary for public safety, such as liability, security, and health. Compliance with defined standards and regulations, although critical, is only one small step in the journey to establishing quality and best practice.

Quality requires an examination of a variety of features, such as the setting, equipment, program, how the children engage or experience the program, and how the program is experienced by families, early childhood practitioners, administrators, and the community. All of these elements affect children's experiences and opportunities for their needs to be met. For example, Catron and Allen (1999) indicate there is substantial evidence that the quality and quantity of materials and the quantity and quality of space predict program-quality factors. When there is sufficient space for children to play, there are more options for children to expand their play materials in either horizontal or vertical directions, each of which has an impact on how children solve problems and think critically. Less crowding reduces noise levels and increases children's ability to engage in dialogue with other children and adults, which contributes to early childhood practitioners being able to more easily establish a responsive environment. Early learning and child care leaders work with stakeholders, including parents, boards of directors, children, community partners, and funding bodies, to determine the meaning of *quality* and the strategy for measuring quality.

Conversation Café

Economists Gordon Cleveland and Michael Krashinsky found in their study of quality ratings from 325 early learning centres across Canada that non-profit child care centres scored, overall, 10 percent higher than their for-profit counterparts (Cleveland & Krashinsky, 2003). Why do you think this would be so?

Models for Assessment and Evaluation

Assessing and evaluating early learning and child care programs requires the examination of a wide range of areas. Each area examined is interrelated and builds upon the other. No matter which assessment and evaluation model is chosen, the early learning and child care team have input into the types of questions posed, and they continuously ensure child-development and developmentally appropriate principles and practices are adhered to.

Katz (1993) indicates five different models that may be considered in early learning and child care settings to assess quality. Each will be described.

The "Top-Down" Model   This model examines the setting, the equipment, and the adult's perspective of the program. For example, the assessment team examines the space's square footage, the number of experience-centres available to children, as well as the variety of materials and equipment.

The "Bottom-Up" Model   This model focuses on attempting to determine how each child experiences the program. As a result, the team examines children's feelings within a particular environment. For example, they would examine the experience-centres, materials, and interactions that each child engages in.

The "Outside–Inside" Model   This model requires the assessment team to examine how the program supports families who use the service; as well, the team examines the parent/family–practitioner relationships, and measures the number of support services and the number of families using them.

The "Inside" Model   This model examines colleague relationships, staff–parent relationships, and relationships with sponsoring agencies. For example, this model examines the ways in which family members are involved in components of the program design and governance structure.

The "Outside" Model   This model examines the centre's relationships with outside agencies and support networks. For example, this model determines the number of partnerships the centre has with outside agencies that support the centre's families.

The Progressive Best Practice Model

Another model used extensively in our work with early learning and child care programs is identified as the *Progressive Best Practice Model*, as illustrated in Figure 8.3. This model has levels: each level is a foundation for the next, and achieving each level supports the early learning and child care program to move toward achieving best practice. The levels contain a series of detailed or specific elements that support the program design and requirements for developmentally appropriate outcomes.

In addition, this model requires early childhood practitioners to examine all of the elements within each level. The linkages between each element and level are also examined. This determines the functioning level at each phase, and what the potential impact may be if an early learning and child care centre is missing key elements within each level or if it is performing below expectations. For example, if the only art-experiences available to children are at the easel, then the opportunities for creative expression are hindered. When children engage in art in their natural environment, they increase their observation skills and their understanding of natural products versus man-made, and they expand their vocabulary. Children become more aware of the colour, context, mediums, and options they may use to create an image when materials and the environment provide choices.

Level One—Physical Play Space   The foundation layer of the model includes the physical dimensions and equipment within the indoor and outdoor early childhood physical play space. Such things as materials, appropriate toys, playground equipment, display materials, physical layout, and bathroom facilities occupy this level. These physical elements respond to requirements such as safety, health and security, child capacity, the amount of floor and ground space, play equipment and materials, floor- and ground-space design, maintenance and hygiene practices, and supplies and environmental factors, including lighting and air quality. Frequently, early childhood practitioner students begin the process of

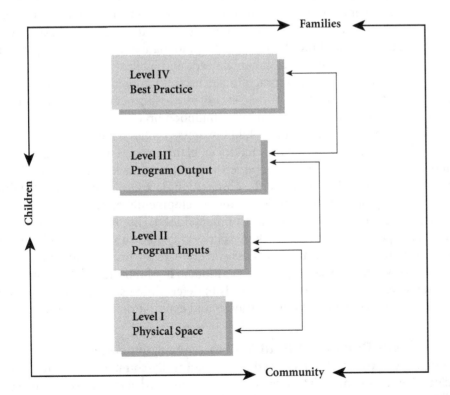

Figure 8.3 *Progressive Best Practice Model*

assessment and evaluation by examining early learning and child care environments.

The physical play space and equipment are necessary to support a centre's programming outcomes. Provincial- and territorial-government standards and regulations tend to address the elements in this first level.

Many programs use the various Environmental Rating Scales by Harms, Clifford, and Cryer (1998) and Harms, Jacobs, and White (1996). These rating scales examine personal-care routines, furnishings, displays for children, and programming components. There are specific rating scales for preschool environments, family daycare, infants and toddlers, and school-aged children.

However, identifying true program quality and achieving best practice extends beyond the physical elements of an early learning and child care centre, which we describe in the next three levels.

Level Two—Program Inputs The programming and experience elements are divided into two separate levels—the program inputs and the program outputs. Level two is the programming-input layer. It builds on and connects to the physical play space and equipment described in level one. Typical program inputs in level two of the model include the process of programming to meet the children's needs, leadership practices, and the knowledge and skills of the early childhood practitioners and families. Other important elements include the quality and frequency of the early childhood professional development and training provided to the staff, the role modelling and mentoring offered to new practitioners, the quality of the children's program, the academic achievement and practical experiences of the practitioners, and the ability of the team to plan and implement a program that is based on children's developmental needs and interests.

As early childhood student practitioners begin to implement experiences with children, they will participate in this level of the assessment and evaluation. For example, a student practitioner and early childhood practitioner observe a child in her play. Discussion occurs on the child's expressed interests, needs, and developmental level. Then, the student practitioner plans an experience to support the child in the identified area. The experience is implemented. The early childhood practitioner and student examine the observation data and discuss the following: the child's response to the experience, the developmental appropriateness of the experience relative to the child's developmental level, the process used to implement the experience, and how further experiences could support the child's interests. Early childhood practitioners assess and evaluate the program input on a continuous basis. This process supports practitioners in obtaining information about children's needs and interests, and it leads to determining strategies that a practitioner may use to spark children's curiosity and exploration in new ways.

Level Three—Program Output The programming-output level represents how the inputs compare to the identified best practices. By comparing the inputs with children's interests and points of view, as well as with predetermined standards, early childhood practitioners determine where the experiences may be improved.

For example, each of the experiences is examined relative to satisfying children's curiosity, being appropriate to children's needs, being season- and child-appropriate, being culturally sensitive, being aesthetically pleasing to children, and being designed for children's convenience. Experienced early childhood practitioners and administrators undertake this level of examination. They guide less experienced practitioners in connecting program inputs with program outputs.

Level Four—Best Practice   Early learning and child care practitioners and leaders who establish strategies to achieve the first three levels have a solid programming foundation established. This is essential to proceed to examine how practices may be adjusted to reflect the next level of quality, known as *best practices*.

Best practice refers to evidence-based outcomes that describe an ideal early learning and child care practice. It assumes all of the appropriate physical and programming dimensions are in place, are active, and are responding to children's cultural and developmental levels and needs. Best practice requires observation, learning, adaptation, analysis, and reflection about similar actions among individual children, either inside or outside of the group and in the overall early learning and child care environment.

To achieve best practice, early childhood administrative leaders and practitioners are continuously committed to change and to improvement (see Table 8.2). This facilitates the delivery of best-possible performance, effective feedback, appropriate reflection, and analysis of the program delivery with the resources available. The most knowledgeable staff person who has a combination of theoretical and application skills in program design, child development, and assessment and evaluation strategies leads the assessment and evaluation process at this level. It is not unusual for some early learning and child care centres to contract external reviewers to conduct assessments at this level. An independent external assessment and evaluation filters out any operating bias, personal filter, or comfort or prejudice factors that may be quietly and secretly limiting the objectivity of the assessments completed within a centre by staff.

As practitioners examine each level and progress to the next one, each successive level becomes more involved in its content and requires a greater level of staff effort, training, and innovation to achieve quality and reach successful outcomes. Each program attribute is examined in depth at each level. Failure to do so may result in a program with attractive packaging but program experiences that are not applicable to children's developmental needs in the early learning and child care environment.

Early childhood practitioners strive to provide the widest-possible variety of resources and experiences at each level to accommodate children's changing needs and interests. Early childhood programs require resources and staff members who are committed to developing a fluid environment. Programs that do not do so are more likely to offer children an overly structured program with repetitive activities.

There are many critical success factors that will either enhance or inhibit progress in achieving best practice. These include financial stability, the attitudes and motivation of staff and administrators, the leadership qualities of the administration and board of directors, the availability of affordable space, the location of the centre, the training of early learning and child care staff, political support, community support, and parents' expectations (Lero & Brophy, 2005).

Early learning and child care programs moving successfully toward best practice offer a wide range of both indoor and outdoor experiences. Practitioners provide children with options and materials that meet children's interests and needs at any point in time. The mix of experiences and the materials within each experience change regularly.

Table 8.2 *Characteristics of Best Practice*

What Is a Best Practice?
A best practice is a process that guides practitioners in delivering measurable improvements to their early learning and child care programs.

A Best Practice Must:
1. **Facilitate a change in quality.** How much a best practice improves quality will determine the maximum standards of practice level that an early learning and child care centre can achieve.
2. **Be illustrated in practice.** The practice must support child-development principles and developmentally appropriate practices to be considered a best practice.
3. **Apply to the overall early learning and child care environment.** The value of best practices is derived from their being applicable to a variety of early learning and child care settings.
4. **Ensure effective leadership.** Best practices require a well-managed learning community that supports and empowers practitioners to participate in continuous learning and development.

Establishing Benchmarks for Assessment and Evaluation

No matter which assessment and evaluation model is used, the process can be a very powerful, stimulating experience for staff. Assessment and evaluation is a dynamic and ongoing process essential to the early childhood practitioner's continuous professional learning and to the centre's movement toward achieving the goals of best practice.

Benchmarks.
Statements of high-quality practices that guide practitioners in examining their levels of practice for each element of an early learning and child care program. Benchmarks guide practitioners in devising plans for program improvement.

Early learning and child care programs establish **benchmarks** to assess and evaluate their service. McClenney (2003) says benchmarking is "generally defined as a process for identifying, understanding, and adapting outstanding practices from other organizations in order to help one's own organization improve its performance" (p. 1). Best practice requires identification of the practices, a strategy for measuring performance, and a commitment to improve practice.

From an early learning and child care perspective, benchmarks provide the map to support staff in implementing developmentally appropriate practices for children and families. Once a benchmark is achieved and maintained, a more demanding benchmark can be set to move the early learning and childcare environment closer to best practice. Progress must be celebrated at each step to reinforce the learning and change that has occurred.

Each benchmark requires a set of quality indicators associated with it that will help the centre determine if appropriate progress is being achieved. All quality indicators linked to a benchmark need to be assessed in light of both cause and effect. This would include responding to questions such as "What is contributing to the outcome for the children?" and "What are the problems preventing the achievement of a benchmark?" and "How should these problems be resolved?"

The purpose of benchmarking is to assist practitioners in implementing better, developmentally appropriate practices. Benchmarking encourages individuals to be innovative and to apply new models of effectiveness, and benchmarks help practitioners understand what standard of practice is necessary to reach a desired outcome. Because benchmarks are sequenced in levels, they allow practitioners to improve practices in small or large increments. Progress against a defined benchmark will set the stage for the definition of a new or modified benchmark.

Assessment and evaluation processes identify opportunities for improvement between the centre's present early childhood practices and a series of benchmarks selected by the centre. Each component of the early childhood program is assessed against a set of determined benchmarks. Assessment processes that are measured against defined benchmarks seldom generate useful evaluations or change in a positive fashion on their own. Practitioners and administrative leaders identify, chart, and monitor the progress toward achieving selected benchmarks to the best-practice standard. Centres need to redefine benchmarks and quality indicators as they achieve continued progress. The navigation along this journey toward best practice will depend on the frequency and honesty of the assessment and evaluation process, as well as on the corrections and changes implemented.

As the centre's assessment and evaluation process evolves, the things that practitioners assess or measure may change. An assessment and evaluation process that is continuous increases a centre's chances of recognizing success, identifying needs for improvement, and establishing new target areas for improvement.

Best practices are characterized as follows:

- The holistic quality-programming ideals that practitioners strive to achieve are on a consistent basis and support the centre's philosophy and mandate.

- Activities are always child-centred and child-initiated, supporting children's maturational unfolding and developmental processes.

- Activities are dynamic and constantly changing and moving an early learning and child care centre forward.

- Programs continuously change as research becomes available on how children learn and develop.

Table 8.3 illustrates how practitioners use best-practice statements and quality indicators to review the current levels of quality being implemented.

Table 8.3 Best Practices and Quality Indicators

Best Practice for Dramatic Play and Storytelling

Through a variety of experience-centres, children develop an appreciation for dramatic play and storytelling.

Quality Indicators

The responsive environment provides:
- Props and materials that promote dramatic play and storytelling (dress-up clothing, story-books, flannel boards, stages, interest-related props).
- A variety of locations and times for children to engage in dramatic play or storytelling (outdoors, small-group time, at various experience centres).
- Sufficient materials, information, and stories that are available about a variety of cultures.
- Opportunities for children to co-operate in dramatic play and storytelling.
- Books, magazines, and story props that are located in various experience centres.

Implementing an Assessment and Evaluation Process

There are multiple dimensions to an assessment and evaluation process. The practitioner's contribution to the process improves the value and effectiveness of children's experiences and activities, and it helps both individual practitioners and the early learning and child care staff collectively to acquire further understanding of the theoretical foundation and application process of implementing developmentally appropriate practices. Administrators and practitioners may wish to explore the *what, where, how, when,* and *why* questions of assessment and evaluation, as illustrated in Figure 8.4, as a way to determine the correct timing to engage in the process.

What to assess and evaluate.

When to assess and evaluate.

Where to assess and evaluate.

How to assess and evaluate.

Why assess and evaluate?

Figure 8.4 The Assessment and Evaluation Process

PARENTING PORTRAIT

How Parents Contribute to the Standards-of-Quality Process

Parents Lucinda, Matt, Nigel, Gunter, and Renatta agree to participate in a focus group that Jennifer and her team are hosting with parents. The purpose of the focus group is to have dialogue with parents to define quality indicators and examine what they would envision as quality indicators for safety.

Jennifer begins the focus group by asking each parent to define what is meant by *quality indicator*. Lucinda says, "It is what parents see, feel, and experience when they enter the early learning and child care centre."

Gunter agrees with Lucinda and adds, "It is how the children talk about their day, how they respond when Mommy or Daddy say it is time to leave for the centre, how they are able to separate from the parent upon arrival, and how they greet Mommy or Daddy at the end of the day."

Jennifer then says, "Children require environments that allow them to take safe risks. For example, they need to be able to climb high, jump, swing, and bounce. Safe risks help children problem solve, predict, and use their bodies in unique ways. As parents, what do you think are acceptable safe risks?"

Renatta responds. She says, "This is difficult for me as a parent. I understand that my Katria should be able to climb and jump as she wishes, but I am afraid of her getting hurt. I would never forgive myself if I sat here and agreed to your allowing the children to climb things other than the climber."

Matt agrees with Renatta, whereas Nigel says, "I think I read in one of Jennifer's newsletters that children will only climb as high as they feel comfortable with. If that is so, then I believe a quality indicator for safe risk would be providing the children with an environment that offers children the freedom to explore and take safe risks in a controlled environment."

The other parents think about Nigel's statement and agree with it. Renatta says, "I like the controlled environment qualifier, because that says to me that children will not be given total freedom and that the children will still be supervised by the practitioners."

At the conclusion of the focus group, Nigel, Lucinda, and Matt make a point of speaking with Jennifer to indicate how much they had learned about standards of quality. Matt says, "I have never been involved in a parental focus group, and I learned so much from the others. I really felt this experience supported me in developing partnerships with other families. I like the bantering back and forth and how each of us was able to contribute to the discussion. This has been a great learning experience for me as a parent." Jennifer replies, "As a practitioner, I too gained new insight into the needs, desires, and knowledge that parents have. By working together, we will increase our quality of programs and standards of practice."

How can focus groups be used to support parents and practitioners in acquiring information about programming? Is there a way to host a focus group with children? If so, how?

What Will Be Assessed A wide range of elements and activities contribute to program outcomes in the early childhood environment. Practitioners and administrative leaders determine what will be assessed. Some of the more common items to be assessed and evaluated include the following:

- Family and community partnerships, including cultural diversity, communication, and community resources.
- Responsive play environments, including the physical environment, daily routines, observation processes of children's responses to the program, children's interests and needs, programming options and experience-centre options, and documentation of children's interests and learning.
- Environmental factors that support developmental tasks, including social/emotional, cognitive, language, physical, problem solving, critical thinking, and communication interaction.
- Health and safety factors, including how children develop an awareness of healthy active-living practices, such as nutrition, self-help, and personal-hygiene skills.
- Programming components that contribute to children's exploring, wondering, and discovering about math, science, language, visual arts, block building, dramatic play, literacy, culture, etc.

When to Assess and Evaluate Practitioners assess and evaluate programming on an ongoing basis each day. The timing and frequency of a more comprehensive assessment and evaluative process will vary according to current levels of service and according to strategies that are in place to support early childhood practitioners in moving toward best practice. Program improvement and practitioner learning are most effective when the assessment and evaluation process is conducted at a time when it is feasible to examine the results and determine a realistic plan of action. Delays to the assessment and evaluative process can negatively affect staff perceptions about the process.

When corrective action is delayed, early childhood staff, children, and parents may assume that assessment is just a "time-waster" and is not a serious component of the centre's program delivery. Delays may also create situations where the individual or group or the process itself has moved well beyond the original state and, in the worst-case scenario, poor practice has actually become embedded in new or subsequent experiences or activities. This requires early childhood practitioners to engage in unlearning inappropriate actions or behaviours. And status quo thinking can be difficult to unlearn in any working environment.

The frequency of program assessment is determined by both internal factors and external factors. Administrators examine how rapidly program changes occur to determine the frequency of assessment. Administrators consider changes to the program, such as new staff, as a guide to determine the frequency and type of assessment. For example, if two experienced early childhood practitioners resign from their positions, and an administrator hires two new college graduates, the frequency of assessment needed and the type of assessment required may differ from previous assessments because of the experience levels, the currency of the theory and application processes, and the personal attributes that each new staff member brings.

External pressures, such as new ministerial changes to operational standards, new playground-safety standards, parental expectations, new centre ownership or leadership, or new research information on children's learning, also affect the timing of an assessment and evaluation process. If there is a major shift in children's socio-economic mix, a change in staff, or a new program design resulting from previous evaluations, the assessment and evaluation process may be frequent, so that the change in service can be measured appropriately.

Where to Assess and Evaluate The assessment and evaluation process occurs where the program delivery takes place. Observations occur in the active indoor and outdoor play environments. Assessment and evaluation may focus on a series of single experiences, projects, field trips, group play, or routines, or the process may take a more holistic view by examining the entire program rather than segments of it.

How to Assess and Evaluate The assessment and evaluation process is both objective, with concrete evidence-based measures, and subjective, with a greater emphasis on behaviour, learning, and change. There is considerable flexibility in how the process is conducted and documented. The process will reflect the established program-outcomes documented, and may be completed at the end of an activity (summative evaluation) or throughout an activity's entire time span (formative evaluation), or the process may be cumulative, whereby a centre revisits evaluations on an annual or biannual time frame as a way to document changes and progress.

Why Assess and Evaluate The assessment and evaluation process helps to identify program strengths, areas requiring further development, how change is being achieved, what problems are being overcome, whether critical success factors are operational and successful, what new challenges to desired outcomes are developing, and what new support mechanisms need to be considered or added. The attributes of early childhood practitioners are identified, and a workplace learning-community is formed. Motivators for practitioners are determined, learning from one another is supported, and collectively the team develops new ways of thinking and innovating. These combined elements lead to creating a responsive environment for children and families.

Early learning and child care staff work together to ensure that the desired outcomes are well understood, can be evaluated, and are applicable and relevant to children's needs, respond to their changing needs, and are extendable to meet the diversity needs within the centre. In research and development centres, the assessment and evaluation mechanisms require testing for validity and reliability.

Documenting an Assessment and Evaluation Process

Regardless of how and how frequently practitioners decide to assess and evaluate programs, it is necessary to properly document the process—this creates a body of evidence for reference and evaluation for subsequent assessments. The documentation process includes material on previously defined goals and desired outcomes, any clarifying context notes, notes on how observations were completed during the assessment, a summary of items for follow-up action with completion timelines, a summary of any learning that is clearly occurring, and, where appropriate, a scoring system to measure and document progress. The documentation process includes clear ownership tags in the notes so real people have a stake in and defined personal accountability for the ongoing progress. This information becomes part of the annual work-planning and review process with practitioners.

The Early Learning and Child Care Climate

The early learning and child care climate influences how each practitioner deals with change, innovation, attention to detail, willingness to learn and experiment, people engagement, and people respect (including children). Concern for the services delivered is given priority. Setting the climate and maintaining it is essential to ensure that assessment is proactive.

Some early learning and child care centres establish processes for assessment and evaluation, while others may take a less systematic approach. Beginning practitioners need to understand the assessment and evaluation process, because never before has such emphasis been placed on quality programming and accountability. The process guides practitioners in understanding the range of options open to them to improve children's experiences. When practitioners think of assessment and evaluation as a form of continuous learning, the process becomes integrated in all of a centre's actions and in the practitioners' professional practice.

"We meet all the standards," "the parents seem happy with the program," "we don't have the resources to do that," "we have always done it this way," "that new idea is too messy or will take too much of my time" are typical responses to rationalize a centre's status quo actions, and may actually move staff *away* from the journey toward best practice. Quality early learning and child care programs cannot be static; rather, as you begin your practice as a practitioner, you must think about how you can strive to constantly change the programs to positively reflect children's needs and how the play space may be created to support those needs—for doing so will increase quality and best practices.

Points to Ponder

Is an assessment only as good as the person doing the assessment? Should an assessment be both formal and informal? Why or why not?

SUMMARY

Quality

- There is no single term that describes *quality*. Quality is, however, influenced by a number of factors, including program philosophy, family needs, cultures, community perspectives, accessibility, affordability, and staffing.
- Early childhood practitioners' past experiences, values, and beliefs about how children learn, grow, and develop influence how they define *quality*.

Indicators of Quality

- There are many factors that affect quality, including suitability and training of early childhood practitioners, child-development and learning environment, group size and ratios, adult interactions, health and nutrition, safety, partnerships, respect for cultural values and diversity, assessment and evaluation, and families.
- Staff morale, wages, staff turnover, financial resources, stress, and access to professional development are internal factors that also affect quality.

How Quality Is Determined: The Assessment and Evaluation Process

- The level of early learning and child care programs is determined by continuous assessment and evaluation processes.
- The three primary objectives of program assessment and evaluation are to document program effectiveness, to provide information for program improvement, and to align program practices with program standards and benchmarks leading to best practice.

The Roles of Administrators and Practitioners in the Assessment and Evaluation Process

- Administrators use the assessment and evaluation process to determine trends in child learning, to evaluate the program's effectiveness, and to evaluate practices, service delivery, funding, resources, and professional and policy development.
- Early childhood practitioners use the assessment and evaluation process to determine individual child needs and interests, to plan experiences for individuals and groups of children, to examine children's developmental levels, and to identify areas of the program and personal skills requiring further development.

The Process of Assessing and Evaluating Quality

- Quality extends beyond the provincial/territorial licensing-standards and regulations. Some of the more common features assessed are the setting, equipment, and program, how children engage in experiences, as well as the roles of practitioners, administrators, families, and community.

Models for Assessment and Evaluation

- There are a number of assessment and evaluation models available to practitioners and administrators. Early learning and child care teams must have input into the types of questions posed, and they must adhere to child-development principles and developmentally appropriate practices.

The Relationship of Benchmarks and Quality Indicators to Best Practice

- Early childhood practitioners establish benchmarks and quality indicators as part of the assessment and evaluation process. Benchmarks are the reference points for examining measures or performance. Quality indicators are the components necessary to determine if appropriate progress is being made. The combined benchmarks and quality indicators lead to best practice.

Implementing an Assessment and Evaluation Process

- Administrators and practitioners explore the *what, where, how, when,* and *why* questions to determine when the timing is right for implementing an assessment and evaluation process.

The Early Learning and Child Care Climate

- The early learning and child care climate is an important consideration before undergoing an assessment and evaluation process. The climate influences the staff's commitment to examining the issues and to making the changes necessary to move the program forward to meet identified benchmarks and to perform best practice.

FURTHER OPPORTUNITIES FOR ENRICHMENT

Research

1. Choose three of the following best practices and research quality indicators that would be suitable for children at age 2 and at age $3\frac{1}{2}$.
   - Children develop knowledge of spatial concepts—e.g., shape, size, measurement.
   - Children develop inquiry skills, such as problem solving and decision making.
   - Children participate in experiences that reflect the cultures within the learning environment and their community.
   - Children demonstrate self-confidence.
   - Children exhibit positive interaction with other children and adults.
2. The quality of early learning and child care centres affects children's experiences and the benefits to them. Research how quality may differ in rural versus urban

centres, profit versus non-profit, military centres versus Aboriginal centres. Who should address the differences—the federal government or provincial/territorial governments? Why?

Group Investigation

1. One of the core contributors to quality in early learning and child care is professional development for early childhood practitioners. Survey three early learning and child care centres to determine the types of professional development opportunities available to practitioners. How frequently is it available? Who provides it? What is the average cost? How is the new information transferred to practice?
2. As new practitioners, what knowledge, skills, and abilities do you bring to an early learning and child care centre that will support the centre in examining quality? What assessment and evaluation strategy would you suggest? Devise a plan of action that illustrates how you would begin an assessment and evaluation process.

Making Connections

1. Examine Table 8.3, Best Practices and Quality Indicators. Devise five potential experiences that would support each of the quality indicators. Specify the age of the child that the experiences are being developed for and how the experiences support the child's interests and needs.
2. In Chapter 7, we discussed responsive environments. How do the characteristics of responsive environments support quality? Explain your answers.

ADDITIONAL READING

Berk, L. & Winsler, A. (1995). *Scaffolding Children's Learning: Vygotsky and Early Childhood Education.* Washington, DC: NAEYC.

Canadian Child Care Federation (1991). *National Statement on Quality Child Care.* Ottawa: Author.

Fennimore, B. S. (1997). "Moving the Mountain: Assessment and Advocacy for Children." In A.L. Goodman (Ed.), *Assessment for Equity and Inclusion* (pp. 241–259). New York: Routledge.

Jones, E. (1984). "Training Individuals: In the Classroom and Out." In J. Greenman & R. Fuqua (Eds.). *Making Day Care Better: Training, Evaluation, and the Process of Change.* New York: Teacher's College Press.

Jones, E. (1993). *Growing Teachers: Partnerships in Staff Development.* Washington, DC: National Association for the Education of Young Children.

WEBLINKS

www.atkinsonfoundation.ca: *Atkinson Foundation.*
www.childcareadvocacy.ca: *Child Care Advocacy Association.*
www.hsnrc.org/CDI/pdfs/CAUserGuide.pdf: *Curriculum and assessment.*
www.voices4children.org: *Voices for Children.*

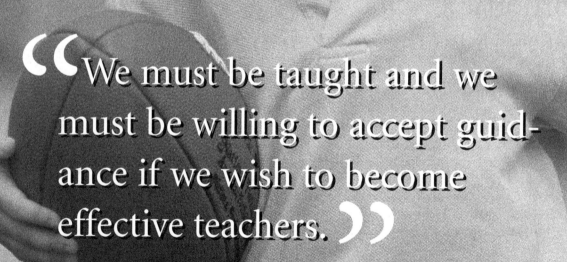

"We must be taught and we must be willing to accept guidance if we wish to become effective teachers."

Maria Montessori, 1966

9

How Philosophy Informs Practice

A Day Begins in an Early Learning and Child Care Centre

Reflecting on Beliefs, Values, and Roles

Jennifer is preparing for her annual performance review with her director. She identifies to her mentor, Suzanette, that her beliefs about children and families have changed since she left college.

Suzanette is interested in her comment and says, "Jennifer, are you able to explain to me what some of the changed beliefs are?"

Jennifer replies, "I don't know if I can explain it. I just feel differently."

Suzanette then asks, "Jennifer, have you examined your philosophy statement that you prepared when you came to us? Is it still current?"

"No, I have not," replies Jennifer. Then Suzanette and Jennifer begin to examine the philosophy statement. As soon as Jennifer reads the statement, she determines some definite changes in her thoughts and beliefs. For example, Jennifer's philosophy statement identified that the early childhood teacher has the most important role in children's lives. Jennifer laughs and says to Suzanette, "Wow, how things change. I believe children's families are the most important teachers and guides in children's lives. The role of the early childhood practitioner is to support children and their families by creating an environment responsive to children's needs."

Jennifer turns to Suzanette and says, "I struggle with the label 'teacher' because I associate that role with structure, prescribed curricula, and a rigid rather than spontaneous environment. I have come to appreciate the power of play."

Suzanette says, "If you are not a teacher, what are you?"

Jennifer thinks for several minutes before responding, then says, "My official title is 'early childhood practitioner.' For me, that means that I am children's play-facilitator. I examine the needs of each child, I examine the play environment, and, with my colleagues, I set up an environment that is responsive to children's needs, interests, and abilities. This may mean that one day children will be intrigued by rain sticks and another day they will be exploring butterflies, rocks, and blocks. My role is to observe, question, and determine children's interests and then design an environment that offers them the appropriate guidance, materials, and opportunities to play and engage in wonderment. The more I observe children and play with them, the more I believe that children learn through play, not through a prescribed or planned program."

Suzanette says, "Jennifer, remember, your philosophy evolves. It will change several times over the course of your career."

Practitioners require time, space, and opportunities to reflect on their practice.

Looking Ahead

Experience with children and personal development are intertwined in the process of becoming an early childhood practitioner. Using life experience, in fact, is the basis for self-reflection, learning (Lindeman, 1989), and further development. And self-reflection is necessary in determining one's beliefs and attitudes. Early childhood practitioners who develop critical thinking and reflective skills are better able to model the interactive skills necessary to deal effectively with children, families, and colleagues. Personal development, codes of ethics, and self-reflection help us determine the various components that influence our philosophy. This chapter is about making connections between our personal beliefs and our practice.

Examining Our Personal Ecology

In the opening vignette, Jennifer recognized that her thoughts and beliefs about how children learn and develop have changed since she first entered the field. These changes in ideas and beliefs are significant to practitioners' practice. As practitioners gain more experience with children and families and take segments of theory and connect it to application, new knowledge and skills evolve that lead practitioners to think about children and programming in different ways.

Our experiences as well as our current situations influence learning. Zachary (2000) suggests that there is a whole ecology that occurs in creating a climate for growing. She describes *ecology* as a constellation of forces that are always present—pushing, pulling, and directing our personal actions and beliefs. Our personal ecology is interwoven among the relationships within our personal and professional environments. Our ecology affects how we approach risk-taking opportunities, the level of risk that we are willing to take to try new things, whether we participate in new learning, how we participate in new learning, and the strategies we use to develop new relationships.

Each of us has a personal ecology (Helgeson, 1995). This network of relationships is at play at any given time in our life. As illustrated in Figure 9.1, early childhood practitioners' personal ecology influences who they are, what they believe in, and what their attitudes are about issues related to children, families, community, and cultural and individual diversity. Furthermore, personal ecology affects how practitioners work with children and families. For example, think about whether guns—or sticks being used as guns—belong in child's play. Are there particular communities or situations where guns would be acceptable in child's play? If you disagree with guns but they are part of a child's family culture, does an early childhood practitioner have the right to disallow guns in a play episode? If so, what message are we sending children about their family values and culture? How do you support children and families when some elements present ethical dilemmas? Conversely, how does examining this issue and reflecting on it lead practitioners to acquire new perspectives and change their beliefs, values, attitudes, and behaviours?

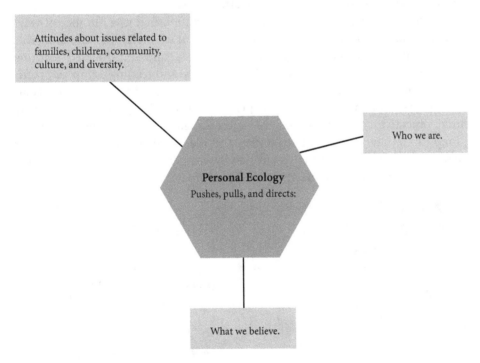

Figure 9.1 *How Personal Ecology Is Developed*

Developing Stretch Goals

We often think of stretching as an exercise for the body, but, in fact, stretching is as important for the mind as it is for the body. Stretching is best described as a learning process that causes one to be pulled or to exert force in new directions or dimensions that cause an individual to gain greater depth of knowledge and application skills. Say, for example, that an early childhood practitioner has worked in an early learning and child care centre that uses an eclectic approach to programming. That practitioner, after six years, decides to move to a program using a Montessori model; however, the practitioner has not studied the Montessori programming approach. The practitioner will have to be "stretched" to learn about Montessori materials and the ways in which the materials are sequentially presented to children.

The saying "Stretch yourself today so you'll be in better shape tomorrow" (Pritchett & Pound, 1995, p. 30) reinforces the importance of lifelong learning. Stretch goals broaden experience or knowledge base. They are "the difference between where one wants to be and where one is" (Zachary, 2000, p. 79). Early childhood practitioners with well-defined career and personal goals tend to be able to determine their learning and developmental needs. Those who are able to define the desired area of stretching are better able to examine potential learning opportunities and determine the strategies needed to reach their learning need. Conversely, practitioners who do not set learning goals may miss valuable learning opportunities. Generally, by determining their personal and professional vision, practitioners are able to identify potential stretch goals.

As Figure 9.2 illustrates, stretching can be accomplished in a number of ways because learning takes place in a variety of venues. For example, self-reflection, role modelling, mentoring, participating in conferences, and self-directed learning (attained through journals, professional associations, and reading) support practitioners on their learning journey. And practitioners achieve their stretch goals most effectively when they identify a plan of action. The plan of action may include objectives, measurements of success, learning strategies, resources required, and time frames for achieving the identified learning. Learning, or stretching, is a lifelong event that is affected by our personal ecology and learning style, and it is a fundamental need in our development.

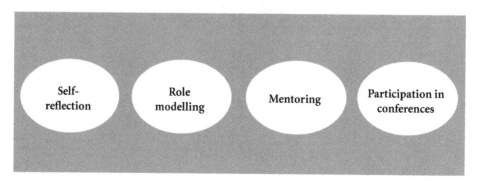

Figure 9.2 *Ways of Expanding Learning and Development*

Self-Reflection

Reflective practice is an interesting and important concept for early childhood practitioners. The process of reflective practice dates back to John Dewey, who emphasized the importance of reflecting on what you are doing and why you are doing it. This self-reflection requires that practitioners think about and learn from their practice and from the practice of others. Reflection is "a natural process that facilitates the development of future action from the contemplation of past and/or current behaviour" (Han, 1995, p. 228). Reflection is, furthermore, "a self-conversation or an inner conversation in your mind" (Mayfield, 2001, p. 123). Stretching and self-reflection are interconnected. Practitioners begin the process of reflection by examining their own practices and beliefs about children as well as the beliefs and practices of others. Then, they share their thoughts, ideas, insights, and possible solutions with others. The sharing helps to solidify ideas and beliefs and to identify areas for further exploration or stretching.

Atherton (2003) suggests the need to reflect *in* action (while doing something) and *on* action (after you have done it). This reflective process helps practitioners to identify discrepancies between their beliefs and their actions. When early child-hood practitioners examine beliefs and new perspectives on the dilemmas and contradictions inherent in early learning and child care settings, they improve their judgment and increase the probability of making appropriate decisions when situations are new or complex. This is reflective practice.

Atherton (2003) suggests that beginning practitioners have a mentor or guide "who can ask appropriate questions to ensure that the reflection goes somewhere, and does not get bogged down in self-justification, self-indulgence or self-pity" (p. 1). Colleagues and mentors who observe and engage in conversation and exploration can help practitioners identify aspects of their practice that they may not be aware of. When practitioners understand how beliefs influence actions, they are better able to modify actions to ensure they are consistent with their beliefs (Arrendondo et al., 1995).

Point to Ponder

Sometimes my beliefs about how children learn and develop, and, as a result, about my role as a practitioner, differ from my colleagues'. Is that OK or should I be trying to conform to the group? What are the advantages of keeping my thoughts and beliefs? What are the disadvantages?

As illustrated in Figure 9.3, journals, peer discussion groups, story recordings, and portfolios are effective strategies for documenting these reflections. Some questions that may help beginning early childhood student practitioners begin the reflective process include the following:

- What did I observe today?
- What did I like about the environment?
- What did I like about what I did with the children and in the environment today?
- What could I have done differently today? How might I have handled the situation differently? Why do I think that now?

Figure 9.3 *Strategies for Developing Stretch Goals*

- What do I like about being with the children and in the environment?
- How might I better meet the needs of a particular child?
- When do I feel comfortable working with children? In what situations do I question whether this is what I wish to be doing?

Table 9.1 provides an example of a reflection entry from a beginning practitioner. As you read the example, think about one of your experiences. What did you learn from it? How will it change your practice? How will you know that has occurred?

Self-reflection requires practitioners to examine both positive and negative learning experiences. For example, this examination helps practitioners to understand why they may gravitate to some program models and avoid others. Assume you have a field placement in a program that focuses on structured indoor group experiences, and you feel distressed. The distress may be because of the structure, the indoor group experiences, or the combination of both. Initially, you may say to your college supervisor that you are not learning anything. But in fact you are. By examining both positive and negative learning experiences, you are able to identify and communicate your beliefs and rationale about how children learn. This, in turn, helps you to prioritize what is really important in your work with children and families. It informs the actions you take—based on your core beliefs, values, and assumptions about why you do what you do. Figure 9.4 illustrates the relationship between self-reflection and learning.

Self-reflection and self-understanding are important tools in developing a personal **philosophy** (Crossley, Dietze, & Hume, 2001). "New and experienced members of the early childhood workforce benefit from understanding themselves" (Gestwicki & Bertrand, 1999, p. 140).

Philosophy. A set of beliefs about how children learn and develop and what the role of the early childhood practitioner is in supporting children's learning.

Table 9.1   My Reflective Entry

Last week at my field placement I set up an outdoor play experience. I had never done that before, and outdoor play is not my favourite time in the program. I decided I would take a table outside and offer children opportunities to cut and paste anything they wanted.

When the children first came to the play area, two children participated for about three minutes. I wondered why more children didn't participate. I asked some children if they would like to come to my experience-centre, but they all said "no." At the end of the outdoor play only the two children had participated. I didn't feel really good about it, but I did not know why.

Yesterday I observed one of my peers setting up her outdoor play experience. She placed some orange pylons in interesting patterns and she placed other pylons and large balls nearby.

As five of the 3-year-old group came into the play area, they ran over to the pylons. One child started to lift a pylon, while another took a ball. Other children joined in. One child walked the pattern, touching each pylon as he followed the path. Another child brought a wagon over and pulled it down through the path. At one point he had some pylons in his wagon. And another child ran in and out of the pylons. The children appeared to be intrigued by these pylons.

Suddenly I reflected back on my activity and compared it to this experience. My peer used something new to the children. She initially set some of it up, and left some pieces for them to use on their own. It was an unstructured activity and it inherently supported the children in their physical movement. My activity didn't have any element of curiosity or intrigue to it. It didn't require the children to explore or try new ideas. I need to think about those three important words—curiosity, wonder, and intrigue.

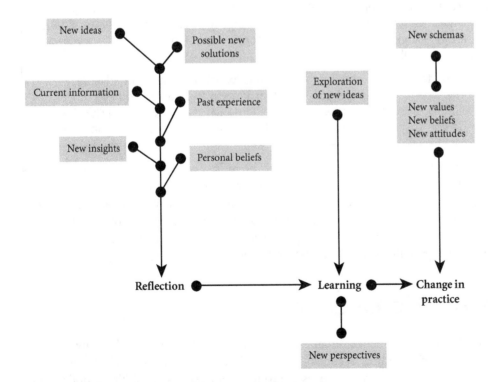

Figure 9.4   The Relationship between Self-Reflection and Learning

PARENTING PORTRAIT

Finding the Right Program-Fit for My Children

Tamara and Ali are starting their 3-year-old twin girls, Jamala and Huda, at an early learning and child care centre. They have chosen this particular centre because of the good feelings they acquired when they met with the staff, especially Jennifer. During the first week, the girls are excited to be going to "school." But, as the weeks go on, Jamala's behaviour begins to change. She wets the bed each night before preschool, she is lashing out at her sister, and there are now frequent outbursts at home and at the preschool. After several weeks, Jamala's behaviour is upsetting to her parents and preschool teachers. Jamala's mother wonders if the program is the right fit for her. The situation is difficult because Huda is flourishing in the preschool.

Jennifer meets with Jamala's parents and suggests that she observe Jamala to try to determine what in the environment is triggering Jamala's unacceptable behaviour. As Jennifer observes, she quickly realizes that Jamala becomes agitated when she is required to return indoors. However, she appears to enjoy the play outdoors: she is active and articulate and frequently plays with other children. Indoors, Jamala is less engaged in play and is, in fact, destructive to the other children's play.

By December, even though Jennifer has tried many strategies, Tamara, Ali, and Jennifer agree that Jamala would probably be happiest at the new outdoor early learning and child care program. Because Tamara and Ali are such strong advocates of using the outdoors as a learning place for their children, they move Jamala to the new centre. Huda continues to attend Jennifer's preschool. Despite missing her sister, Jamala regains her self-confidence and language skills. Her creative work takes on new directions, and she begins to identify an interest in music. This is a win–win situation for both girls.

How do you feel about separating the twins? What are the advantages? The disadvantages? Do you think that Tamara and Ali should have moved Jamala, or should she have been required to develop coping skills? What do you suspect may be Jennifer's philosophy about children and families?

Examining beliefs, past experiences, the influences of others, and current ideas about how children play and learn helps practitioners to make sense of how children's backgrounds and families, program design, and early childhood practitioner roles affect practice (Bullough & Gitlin, 1995; Bullough, 1994; Mayfield, 2001).

Practitioners who understand themselves and who engage in stretching and visioning are cultivating a foundation for developing their philosophy.

Professional Ethics

Code of ethics. A position statement developed by an organization that outlines guidelines for acceptable professional practices and sets forth a common base for resolving ethical dilemmas in the early learning and child care sector.

Another major influence on an early childhood practitioner's philosophy is a professional **code of ethics**. A code of ethics, as described by Mayfield (2001), is "reflective thinking by a profession as a group about its responsibilities, obligations, values, and practices relevant to children, families, other professionals, and society.

Ethics illuminate what a profession perceives as valuable and worthy" (p. 133). Codes of ethics for early childhood practitioners are a statement of responsibilities, values, and practices adopted by either a provincial or national organization.

A code of ethics provides early childhood practitioners with the following:

- Professional guidelines expected of practitioners working with children, families, and community.
- A reference point when making decisions in areas that are potentially difficult or ethically challenging.

Most provincial associations of early childhood educators have a code of ethics. In addition, the Canadian Child Care Federation (CCCF) has adopted a comprehensive code of ethics (2000) (see Table 9.2). Other associations may have briefer codes of ethics. Note that the CCCF's code of ethics has eight core principles, as well as the expected standards of practice. As you read it, think about it in terms of your beliefs and values. Are there aspects of it that you feel you would like to transfer to your own philosophy and practice? If so, think about what the statement says to you in relation to your values and beliefs.

Why Have a Code of Ethics?

Early childhood practitioners are expected to work in partnerships with children, families, and colleagues, which requires a considerable professional standard of practice in skills, communication, and expression of empathy and understanding. Ethics are part of these working relationships because relationships are based on value choices. Children do not choose their practitioners or the early learning and child care centre, and sometimes parents have limited choices for their children. As a result, practitioners have "power" over children and families, and the child is in a position of vulnerability. The code of ethics guides practitioners in their professional decision-making process.

Table 9.2   Code of Ethics of the Canadian Child Care Federation

Child care practitioners work with one of society's most vulnerable groups—young children. The quality of the interactions between young children and the adults who care for them has a significant, enduring impact on children's lives. The intimacy of the relationship and the potential to do harm call for a commitment on the part of child care practitioners to the highest standards of ethical practice.

Child care practitioners accept the ethical obligation to understand and work effectively with children in the context of family, culture and community. Child care practitioners care for and educate young children. However, ethical practice extends beyond the child/practitioner relationship. Child care practitioners also support parents as primary caregivers of their children and liaise with other professional and community resources on behalf of children and families.

The Canadian Child Care Federation and its affiliate organizations recognize their responsibility to promote ethical practices and attitudes on the part of child care practitioners. The following principles, explanations and standards of practice are designed to help child care practitioners monitor their professional practice and guide their decision-making. These ethical principles are based on the Code of Ethics of the Early Childhood Educators of B.C. They have been adapted for use by adults

continue **Table 9.2**

who work with children and families in a variety of child care and related settings. They are intended both to guide practitioners and to protect the children and families with whom they work. Professionalism creates additional ethical obligations to colleagues and to the profession.

Eight ethical principles of practice are presented. These principles are intended to guide child care practitioners in deciding what conduct is most appropriate when they encounter ethical problems in the course of their work. Each principle is followed by an explanation and a list of standards of the principle in a child care or related setting.

The ethical practice of child care practitioners reflects the eight principles. However, the resolution of ethical dilemmas can be difficult and there will be circumstances in which the ethical principles will conflict. In these difficult situations, it is recommended that child care practitioners carefully think through the likely consequences of giving priority to particular principles. By evaluating the consequences, it may become clear which principle ought to be given more weight. The preferred action should be the one which produces the least amount of avoidable harm. Child care practitioners are also encouraged to consult with colleagues to obtain different perspectives on the problem, always being mindful of confidentiality issues. However, the individual practitioner facing the ethical dilemma will make the final decision.

The Principles of the Code
- Child care practitioners promote the health and well-being of all children.
- Child care practitioners enable children to participate to their full potential in environments carefully planned to serve individual needs and to facilitate the child's progress in the social, emotional, physical and cognitive areas of development.
- Child care practitioners demonstrate caring for all children in all aspects of their practice.
- Child care practitioners work in partnership with parents, recognizing that parents have primary responsibility for the care of their children, valuing their commitment to the children and supporting them in meeting their responsibilities to their children.
- Child care practitioners work in partnership with colleagues and other service providers in the community to support the well-being of children and their families.
- Child care practitioners work in ways that enhance human dignity in trusting, caring and co-operative relationships that respect the worth and uniqueness of the individual.
- Child care practitioners pursue, on an ongoing basis, the knowledge, skills and self-awareness needed to be professionally competent.
- Child care practitioners demonstrate integrity in all of their professional relationships.

Child care practitioners promote the health and well-being of all children.
Child care practitioners are responsible for the children in their care. They create environments for children that are safe, secure and supportive of good health in the broadest sense. They design programs that provide children with opportunities to develop physically, socially, emotionally, morally, spiritually, cognitively and creatively. A healthy environment for children is one in which each child's self-esteem is enhanced, play is encouraged and a warm, loving atmosphere is maintained.

In following this principle, a child care practitioner:
- Promotes each child's health and well-being;
- Creates and maintains safe and healthy environments for children;
- Fosters all facets of children's development in the context of the child, their family and their community;
- Enhances each child's feelings of competence, independence and self-esteem;
- Refrains from in any way degrading, endangering, frightening or harming children;
- Acts as an advocate on behalf of all children for public policies, programs and services that enhance their health and well-being; and
- Acts promptly in situations where the well-being of the child is compromised.

continue **Table 9.2**

Child care practitioners enable children to participate to their full potential in environments that are carefully planned to serve individual needs and to facilitate the child's progress in the social, emotional, physical and cognitive areas of development.

Child care practitioners understand the sequences and patterns of child development and cultural influences on those patterns. They use this knowledge to create environments and plan programs that are responsive to the children in their care. Child care practitioners implement programs and use guidance techniques that take into account the ages of the children and individual variations in their development.

In following this principle, a Child care practitioner:
- Considers cross-cultural variations in childrearing approaches when assessing child development;
- Applies the knowledge that the stages of physical, social, emotional, moral and cognitive development of each child may be different;
- Determines where each child is on the various developmental continua and uses that knowledge to create programs that allow for individual differences and preferences; and
- Uses developmentally appropriate methods and materials in working with children.

Child care practitioners demonstrate caring for all children in all aspects of their practice.
Caring involves both love and labour. Caring is at the core of early childhood education and is reflected in the mental, emotional and physical efforts of child care practitioners in their interactions with all children. Being cared for and cared about is consistently communicated to all children.

In following this principle, a Child care practitioner:
- Responds appropriately to each child's expressions of need;
- Provides children with experiences that build trust;
- Expresses warmth, appropriate affection, consideration and acceptance for children both verbally and non-verbally;
- Communicates to children a genuine interest in their activities, ideas, opinions and concerns; and
- Supports children as they experience different emotions and model acceptable ways of expressing emotions.

Child care practitioners work in partnership with parents, recognizing that parents have primary responsibility for the care of their children, valuing their commitment to their children and supporting them in meeting their responsibilities to their children.
Child care practitioners share joint interest in the children in their care while recognizing that parents have primary responsibility for childrearing and decision-making on behalf of their children. Child care practitioners complement and support parents as they carry out these responsibilities. Through positive, respectful and supportive relationships with parents, child care practitioners advance the well-being of children.

In following this principle, a Child care practitioner:
- Promotes considerate relationships with the parents of children in care;
- Respects the rights of parents to transmit their values, beliefs and cultural heritage to their children;
- Supports parents with knowledge, skills and resources that will enhance their ability to nurture their children;
- Encourages and provides opportunities for parents to participate actively in all aspects of planning and decision-making affecting their children; and
- Builds upon strengths and competencies in supporting parents in their task of nurturing children.

Child care practitioners work in partnership with colleagues and other service providers in the community to support the well-being of children and their families.
Child care practitioners recognize that nurturing family environments benefit children. Child care practitioners work with other helping professionals to provide a network of support for families.

continue **Table 9.2**

In following this principle, a Child care practitioner:
- Supports and encourages families by developing programs that meet the needs of those families being serviced;
- Assists families in obtaining needed specialized services provided by other professionals; and
- Advocates public policies and community services that are supportive of families.

Child care practitioners work in ways that enhance human dignity in trusting, caring and co-operative relationships that respect the worth and uniqueness of the individual.
Child care practitioners welcome and cherish children unconditionally. They respect the dignity of children, parents, colleagues and others with whom they interact. They demonstrate respect for diversity by valuing individuality and appreciating diverse characteristics, including ideas and perspectives.

In following this principle, a Child care practitioner:
- Communicates respect by practicing and promoting anti-bias interactions;
- Supports and promotes the dignity of self and others by engaging in mutually enhancing relationships;
- Plans inclusive programs that communicate respect for diversity regarding ability, culture, gender, socio-economic status, sexual orientation and family composition; and
- Provides opportunities for all children to participate in childhood activities.

Child care practitioners pursue, on an ongoing basis, the knowledge, skills and self-awareness needed to be professionally competent.
Early childhood professional practice is based on an expanding body of literature and research. Continuing education is essential. In-service skills training and self-awareness work prepare child care practitioners to fulfill their responsibilities more effectively.

In following this principle, a Child care practitioner:
- Recognizes the need for continuous learning;
- Pursues professional development opportunities;
- Incorporates into practice current knowledge in the field of early childhood care and education and related disciplines;
- Assesses personal and professional strengths and limitations and undertakes self-improvement;
- Articulates a personal philosophy of practice and justifies practices on the basis of theoretical perspectives; and
- Shares knowledge to support the development of the field.

Child care practitioners demonstrate integrity in all of their professional relationships.
Child care practitioners are truthful and trustworthy. They communicate honestly and openly and endeavour to be accurate and objective. Child care practitioners treat as confidential information about the children, families and colleagues with whom they work. The information may be shared with colleagues and other helping professionals as required for the care and support of the children or as required by law. Child care practitioners acknowledge real core potential conflicts of interest and act in accordance with the principles of this code of ethics.

I Believe Statements
In following this principle, a Child care practitioner:
- Communicates with children, parents, colleagues and other professionals in an honest, straightforward manner;
- Conscientiously carries out professional responsibilities and duties;
- Identifies personal values and beliefs and strives to be objective;
- Treats as confidential information concerning children, families and colleagues unless failure to disclose would put children at risk; and
- Recognizes the potential for real or perceived conflict of interest and acts in accordance with the principles of the code where dual relationships with colleagues or families exist and/or develop.

Source: Canadian Child Care Federation

How a Code of Ethics Informs Practice and Philosophy

Many early learning and child care programs provide parents and visitors with a copy of their own program philosophy, which identifies the values and principles that they adhere to when working with families. "Most importantly, [practitioners are stating] their intent to work toward fulfilling these tenets on a daily basis. These principles apply to everyone who is involved at the centre" (Wylie, 2004, p. 8.).

A code of ethics, combined with one's personal philosophy and a program philosophy, is intended to guide early childhood practitioners in making decisions in the interest of children and families. For example, assume your personal philosophy is that children's play is how children learn and develop. You have been assigned to complete a four-week placement at an early learning and childhood centre. During the third week, you are asked to prepare stencils for the children to colour for the following day. You struggle with this for two reasons. First, stencils do not provide children with the opportunity to be creative. Second, if you do not prepare the stencils, how will your grade be affected?

In another example, assume a father asks the program director to keep his child indoors because he does not want his snowsuit to get dirty. Ethically, the director is required to ensure the child has a minimum of two hours of outdoor play daily. But what are the consequences for the child if he does go outdoors? Will the child be punished at home? How will this affect the parent–practitioner relationship? On what does the director base her decision?

Early childhood practitioners enter this field to support children's healthy growth and development. Ethical dilemmas such as in the preceding examples surface from time to time. Philosophies and codes of ethics, therefore, are essential in guiding practitioners in their decision-making process.

Developing a Personal Philosophy

A personal philosophy means many things to many people. Crossley, Dietze, and Hume (2001) indicate that a philosophy statement for early childhood practitioners "presents the ideal toward which [a practitioner] strives. It establishes a basic premise from which all actions and experiences emanate. It is a returning point, a centering, in a time of crisis" (p. 1). As illustrated in Figure 9.5, an early childhood practitioner's personal philosophy is based on core values, related to what practitioners believe about children, the purpose of life, their role in their own lives and in the lives of others, and their responsibility as members of society. Examples of core values include the following:

- Each child is unique and is respected for what he brings to the environment.
- Early childhood provides each child with the foundation development for later learning.

- Children's play is their venue for learning.
- Early learning and child care support the development of the child and family by creating a responsive environment.
- Early childhood practitioners respect children, families, and colleagues.

Examining their thoughts and priorities about how children play, learn, and develop is necessary as a beginning point in practitioners' developing a personal philosophy. What practitioners believe about themselves, about others, and about life influences their beliefs about children, play, and learning. In addition, exploring how other practitioners feel, how they practise, and how they support personal development also contributes to practitioners' forming their ideas, ideals, and approaches to working with children and, hence, their personal philosophy. Table 9.3 provides one process that is used in developing a personal philosophy.

Thinking about a personal philosophy requires early childhood practitioners to engage in a self-reflective process. Begin this reflective process by examining questions such as the following:

- How does play support children's development?
- What do you think is important in a responsive environment for young children?
- What do you want children to feel when they enter your play environment?

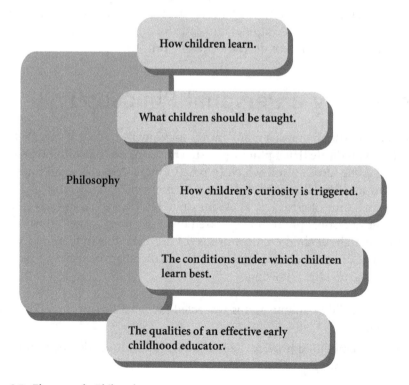

Philosophy

How children learn.

What children should be taught.

How children's curiosity is triggered.

The conditions under which children learn best.

The qualities of an effective early childhood educator.

Figure 9.5 *Elements of a Philosophy*

- What best practices and quality indicators are essential for children?
- What do you want families to say about the play environment for their children?
- What skills and talents do you wish to project in the play environment?
- How do your ideas influence what you do with children in early learning and child care environments?
- How do you implement your philosophy?
- How do your experiences reflect your philosophy?

There are many other questions that you may wish to explore. Questions and answers will evolve, change, and be replaced as you become partners with children in their play environments. Your personal philosophy today may be very different in two years, four years, and in ten years. As your career evolves, so will your beliefs about how children's play is learning. Experience and lifelong learning affect the direction in which one's philosophy evolves. Although others may influence your philosophy, you determine your beliefs and values. Table 9.3 provides statements that may help you in beginning to formulate your personal philosophy.

A personal philosophy informs practice. In fact, each day that practitioners participate in an early learning and child care environment, their personal philosophies are being put into practice (Driscoll & Nagel, 2005). When their philosophy is clear, practitioners are able to articulate and practise their beliefs about what is best for children, which influences how practitioners organize and execute a responsive environment for children and families. A personal philosophy creates a vivid portrait of who practitioners are, the practices they cherish, and the commitment they bring to children and families.

Philosophy statements, such as the one illustrated in Table 9.4, require periodic evaluation. Some of the points to examine when evaluating philosophies include the following:

- Does your philosophy accurately relate to your beliefs about children and learning?
- Is it understandable to you and to others?

Table 9.3 *Philosophy Statement Considerations*

My Personal Philosophy

I believe the purposes of early learning and child care are ....
I believe that children learn best through play experiences that........
I believe a responsive environment is one that ....
I believe any early learning and child care environment offers children .....
I believe that children and families are........
I believe the feeling tone I wish to create will....
I believe I bring qualities such as.............

Table 9.4 *A Sample Philosophy Statement*

PERSONAL PHILOSOPHY

I believe that:
- All children are unique individuals who develop in their own way and at their own pace. All children have the right to be respected and included.
- Children learn through play. Play gives children the method to practise social roles, express feelings, and solve problems.
- Children are active learners who learn best when they are given the freedom and time to explore, examine, question, and experiment.
- Children learn best in an environment that is safe, nurturing, consistent, stimulating, and aesthetically pleasing.
- Observation of children and knowledge of child development are the tools caregivers require to develop experiences that are based on the child's interests, needs, and abilities.
- Children should be involved in the development of experiences. Experiences should enhance children's social, emotional, physical, and cognitive development.
- Children's families are unique; their values and goals must be respected. Partnerships between the family, caregivers, and the community are necessary for the optimal development of the child.

"The time has come," the Walrus said,
"To talk of many things:
Of shoes—and ships—and sealing-wax—
Of cabbages—and kings—
And why the sea is boiling hot—
And whether pigs have wings."

Lewis Carroll, *Through the Looking-Glass, Chapter iii*

- Does it provide practical guidance for practice?
- Does what I believe make good sense?
- Have I been comprehensive, stating my beliefs about
  - How children learn?
  - What children should be taught?
  - Under what conditions children learn best?
  - The qualities of a good early childhood practitioner?

As a student practitioner, your philosophy is put into practice each day you work with children. Articulating your philosophy guides your practice and helps you to become aware of your beliefs, biases, and goals for future development. Your philosophy helps you determine how your decisions impact children, families, and colleagues. Examining your philosophy, adjusting your philosophy, and making conscious choices about what is best for children help you to be authentic. It improves your professional practice and your commitment to providing children with quality environments.

Early childhood practitioners face ethical decisions almost daily. By combining your knowledge about codes of ethics with your personal philosophy, you will develop effective practices that will guide you in making the best decisions for the children you serve.

SUMMARY

Personal Ecology

• Our personal ecology affects how we approach risk taking, our ability to try new things, how we participate in learning, and how we develop relationships. These all impact our beliefs and values, which form the foundation of our philosophy.

Stretch Goals

• Stretch goals broaden our potential learning opportunities and strategies needed to reach learning goals. Self-reflection, role modelling, mentoring, participation in conferences, self-directed learning, and reading support practitioners in their learning journey.

Self-Reflection

• Practitioners begin the process of self-reflection by examining their own practices and beliefs about children and the beliefs and practices of others. Reflection helps to identify discrepancies between beliefs and practices when practitioners explore both positive and negative learning experiences.

Professional Ethics

• A professional code of ethics influences an early childhood practitioner's philosophy. It serves as a professional guideline for practitioners working with children, families, and communities. A code of ethics, combined with a personal philosophy, guides practitioners in making good decisions in the interests of children and families.

Considerations of a Personal Philosophy

• A personal philosophy is a statement that describes the ideal that the practitioner works toward. It is based on a practitioner's personal ecology, stretch goals, self-reflection, and ability to combine an association's code of ethics with a practitioner's personal beliefs about how children play and learn.

FURTHER OPPORTUNITIES FOR ENRICHMENT

Research

1. Identify two or more associations established to support the development of early learning and child care in your province or territory, as well as on a national basis. How many of those organizations have a code of ethics? What are the core components of their codes of ethics? Are there particular elements of the codes of ethics that you agree with or question?
2. Examine the concept of self-reflection. Why has this concept become part of educational programs and business practices? What conditions are necessary to begin the process of self-reflection? How does self-reflection support personal development?

Group Investigation

1. Obtain a code of ethics from a provincial Early Childhood Education Association and examine it in relation to the *Canadian Child Care Federation Code of Ethics*. Identify which elements are similar and which are different. Are there specific elements that are contradictory?

   Based on the theory presented throughout this text and from other reading in your studies, are there components of either of the codes of ethics that are now dated and that do not fit with today's society?
2. There are those who argue against the need for a profession to have a code of ethics. They suggest that ethical behaviour is a matter of individual ethical values and beliefs and therefore codes are irrelevant and unnecessary. Others argue that individual early childhood practitioners and groups make ethical choices that affect children and families. The code of ethics can provide the context for that type of decision making. After reviewing a minimum of three codes of ethics, what is your perspective? Justify your position.
3. Examine the "Ethics Corner" in two issues of *Interaction*, published by the Canadian Child Care Federation. Write a response to the ethical issue. Justify your answer. Go to **www.cccf-fcsge.ca/publications/interaction_en.htm** to choose an *Interaction* edition.

Making Connections

1. Write your philosophy statement, reflecting your beliefs about how children learn and what kinds of environments children require. As you do so, record the various elements that you explore as you determine your philosophical perspective. What did you learn about your beliefs as you engaged in the process?
2. Identify four areas that you believe may be areas requiring "stretching." Identify why you think these areas need stretching, and determine potential processes that you may use to begin the stretching process.

ADDITIONAL READING

Canadian Child Care Federation. *National Ethics Training Program on Best Choices: Guidebook to the Ethical Journey.* Available at **www.cccf-fcsge.ca/projects/ethics_en.htm**

Feeney, S. & N. K. Freeman. (1999). *Ethics and the Early Childhood Educator: Using the NAEYC Code.* Washington, DC: NAEYC.

Mackay, H. (2004). *Right & Wrong.* Sydney: Hodder.

WEBLINKS

www.cfc-efc.ca/ecpaa: *Alberta—Early Childhood Professional Association of Alberta.*

www.cfc-efc.ca/ecebc: *British Columbia—Early Childhood Educators of British Columbia.*

www.mccahouse.org: *Manitoba—Manitoba Child Care Association.*

www.eccenb-sepenb.org: *New Brunswick—Early Childhood Care and Education New Brunswick.*

www.cfc-efc.ca/aecenfld: *Newfoundland and Labrador—Association of Early Childhood Educators, Newfoundland and Labrador.*

www.cfc-efc.ca/ccecens: *Nova Scotia—The Certification Council of Early Childhood Educators of Nova Scotia.*

www.cfc-efc.ca/aeceo/index.html: *Ontario—Association of Early Childhood Educators, Ontario.*

www.childcareontario.org/index.html: *Ontario Coalition for Better Child Care.*

www.ecda.pe.ca: *Prince Edward Island—Early Childhood Development Association of PEI.*

www.aqcpe.com: *Quebec—Association québécoise des centres de la petite enfance (Quebec association of child care centres).*

www.sasktelwebsite.net/saskcare/index.html: *Saskatchewan—Saskatchewan Early Childhood Association.*

www.cfc-efc.ca/ycca: *Yukon—Yukon Child Care Association.*

"Today's graduates of ECE programs have the opportunity to play a key leadership role in the development of a truly pan-Canadian system of early learning and child care. The success of this system and the well-being of the children it serves starts with you."

Barbara Coyle, Executive Director, Canadian Child Care Federation

10

The Future of Early Learning and Child Care

Learning Objectives

In this chapter you will:

1. Examine the three processes that will influence the future of early learning and child care.

2. Discuss the key attitudes that will make the difference in the future of this field.

3. Identify the seven areas where change will occur in the field in the next 10 years.

4. Examine 21 key trends that will emerge in an early childhood professional's life.

A Day Begins in an Early Learning and Child Care Centre

Jennifer Designs Her Destiny

Jennifer has now been in her position for five years and is feeling the need for a new challenge. She realizes that it will be difficult to leave the children and her colleagues, but she also knows that she will not maximize her knowledge and skill development if she does not take the risk of seeking new horizons. She feels this is a good time to pursue a new direction because she is considering marriage and a family. Both she and her future husband are examining whether her current income is sufficient to support their values and their vision for themselves and their children.

Jennifer is preparing for her monthly program-discussion session with her director, Gail. Jennifer knows that Gail would be a wise mentor to raise her concerns with. At her meeting with Gail, she says, "Gail, I like my work here, but I am exploring my options. I am feeling the need for further challenge, and I am thinking of moving on. I am even considering going back to school to upgrade my credentials so I can learn more about our field and ultimately increase my income."

Gail responds, "Jennifer, you are a valuable asset to our organization, and we would hate to lose you. However, I appreciate your dilemma. It is difficult to make a living in this field at this time. We are underpaid."

Jennifer replies, "I want to find a way to continue learning and to build a meaningful career in this field. But I am at a crossroads. I am in a phase of self-reflection."

Gail comments, "I think this is a phase of re-clarification and professional realignment that challenges early childhood practitioners to examine their beliefs, philosophies, and aspirations. It is a journey that each practitioner must take. I can't help you make your decision; I can only offer you my perspective on what I have learned, if that would interest you."

Jennifer says, "Gail, I admire your expertise in the field, and yes, I would appreciate your perspective."

Gail responds by saying, "Jennifer, I have learned that this field is somehow connected to who I am as a person. As I nurture children, I feel that I am doing what I was intended to do. When I am involved with children, time and space seem to disappear. I probably learn more from them than vice versa. It is sort of a magical time for me. I have watched this field struggle and grow through many stages over the years. I am mostly optimistic at this point. I believe it has a viable and exciting future. I am excited to be part of helping the field evolve to its next phase. The signs of development that are occurring nationally and internationally excite me. I am not sure what the future of early learning and child care holds, but I know that it will be challenging and it will continue to test our commitment. And it will demand that we evolve in the process."

Jennifer responds, "Gail, your thoughts help me keep things in perspective. I think I need to reevaluate all my options for the future and then decide my next course of action. Your thoughts and perspective have been very helpful, thank you."

Assimilation, accommodation, and efficiency are demonstrated in all systems in nature, including these apples and our profession.

Looking Ahead

In this chapter, we will acquaint you with the potential future of early learning and child care. Margaret Norrie McCain is one of the most visible advocates for a Canada-wide early learning and child care system. She identifies that by adopting a national system that is done well, Canada will be in a position to address child poverty, school performance, and workforce productivity. McCain cautions governments that a poorly developed system will waste scarce funds and "we will forgo an opportunity to further reinforce the core values of what it means to be a Canadian" (McCain, 2005, p. 1). In essence, early learning and child care is in a "paradigm shift."

This chapter differs from our previous chapters, which provided clear theoretical and application information. This chapter, instead, incorporates information gained from various regional, national, and international studies and determines some of the core changes that will be needed in order for this paradigm shift to evolve.

We know from the media and various levels of government that changes are coming within the early learning and child care sector. Some of the changes are as simple as converting the terminology from *early childhood educator* to *early childhood practitioner*, or *early childhood education* to *early learning and child care*. Other changes, such as amalgamation of services, will affect how services to children are offered and the roles of early childhood practitioners. For example, as the federal government and the provinces and territories sign early learning and child care agreements, early childhood services in provinces and territories will change. Demand for quality service and accessibility and the need for parental choice will increase. As well, changes to the educational preparation of early childhood practitioners will change. As you explore this chapter, examine the themes and make connections with the previous information presented throughout the book. As identified in Chapter 1, this is an exciting time to be entering the early childhood sector, and the future holds the promise of an enriching career.

In the Future

What if in the next 20 years the field of early learning and child care continues to evolve in the same dramatic way as it has in the past 20? What if this field continues in its development in the same dramatic fashion as the children it serves? What if the field of early childhood follows a similar, yet unique, path that other emerging professions have over the last century (e.g., education and health care)?

Think of Jennifer. She identified her need to continue to learn about the field and to increase her salary. What Jennifer does not know is how the field will evolve. We know that in the 1950s, teachers across Canada were poorly paid and worked in challenging conditions. As their profession has evolved, they have become highly recognized, respected, and compensated for their contribution to Canadian society.

We know that Canadian demographics have and will in the future continue to have a profound impact on the early learning and child care sectors. Canada is experiencing a declining birth rate, while continuing to attract an increasing number of immigrants—most of whom are settling primarily in the large urban areas of Toronto, Montreal, and Vancouver. We continue to have a high rate of participation in the labour force by mothers with young children, and single-parent families with young children are increasing. As well, child poverty in Canada continues to grow, as does the incidence of non-traditional work hours.

We will continue to have a high rate of mothers in the labour force, which will drive us as a community to meet the needs of those families.

The Natural Laws of Evolution

Studies in organizational and community development and history in general suggest that, as part of modern society, this profession will evolve or follow a specific natural law of evolution. This process has been and is currently exemplified in related fields such as education and health care. So we can be confident that the early learning and child care sector will very likely respond to society's evolution in three specific ways (see Figure 10.1).

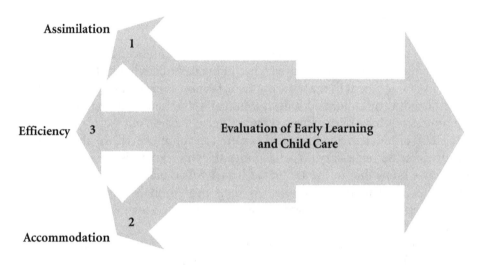

Figure 10.1 *The Natural Laws of Evolution*

First, the field of early childhood will tend toward greater *assimilation*, taking from its surroundings what it needs to move forward and respond to the needs of families living in Canada. Second, the field of early childhood will tend toward greater *accommodation*, adjusting itself to the current and emerging demands of Canadian society in general. Third, the field of early childhood will move toward increased *efficiency* or overall balance to ensure its long-term viability in Canada's future social-service system.

Charles Darwin described the early evidence of three evolutionary processes in his seminal work *The Origin of the Species,* and demonstrated their application in the natural world. For example, a crow that you see in your backyard is the systematic culmination of all the generations of its ancestors who assimilated, accommodated, and thereby achieved greater efficiencies in coping with their environment. These same processes apply to you and your ancestors. And these processes equally apply to collections of systems, such as groups or organizations or professions or communities.

So, these three processes—assimilation, accommodation, and efficiency—while not unique to early childhood, will manifest themselves in special ways unique to this field and will impact Canadian society at many levels, including children, families, neighbourhoods, communities, villages, towns, cities, and provinces and territories.

The Drive for Change

The drive for change and evolution in the early learning and child care sector has been emerging for some time from many influences and sectors. There have been numerous studies, reports, and recommendations over the past 30 years calling for action to address the needs of Canada's families. As Stephen Lewis (2004), former deputy director of UNICEF, noted in his remarks to the *Child Care for a Change!* conference, "I have never seen an issue so extraordinarily well-documented. The materials are superb, every single aspect of this issue, of this objective, of this remarkable cause, has been analyzed and documented and thought about and written about ad infinitum" (p. 5).

Internationally, the Organisation for Economic Co-operation and Development (OECD) (Bennett et al., 2004) has assessed the state of early childhood education and care in Canada, supplemented by the OECD *Thematic Review of Early Childhood Education and Care—Canadian Background Report* (Doherty et al., 2004). This prestigious international research-organization has described Canada's child care system as a disjointed, inefficient collection of programs and services that provide child care for working parents but ignore the dramatic and increasing evidence that shows that educating preschoolers provides lifelong dividends to all concerned. They summarize their recommendations as follows:

> During the 90s, growth in early childhood services slowed significantly in Canada, despite profound economic and social changes that affect the capacity of many parents to support early childhood development. The result is a patchwork of uneconomic, fragmented services, within which a small "child care" sector is seen as a labour market support, often without a focused child development and education role. In the same period, other OECD countries have been progressing toward public managed, universal services focussed on the development of young children. In these countries, services are also expected to play a significant role with respect to social cohesion, the alleviation of the effects of child poverty, improved child health and screening, better parenting, and family engagement in education.

(Doherty et al., 2004, p. 6)

Such significant research findings and others like them become the catalysts and the impetus for the evolution of the field of early childhood. We cannot stay where we are; evolution is inevitable. What is unclear is the form that the change or evolution will take. We have focused primarily on the likely impact on service providers—the early childhood practitioners who are tasked with nurturing the next generations of children. But one cannot talk about part of the system without relating it to the whole.

Let us first consider the dimensions of early childhood practitioners, what the Child Care Human Resources Sector Council (CCHRSC) terms the people in early childhood education and care (ECEC) in their recent *Labour Market Update Study* (2004).

Its authors note that in 2001 there were approximately 137 000 early childhood educators and assistants. Of this number, 93 000 worked outside the home in a child care centre or nursery program, and 60 500 of these were employed full time. Another 44 000 worked at home, and 33 000 of these offered care on a full-time basis. And not surprisingly, 96 percent were women. The study also noted that childhood educators are an aging group, more so than the general population in the last 10 years (p. 1).

Clearly, dramatic evolutionary change for this group is overdue in many ways. What is unclear is what forms this change will take and how quickly. From new practitioners' perspectives, it is interesting to explore what the future holds as they prepare to enter this interesting and dynamic field of community service.

Vancouverite Frank Odgen, a professional futurist, author, and public speaker known as "Dr. Tomorrow," remarked during an address to a community-college audience that the future of education belongs to Walt Disney. He pointed out that, in the past, "You needed to know the three *R*s of the Industrial Age—reading, 'riting, and 'rithemetic—to survive. Today, if you have not acquired the knowledge of the new three *R*s—RAM, ROM, and run—you are electronically illiterate. Our schools, instead of preparing students for the future, imprison them in the past" (2005). He argued convincingly that children of the future will not be interested in being taught; rather, they will be interested in being entertained. Consequently, Odgen believes that increasingly, what we call *teaching* will need to be reworked to be much more entertaining and therefore much more directly need-fulfilling to the learners. Teaching will also need to reflect the technical advances that are occurring daily all around us. Early childhood practitioners have long recognized the need for active learning, which is now being recognized as the foundation needed to lead the charge in innovative educational methodology for older children and adults. The popularity of learner-centred educational models is a case in point.

Odgen (2005) contends that because knowledge now travels at the speed of light and doubles every several months, old methods of education are quickly disappearing. And while our schools, colleges, and universities have probably changed more in the last 20 years than in the last two centuries, they will need to change much more and much faster to meet the future that awaits us. Odgen believes that the critical factor in all of this is a special attitude. He notes that 150 years ago, when North American immigration skyrocketed, it was mainly ordinary, unskilled, and uneducated people who took the risk to relocate to a new world. Their special attitude was generally one of openness to change, a desire for a new life, and a relish for adventure. This same attitude is often evident in today's new immigrants to Canada and certainly in most young children. This same attitude is required of early childhood practitioners; this same challenge faces each of us as we journey further into the "information age of the 21st century." It is not difficult to see this special attitude in early childhood educators; it is often contended that this same special attitude that Odgen refers to is actually essential to someone entering the field in its current state of development. Like other careers, early childhood practitioners will be required to take into consideration the realities of the information age in which we live and serve our communities (Milliron & Prentice, 2004).

The Seven Areas of Professional Evolution

The fundamental question that arises is, What forms of change or evolution can we expect based on the impacts of these three natural processes—assimilation, accommodation, and efficiency? And then, What are some of the more obvious examples of pending change that practitioners can prepare themselves to meet? We will consider this question from seven perspectives or domains that relate to the life of an early learning and child care practitioner, beginning with the intellectual domain, then moving to the career domain, then on to the financial, social, family, and health domains, and culminating in the spiritual domain (see Figure 10.2).

Each domain considers one important aspect in which evolution is both expected and anticipated with both curiosity and excitement. And as illustrated in Table 10.1, each domain identifies three likely evolutions that will occur within the next decade.

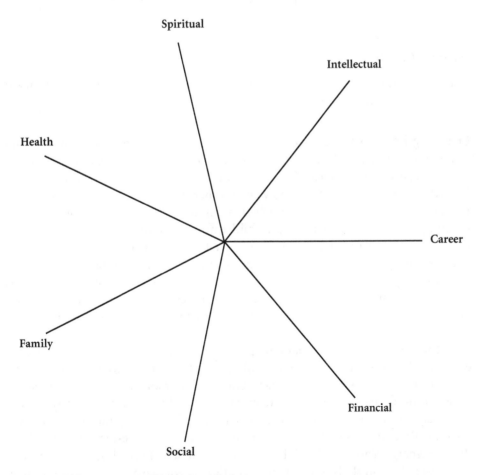

Figure 10.2 *The Seven Areas of Professional Evolution*

Table 10.1 *Future Trends*

Domain	Trend 1	Trend 2	Trend 3
Intellectual	Lifelong Learning	Research Ability	Increasing Specialization
Career	Technological Advancements	Service Integration	Growing Globalization
Financial	Increasing Funding Stability	Professional Credibility	Better Employee Benefits
Social	Universal Access	Public Recognition	Greater Public Accountability
Family	Increasing Time-Management Expectations	Family Appreciation	Self-Appreciation
Health	Stress Management	Role Modelling	Hygiene and Disease-Prevention
Spiritual	Stronger Professional Identity	Professional Certainty	Love of the Profession

Intellectual

There are at least three obvious intellectual trends that have emerged that impact early childhood practitioners.

Lifelong Learning First, *lifelong learning* has quickly become the byword of the past decade, driven by the system's need for efficiency. Early childhood practitioners can expect to be in a learning environment of some sort for their entire lives. Indeed, everyone will be. New knowledge is increasing so fast that we will have to pursue a lifelong learning curve, which is unlikely to ever flatten out. Lifelong learning in the early learning and child care environment is essential to keep abreast of the new research and how it impacts our particular field and our practice. Because practitioners deal with the next generation, they have an increased responsibility to ensure that current practices reflect best practices. And because access to new knowledge and information continues to accelerate, practitioners are not merely being changed, they are being transformed in ways that they could never have anticipated.

Moreover, learning and changing practices to support new knowledge require early childhood practitioners to not only accept the importance of lifelong learning, but to actually *want* to learn new information, motivating them to seek out typical professional-development activities provided by professional associations and local educational institutions, as well as to find new ways and new sources of learning. Practitioners will have to actively search out the latest cutting-edge ideas that are emerging around the globe and then assimilate those ideas into their existing knowledge and skills base. Then, practitioners will have to make accommodations to enhance their overall efficiency. It will not be unusual for early childhood practitioners to spend at least 20 percent of their time exclusively on engaging in various types of professional-enhancement opportunities, which already occurs in the information-technology industry.

Research Ability Early childhood practitioners require research abilities. Practitioners will require efficient skills in finding accurate information quickly. To be accountable for the developing needs of young children in a quality early learning and child care environment, access to up-to-date, accurate information is essential. The ability to assimilate the new knowledge and transfer it to learning environments is a key role of upcoming early childhood practitioners. Lifelong learning requires a combination of examining monthly professional books, magazines, and journals, as well as developing sophisticated research skills that give you access to the world of information. As a result, early childhood practitioners must be computer literate and in regular touch with key relevant Web sites. These sites will reflect the diverse range of interests that all professions require of their members, such as research results, public-policy developments, methodological advances, special-interest topics, and so on. *Research ability* means knowing how to find out about the polar bear population of Iqaluit. It means knowing how to find the instructions for writing a funding proposal. It means discovering the origin and meaning of the word *universality*. It means knowing how to find answers to questions that children have not even thought of yet. It also means scanning fields related directly and indirectly to your professional interests—e.g., finding out what is going on in the fields of biology, particle physics, or cosmology that relate to early learning and child care. Assimilating and accommodating emerging information from a wide variety of fields will be the norm in the future.

Increasing Specialization A third intellectual trend that is also inevitable is increasing specialization. Specialization is a form of accommodation and assimilation that is required of efficient systems throughout society. Historically, early childhood education comprised daycare centres and kindergartens. Then, in response to the changing needs of families and society, early childhood education started to expand into areas such as family daycare, infant care, junior kindergartens, rural daycare, high school daycare, workplace daycare, 24-hour daycare, and so on. Early childhood services will continue to subdivide as the system evolves to respond to society's changing needs, resulting in early childhood practitioners choosing areas of specialization. New areas of increasing specialization will provide new opportunities for practitioners to broaden their career aspirations, and will also place increased responsibility on them to expand their knowledge and skill levels to reflect the emerging developments that will occur. For example, public-school educators now specialize in narrower areas of study and service delivery, such as elementary, junior high, high school, or post-secondary schools. Health-care providers also select from such specialities as pediatrics, gynecology, or cardiology. Similarly, early learning and child care providers will have to specialize, which will require them to consciously select narrower areas of study and employment to reflect their interests and priorities. For example, practitioners may specialize in programs for children with special learning needs or special learning interests, such as music, sports, art, multiculturalism, computers, languages, etc. As we continue to gain information about how children learn and develop, more areas of specialization will emerge.

Career

Within the realm of an early childhood practitioner's career, there are also some interesting trends emerging.

Technological Advancements A career trend driven by the system's ongoing need for balance and efficiency that is also inevitable is technological advancement. Technological advancements are changing, and will continue to change, early learning and child care services. In some centres, for example, preschool children carry cellphones, and we suspect that soon this will be a common occurrence. It is likely that hand-held computers and digital cameras are not far behind. Some urban workplace early learning and child care environments have on-site cameras, allowing parents to check on their children from their workstation whenever they wish during their workday. Are you ready to be on camera all the time?

Early childhood practitioners will be required to be familiar with and comfortable with ever-increasing technology. Although we view early learning and child care primarily as a community service-delivery system that is non-technical, technological advances will increase as part of the evolutionary process. For example, children increasingly attend early learning and child care centres with various technological devices intended to enhance or support their development in such areas as security, language, hearing, vision, and motor coordination. For example, we now commonly see children with eyeglasses, hearing aids, and body braces of various kinds. We already have sound and video monitors for infants' bedrooms. What technology will offer in the future is anybody's guess, but with our current focus on personal security, it is likely that children will soon carry GPS (geographical positioning systems) that their parents and early childhood practitioners will monitor simultaneously. In fact, surgically implanted tracking monitors are already on the market. These are examples of this ongoing accommodation principle in action.

Service Integration Another career trend that will continue is service integration, which has been occurring, and continues to occur, between the overlapping services of early learning and child care and the education sector. Stephen Lewis (2004) listed it as a first premise not just within Canada but internationally:

> Number one: everyone understands, I think, and this is an international understanding, it is not merely a Canadian understanding, that early learning and child care fused together is the kind of objective which any civilized society strives for, and that it becomes an indispensable and vital dimension of a child's life, enhancing all of the family characteristics which shore up the child by profoundly influencing in the most positive imaginable way the opportunities for the child.

(p. 2)

As identified in Chapter 1, the United Nations General Assembly Special Session on Children resulted in "the nations of the world adopting by unanimity a declaration and plan of action called *A World Fit for Children.*" *A Canada Fit for Children* represents Canada's plan of action to improve the lives of children living in Canada and in the world. It calls for children living in Canada to have access to child-centred, multi-sectored, forward-looking, and collaborative services.

This service integration will continue in new and varied forms throughout the sector. We have seen the assimilation process of service integration occur in many venues in society, from one-stop shopping in malls to individual stores that will do your hair and dry clean your clothes while you wait. Workplace daycare and child care centres located in high schools are current examples of this convenience phenomenon. In Charlottetown, P.E.I., there are two health spas with a daycare service located in the facility that provides service to both members and the public. This is efficiency in action through the combined processes of assimilation and accommodation.

Across Canada, a number of provincial, municipal, and local initiatives are evolving that combine early learning and child care services in one locale. For example, consider the emergence of family resource centres (FRC). These centres offer parent-education programs combined with a variety of other child care services. Program models such as the Toronto-based First Duty programs may become prevalent. First Duty programs, located in local schools, provide a range of family support services, with staff that include teachers, health-care providers, and early childhood practitioners. In the future, perhaps dentists, psychologists, social workers, dry cleaners, grocery stores, clothing stores, and fast-food outlets will be added to the local school, making schools community hubs. There are such models already in place in the North, a trend that will place increasing pressure on early childhood practitioners to work more closely as members of an interdisciplinary team. Early childhood practitioners will have to develop advanced communication skills and regularly enhance them in order to deal with the wider variety of people and occupational groups that they will come to interact with.

> ## Conversation Café
>
> As we prepare for change and the evolution of early learning and child care in Canada, what new roles will practitioners play? What additional educational backgrounds will they require? And how will our country's emerging demographics (e.g., lower birth rates and higher immigration rates) affect this community service and the employability of its professionals?

Growing Globalization   The third significant career trend that early childhood practitioners will face is growing globalization. Not only does knowledge travel at the speed of light, so too does interpersonal communication. Never before has it been so evident that we are on a rather small "blue marble" called Earth and that we can connect with just about anyone and anywhere at any time.

The field of early learning and child care is part of a global movement to take better care of the world's children. The first World Summit for Children, held in 1990, the largest gathering of countries ever to meet to address this topic, set specific targets for the year 2000. Then, in May 2002, more than 7000 people from around the world gathered to take part in the United Nations General Assembly Special Session on Children. It was deemed the most important meeting held about children since the first World Summit. In preparation for the General Assembly, Stephen Lewis noted that the primary issues of child poverty, child soldiers, child labour, street children, and other forms of child exploitation all boiled down to early child care and education, basic education, and their integration into every child's life (Lewis, 2004, p. 3).

Growing globalization will provide early childhood practitioners with unique professional development opportunities.

World attention is very closely focused on early learning and child care. Consequently, opportunities for early childhood practitioners to participate in dialogue with a worldwide network of practitioners, researchers, educators, and advocates are possible. For example, early childhood practitioners and students from Holland College in Charlottetown, Prince Edward Island, and Malaspina University College in Nanaimo, British Columbia, are currently involved in a Canada–China workplace exchange so that each can benefit from the other's expertise. This trend will increase, and there will be continued opportunities for practitioners to learn about early childhood practices, as well as cross-cultural activities, at the service, training, infrastructure, and development levels.

In a similar vein, with Canada's demographics indicating the need for increased immigration to meet the country's future needs, and with the anticipated relaxation of our immigration laws, increasing numbers of children from other countries will be entering early learning and child care centres. This influx will increase the opportunities for early childhood practitioners to work in a multicultural setting and will provide networking options to those who are interested in pursuing a professional-development experience by working overseas. Early childhood practitioners with second and third languages will have an advantage in actualizing this career interest.

Financial

The financial realm of early learning and child care has been characterized historically by uncertainty and inadequacy. With the federal government's 2005 commitment to begin the process of developing a national child care program, there is an infusion of more public dollars into the system through various means by federal, provincial, and municipal levels of government.

Increasing Funding Stability As governments increase their financial commitment, increasing funding stability is on the horizon. We are reminded, however, that "as of 2003 there were approximately 690,000 regulated child care spaces for children aged 0 to 12 years—still only enough regulated spaces for a small proportion of children in Canada. There continues to be important differences in the way child care is organized and managed across the provinces and territories"

(Beach et al., 2004, p. 3). For example, as we identified in Chapter 2, each province and territory has different staff–children ratios and staff-training requirements. Currently, the province of Quebec spends more money on early learning and child care than any other province or territory.

The federal government's spending for early learning and child care has risen from $988 million in 1995 to $2.6 billion in 2003, and in 2005 it allocated $5 billion dollars over five years. At the time of writing this book, the provinces and territories and the federal government are negotiating how to use the funding. The federal government has determined that the $5 billion child care fund will not be released without the provinces' agreeing to accountability measures. Determining the allocation amounts and time frames will be an ongoing and difficult journey for all concerned.

Debate continues regarding "for-profit" and "not-for-profit" child care. For example, Cleveland and Kranshinsky (2005) indicate in their study that "non-profit child care centres outscore their commercial counterparts in all aspects of early learning and care" (p. 1). McCain and Romonow (2005) indicate the need to reduce commercial centres and "restrict expansion dollars to public and non-profit child care providers" (p. 2). As the paradigm shifts, the overall child care system will move toward greater levels of predictability. There will be more stability in terms of funding sources and service quality as federal leaders slowly implement national standards. Advocates such as McCain strongly encourage provinces and territories to develop a single early learning and child care centre with multiple functions. "Any agreement should encourage provinces to rationalize their early years services to provide a stable platform for expansion" (McCain & Romonow, 2005, p. 2).

The need to carve out an early learning and child care system that is affordable, accessible, and of high quality continues to reflect the current value-system of Canadian society, as reflected in other social-services systems already in place in health and education.

Professional Credibility   A second financial trend tied to stability will be increasing professional credibility. Financial stability will create increased status and credibility for the early learning and child care sector, which will encourage individuals to choose this profession, get the appropriate training (McCain & Romonow, 2005), and be prepared to invest in engaging in lifelong learning options, including advanced training at the post-secondary and graduate levels. As a result, post-secondary institutions will increasingly offer a variety of ways to enable both new and existing early childhood practitioners to access educational programs. Distance-education programs are one way to support lifelong learning. As a new interest develops in the emerging speciality areas of early learning and child care, there will be additional pressure on Canada's 135 post-secondary institutions to create more accessible ways of participating in lifelong learning. Institutions using traditional teaching models will be challenged to create new methodologies that will reflect innovative educational strategies.

These advances will influence the development of numerous highly sophisticated positions within the early childhood sector. New partnerships with other fields that also have a vested interest in nurturing the children in Canadian society will emerge. These developments will create an exciting and dynamic field of employment and career opportunities.

Better Employee Benefits   The third financial trend we can expect is better employee benefits. Historically, the early childhood sector has been characterized by difficult working conditions, high levels of job insecurity, limited career opportunities, health and safety concerns, and uncertain employment status (Crowther, 2005). "Earned income was about half the national average for all occupations and less than half as much as elementary school and kindergarten teachers. The overall annual income for full and part time early childhood educators and assistants in 2000 was $16,167 while full time early childhood educators earned just over $19,000" (Beach et al., 2004, p. 2). Salary ranges were indeed diverse: " . . . compensation can vary widely (e.g. from just above minimum wages with no benefits, to an annual salary of close to $70,000 with full benefits and a pension plan)" (Beach et al., 2004, p. 2). McCain and Romonow (2005) emphasize the need for early childhood practitioners to be adequately compensated and supported. Many early learning and child care centres have become unionized as a way to address working conditions and salaries. There are currently approximately 31 500 unionized employees in the early learning and child care sector (Beach et al., 2004, p. 5).

The stabilization of the early learning and child care system's financial base, combined with practitioners' emerging credibility, will trickle down to create more attractive career opportunities for graduates and, therefore, more competition for positions. This increased competition will encourage employers to offer more incentives to prospective employees and current staff as a way to attract and retain competent staff, which will translate into significantly improved wages and working conditions. "Steps must be taken to ensure that [early learning and child care] becomes a viable profession so the sector can compete with more financially secure occupations in the broader educational and social service sector" (Beach et al., 2004, p. 5).

A more secure financial future expands employers' capacity to offer wider benefits packages that will include the usual items, such as salary scales, paid vacations, medical and dental packages, and professional development time, as well as some unique new ones, such as subsidized fees for staff children, computer purchases, and travel and cultural programs.

Social

In terms of the broader community, the social trends and corresponding implications for early learning and child care are significant.

Universal Access   The first trend is universal access. It is apparent, after many years of social action by thousands of people, that the federal government acknowledges the need for families to have access to an early learning and child care system. It is, in fact, an essential family support-system in modern society. Ownership of this principle is the result of a long process of assimilation of research, studies, briefs, conferences, and other related analysis, culminating in the addition of this essential service to the Canadian social fabric. The result will be a more balanced social service network to enhance the nurturing of Canadian families. Governments will, however, need to make provision for families who decide not to use the pubic early learning and child care system. Such initiatives may take the form of an expansion of parental tax breaks that historically have been exempted by the child tax benefit program. As stated by Friendly (2004), a well-designed national system must "be at the heart of a renewed social policy mission in Canada" (p. 51), which will require a national approach to identifying goals and objectives, determining who the programs serve, and deciding how they will be delivered.

Public Recognition The second social trend that will continue to emerge is public recognition. Professionalism, unionization, and advocacy are three key elements that increase recognition. Yet in 2003 only about 15 000 early childhood practitioners had any affiliation with a professional organization (Beach et al., 2004, p. 5). This trend will need to change in the future as part of the emergence of this sector.

Members of our Canadian society are increasingly acknowledging that early learning and child care has a dual purpose: to support children's development and enhance labour-market participation. Investments in early learning and child care are necessary to support Canada's ability to be competitive and productive in the 21st century and are "key to labour strategy, the urban agenda, equality for women, social integration of newcomers, strengthening social cohesion and...a social determinant of health" (Friendly, 2004, p. 51). Public attention will increase awareness of the valued service provided to the community and increase appreciation of those who pursue it as a career. As well, there will be greater recognition of the contributions that practitioners can make to related fields like parenting, pediatrics, and community development. And early childhood practitioners will play key roles in various segments of society, such as in research, education, politics, and public commissions, thereby providing a higher profile and recognition for those who work with young children.

Greater Public Accountability The third social trend to emerge will be greater public accountability. Early childhood practitioners have always carried considerable responsibility. In the past, accountability for this came mostly from children, their parents, the licensing agency, and the local community. In the future, society will cast a much closer eye on this important community service. This scrutiny will dramatically increase professional accountability. With the trends and advances in technology, specialization, integration, and globalization comes increased public evaluation of all aspects of the sector, its services, and its members. One example will be in ethics. Early childhood practitioners will be equated with other professionals and held to a similar standard, placing increased pressure on practitioners to ensure that their practice is ethical and that their actions are perceived to be of the highest standard—which will apply to all areas of practice, from professional conduct to service delivery to financial management.

Family

While practitioners' primary work is with families, they are also a part of their own families. The evolution of their professional role will impact directly on their own families in ways that they may not have anticipated. Practitioners can expect more demands—not just on their expertise, but also on the time required to meet those expectations. At the same time, these demands will be counterbalanced by signs of increased appreciation, both from their families and from themselves.

Increasing Time-Management Expectations The first family trend that practitioners can expect is increasing time-management expectations. One of the results of increased responsibility, accountability, credibility, and recognition is that more people will expect more of practitioners' time. They will be asked for their expertise on many issues related directly and indirectly to children, which will affect their time with their families and affect other significant relationships as

Increasing professional demands will put added pressure on practitioners to manage their personal and professional time wisely.

well. Practitioners will be expected to enhance on a continuous basis their ability to determine priorities and set short- and long-term goals and action plans. Without strong skills in this area, important personal and professional relationships can be jeopardized very quickly.

Family Appreciation The second family trend that will strengthen is family appreciation. Early childhood practitioners are often shown signs of appreciation from the children and families they serve, while frequently being unacknowledged at home for their career choice and their work. When a dog-kennel staff person earns a higher hourly wage than many practitioners do, families may find it difficult to appreciate this career choice. Sometimes spouses may feel as if they are subsidizing practitioners' employment with their salary, or children may feel they are doing without or with less than their peers. As the public profile of this service sector rises, family members may gain greater awareness of both the demands of the work and the impact of this profession on the community. For example, our health-care crisis in Canada has opened our eyes to the important role nurses play in health care. As a result, new roles and significant status changes and compensation occurred, a shift in perception that will also take place in the early learning and child care sector.

Self-Appreciation The third family trend to be highlighted is self-appreciation. Each practitioner is a sort of family unto herself, and with that come many varied and interesting roles. When practitioners notice new segments of their extended community honouring them and their contributions to the lives of the people around them, they are motivated to self-evaluate their roles in life. In so doing, they acknowledge and own the knowledge and skills they bring to their work, leading to increased self-esteem or self-appreciation. This increased competence positively affects their work and those around them in ways that can only add more quality to the service they provide to their community.

Physical Health

Practitioners' physical health will also be challenged in terms of how to stay physically and emotionally balanced while increasingly taking on the role of community model and staying on the cutting edge of new developments in the care and prevention of disease in the children in their care.

Stress Management The first health trend is stress management. Stress management has long been a challenge in the early learning and child care sector, stemming from the crucial responsibilities of nurturing children in undervalued and undercompensated workplaces. As early learning and child care programs are carved into Canadian society, there will be increased responsibilities and accountabilities, which will magnify the personal and professional stress that practitioners experience. And managing stress becomes crucial in a demanding career working with children. Early childhood practitioners will require strategies to manage the demands of an expanding role in a balanced way. A specific, detailed plan for monitoring stress and specific actions to reduce stress are necessary. Ongoing mentoring and professional-development support are crucial parts of a successful stress-management plan.

Role Modelling The second health trend is role modelling for personal balance and a balanced lifestyle. Role modelling is somewhat unique to this sector and is not new—children consistently use early childhood practitioners for this purpose. As the role of and profile of early childhood practitioners evolve, there will be increased pressure to model not just professional skills, but also the stress-management skills cited above: general physical-health skills, such as nutrition, exercise, and lifestyle: and, of course, communication skills.

Hygiene and Disease Prevention The emerging focus on hygiene and disease prevention will continue to prevail. The SARS (sudden acute respiratory syndrome) epidemic in Toronto, the AIDS pandemic in Africa, the West Nile fever threat, the rise in sexually transmitted diseases (STDs), the increasing number of pet-related diseases, and others as yet unidentified will put increasing pressure on this sector to protect the children it serves. This growing responsibility will require practitioners to assimilate new technical information and be ready to accommodate new procedures and practices into established routines. Hygiene and disease prevention will involve new protocols at all levels of the sector, from pre-entrance medical examinations for children to personal-hygiene practices for staff, parents, and children. This challenge will test the resources of both the early childhood sector and

Canada's entire health-care system and, indeed, the world's. Early childhood practitioners will play an important role in supporting children in acquiring healthy daily-living practices. Ongoing knowledge and practices to protect themselves and children will be necessary.

Spiritual

With practitioners' roles expanding, their very identity will grow stronger, clearer, and they will display more certainty about who they are as professionals and how they fit into the service matrix of their community, manifested in practitioners' stating with assurance the love they have for the work they do in their community.

Stronger Professional Identity The spirit of this field has been strong for some time and will continue to foster an even stronger professional identity, as manifested in the powerful and successful and ongoing advocacy role carried on by its members. Advocacy has been the hallmark of early learning and child care from the beginning. Advocacy initiatives must be increased and sustained to push the various political systems to nurture and fully integrate this essential service into the community-service network. So, every practitioner, of necessity, will be called upon to serve either directly or indirectly in this task.

Coming together as a national, provincial, territorial, or regional meeting or conference will continue to contribute to the field's synergy. "It is estimated that in 2003 less than 15,000 individuals who work in child care had any affiliation with a child care organization . . . " (Beach et al., 2004, p. 5). But this will change dramatically. As the early learning and child care sector gains status and recognition, practitioners will gain confidence and the ability to contribute to the community-service network. This rising level of appreciation for what practitioners are will support practitioners in articulating and advocating more clearly the kind of profession they desire within the social-service network, and this will drive practitioners to move together into even more dynamic partnerships and coalitions with shared goals. It will also challenge them to use their creativity and genius to find new and innovative strategies and methods to nurture the children of the future in tandem with other community-service providers.

Professional Certainty The second spiritual trend is professional certainty. Early childhood practitioners exhibit this certainty through their confidence in their current roles as early childhood practitioners and in their aspirations for future roles within the field. Certain individuals will, in fact, play a vital role in building and maintaining the kind of advanced, caring society for which Canada is known worldwide. These practitioners know that they couldn't be who they are, doing what they do, and having the relationships they have, without having spent precious time in early learning and child care settings. They know that their service and advocacy efforts in this sector are tied very closely to their purpose in life. They realize that this has been their calling, as if somehow they were destined to be doing this work at this time and in this way. While the form of their work in terms of roles and duties has continually changed, there has also been a constancy of purpose throughout. From this certainty come passion and commitment to themselves, to the children and families of Canada, and to early learning and child care.

Love of the Profession   The third spiritual trend is love of the profession. Wise practitioners who have spent their careers in the trenches of early childhood education often talk about the love they have for the children they served as well as for the parents, colleagues, and communities that have been intertwined in their careers. They have an abiding respect for the exciting future that is on the horizon as well as for the history of this field, which they have been an integral part of. They do not resent past struggles, nor are they infatuated with future successes. They have learned to honour both the successes and the challenges equally, thereby ensuring that the early childhood sector assimilates and accommodates itself in the natural manner required to build a more efficient and balanced system for all families living in Canada. It is these enlightened individuals who will express with genuine affection their love and commitment to the early learning and child care sector. These are the people who have been the catalysts for the evolution of this field and who will serve the same role in its future, with the assistance of the next generation of families.

There will be stronger commitment and spirit comprising a clearer identity, along with a certainty and love of their work and profession.

SUMMARY

The Future

- The three natural processes of assimilation, accommodation, and efficiency will govern the future of early childhood education and care in Canada. As a result, the future will require an attitude of openness, a desire for adventure and learning, and a willingness to grow and evolve.

The Seven Areas of Growth

- **Intellectually,** the challenge will be a commitment to lifelong learning, sound research skills, and increasing specialization of the field.
- **In their careers,** practitioners will have to deal with the ongoing impact of technological advances, the accelerated integration of services with related fields, and the growing globalization of the early childhood education and care community.
- **Financially,** the effects of increasing funding stability, along with growing internal professional credibility and improved employee benefits, will provide new challenges.
- **Socially,** the trends of universal service access coupled with greater public recognition and greater accountability will garner the field's attention.

- For practitioners and their **families,** managing time will become increasingly demanding, which will be countered with greater appreciation from family and friends. As a result, professionals will experience higher degrees of self-esteem.
- In the **health** area of growth, stress management will become an increasing concern, aggravated by the demand for practitioners to become more public role-models and by the new emerging dimensions of health care that are approaching the field in light of such new diseases as AIDS, SARS, West Nile virus, and others.
- Practitioners' **spiritual** area of growth will become clearer and stronger: practitioners' professional identity will be reflected in greater professional certainty expressed by members, in a continued commitment to advocacy, and in a more openly expressed love for this field of community service.

FURTHER OPPORTUNITIES FOR ENRICHMENT

Research

1. Review Frank Odgen's 42 laws, which he argues will govern our future. You will find these laws at his Web site: **www.drtomorrow.com.** Discuss with a group of your colleagues what implications his laws suggest for early childhood education and care.
2. Interview a senior early childhood practitioner who has had at least 20 years' experience in this field. Make a list of 21 significant evolutions that this professional has witnessed and share them with your class.

Group Investigation

1. With a small team of your colleagues, brainstorm and write up the job description and daily duties of an early childhood practitioner in the year 2025. Be sure to include not just the speculations of your fellow students but also the suggestions of seasoned practitioners.
2. Based on the ideas presented in this text and from other reading in your studies, list the three specific reasons why you might choose to devote your life to this field of community service. Compare your reasons with a classmate's and notice the difference in your reasons.
3. Respond to the following questions carefully and then compare your results with two other fellow students'. What do your aspirations have in common and how do they differ? Identify three significant things you learned from this exercise.

My Professional Role in 2025

I will be in the following type of position:

I will be carrying the following responsibilities and duties:

I will professionally have the following:

I will personally have the following:

I will earn annually:

Making Connections

1. Having reviewed the predictions outlined in this chapter, find historical evidence to substantiate that these patterns have occurred previously in this field. Use a variety of research tools, including the web, various policy organizations, professionals, and other sources.

ADDITIONAL READING

Beach, J., Bertrand, J., Forer, B., Michal, D., & Tougas, J. (2004). *Working for Change: Canada's Child Care Workforce—Labour Market Update Study*. Ottawa: Child Care Human Resources Sector Council.

Bennett, J., Buysse, B., Lindberg, P., & Penn, H. (2004). Early Childhood Education and Care Policy—CANADA–Country Note. Paris: OECD Directorate for Education, Organisation for Economic Co-operation and Development.

Darwin, C. (1979). *The Origin of the Species*. (7th Printing). Toronto: Random House Value Publishing.

Doherty, G., Friendly, M., & Beach, J. (2004). *Early Childhood Education and Care Policy—Background Report for Canada—OCED Thematic Review of Early Childhood Education and Care Report*. Paris: Organization for Economic Co-operation and Development.

Lewis, S. (2004). Proceedings of Child Care for a Change! Shaping the 21st Century Conference. Winnipeg, Canada: Canadian Council on Social Development.

Odgen, F. (1994). *The Last Book You Will Ever Read*. Available from **www.drtomorrow.com.**

WEBLINKS

www.ccsd.ca/home.htm: *Canadian Council on Social Development.*
www2.lucidcafe.com/lucidcafe/library/96feb/darwin.html: *Charles Darwin.*
www.ccsc-cssge.ca: *The Child Care Human Resources Sector Council.*
www.childcarepolicy.net: *Child Care Network.*
www.drtomorrow.com: *Frank Odgen.*
www.oecd.org: *Organisation for Economic Co-operation and Development.*
www.un.org: *The United Nations.*

Glossary

Aboriginal Head Start. Centre-based programs designed for First Nations families. These programs offer families early childhood experiences and health-promotion services.

Accessible early learning and child care. All children and parents have access to affordable early learning and child care. One of four early learning and child care principles.

Assessment. The act of observing, gathering or collecting, and recording information relevant to desired program outcomes. Assessment is also the process of judging and documenting the value and worth of the elements of the children's program for the purpose of making recommendations and decisions about current and future program-delivery.

Authentic curriculum/emergent programming. Programming that evolves in response to children's expressed interests, needs, or abilities.

Bank Street model. This program model, based on the work of Lucy Mitchell and Barbara Biber, emphasizes the need for children to have learning environments that support autonomy, expand knowledge, and develop self-concept and interpersonal skills.

Bank Street programs. Based on the work of Eric Erikson, Jean Piaget, and John Dewey, these programs focus on all aspects of child development. The programs encourage both interpersonal interactions and play experiences that support the cognitive, social, and emotional aspects of children's development.

Behaviourist theory. John B. Watson's theory emphasizes that children learn through behaviour-modification strategies. Learning and behaviour occur through responses and consequences.

Benchmarks. Statements of high-quality practices that guide practitioners in examining their levels of practice for each element of an early learning and child care program. Benchmarks guide practitioners in devising plans for program improvement.

Best practice. Refers to evidence-based outcomes that describe an ideal early learning and child care practice.

A Canada Fit for Children. Canada's national plan of action, which is intended to improve the lives of children in Canada and in the world. It lays out a roadmap to guide Canada's collective efforts for and with children. As one element of the monitoring of progress and results, it includes examples of directional signposts and milestones for the federal government. It calls for strategies that are child-centred, multi-sectoral, forward-looking, and collaborative. It also signals emerging issues and identifies ways to promote and protect children's rights, including greater public awareness of the United Nations' *Convention on the Rights of the Child*. *A Canada Fit for Children* contains a declaration of Canada's commitment to children. The plan of action outlines goals, strategies, and opportunities for action on key priorities within four central themes: supporting families and strengthening communities; promoting healthy lives; protecting from harm; and promoting education and learning.

Canadian Child Care Federation (CCCF). A bilingual, non-profit, national, member-based organization established in 1987. There are more than 11 000 members, including early learning and child care practitioners, academics, parents, and policymakers.

Centre-based child care. Care provided to children in a group setting licensed by the provincial/territorial governments. Practitioners are usually not related to the children.

Challenging activities. Experiences that provide new areas of growth to children.

Child care. Government-regulated child care offered in centres and family child care homes.

Child-initiated approach. The experiences and program ideas evolve directly from children or as a result of observations that the early childhood practitioners make of children during play.

Child life programs. Programs located in hospital settings to encourage the physical and psychological care of children while recuperating from illness or injury.

Childminding (LINC). Informal, unlicensed arrangements for children of newcomers while the parents attend language instruction.

Children's health services. Programs designed by health units to support children's health, wellness, and development.

Code of ethics. Is a position statement developed by an organization, which outlines guidelines for acceptable professional practices and sets forth a common base for resolving ethical dilemmas in the early learning and child care sector.

Cognitive developmental theory. Jean Piaget maintained that children develop their intelligence by interacting with their physical environment. Children take new knowledge and adapt it to their current knowledge. Piaget identified four stages of intellectual development: sensorimotor, preoperational, concrete operational, and formal operational.

Community Action Program for Children (CAPA). Serves children and their families who live in conditions of risk. Funds are available for community coalitions that provide information, education, and support-services to families.

Community involvement in program design and implementation. Early learning and child care programs are delivered in the communities where children live. Each family is a member of this community. As children's exposure to people and environments expands to include others beyond the family unit, it is the children's community that offers experiences to support their growth and development. Community members or community organizations partner with early learning and child care centres to provide services and experiences that support young children's development.

Community programs. Nursery schools/preschools and resource programs that are regulated by provincial/territorial governments.

Concrete operational intelligence (6–7 years to 12–13 years). Children begin to think logically and with a more critical perspective. They are now able to understand conservation—e.g., when given a ball of playdough they understand that the quantity remains constant whether the ball of playdough remains in a ball or is flattened.

Constructivist learning environment. Children develop knowledge from the experiences within the environment. The early childhood practitioner facilitates or guides the process of exploration, wonderment, and discovery.

Context. Refers to the environment in which development occurs.

Corporate child care. On-site child care set up at workplaces for the children of employees.

Creative play. This program model encourages and supports children's play that facilitates development in six domains: personal awareness, emotional well-being, cognition, communication, socialization, and perceptual motor skills.

Culture. The underlying beliefs, patterns of behaviour, and assumptions of a group that are passed on from one generation to the next.

Curiosity. A child's desire to explore, discover, question, and wonder.

Curriculum. A prescribed set of learning outcomes presented to a group of children.

Demonstration programs. Full- or part-day programs usually affiliated with a post-secondary educational institution. These programs provide college or university students studying about children with opportunities to observe, participate in placement experience, or collect data for specific assignments.

Developmentally appropriate environments. Those that both support and challenge children with age-appropriate learning experiences.

Developmentally appropriate practice. Programs designed based on child development and play.

Developmental programs. Child-centered, and provide age-appropriate experiences that contribute to improved lifetime outcomes. One of four early learning and child care principles.

Drop-in programs. These programs are designed to provide children with care for short periods while their parents participate in a particular activity or service.

Early childhood. Refers to the period from birth to 8 years of age.

Early Childhood Development Agreement (ECDA). A federal, provincial, and territorial agreement that provides funds to support programs and services for children under 6 years of age and their families in promoting healthy pregnancy, birth, and infancy; improving parenting and family supports; strengthening early childhood development, learning, and care; and strengthening community supports.

Early childhood education. A term used to describe the field that prepares individuals to work with young children in a variety of early learning and child care settings.

Early childhood education and care (ECEC). Programs that support the healthy development of all children by providing each child with access to quality programs that are developmentally and culturally appropriate, regardless of choice of service, age, or developmental needs of children or residence of family.

Early childhood educator. A term used to describe individuals who work with children and hold a post-secondary ECE credential.

Early childhood practitioner. Individuals who have completed early childhood studies in a college certificate, diploma, or university degree program, and who participate in continuous learning about young children.

Early childhood services. Programs provided for children in child care settings, homes, institutions, recreational facilities, or other group settings. In these environments, early childhood practitioners create safe, interesting, innovative play opportunities that are responsive to children's needs, interests, and abilities, while supporting the needs of families.

Early childhood student practitioners. Individuals who participate in early childhood studies in an early childhood apprenticeship, college-certificate, diploma, or university-degree program.

Early intervention programs. Family- or centre-based programs for children who have been identified with atypical developmental patterns.

Early learning and child care. A comprehensive system of early learning and child care programs for children from infancy to 6 years, based on principles of inclusion, affordability, accessibility, quality, and parental choice. In these environments, early childhood practitioners create safe, interesting, innovative play opportunities that are responsive to children's needs, interests, and abilities, while supporting the needs of families.

Eclectic approach. Combining aspects of different theories as a way to guide early learning and child care program design and delivery.

Ecological theory. Bronfenbrenner's environmental-system theory of development. This theory emphasizes the role of social context through the five environmental systems: microsystem, mesosystem, exosystem, macrosystem, and chronosystem.

Emergent program. Describes the experiences that are offered to children as a result of children's exploring ideas and interests that are cognitively challenging and meaningful to them.

Environmental aesthetics. Focuses on how individuals experience their world through their senses, by incorporating their environmental perceptions and their aesthetic preferences of their environments, cultures, and seasons (Carlson, 2002).

Ethnicity. Refers to cultural heritage, nationality characteristics, race, religion, and language.

Evaluation. The process of forming or making judgments from the information gathered and making recommendations based on the results during and after an assessment process or event.

Family-centred practices. Programs whose practices are responsive to the needs of children and families. Families are appreciated for the diversity and uniqueness that they bring to the learning community.

Family child care. Child care offered on a full- or part-time basis for small numbers of children and provided by a non-relative caregiver in a home setting. This may or may not be government-regulated.

Family partnerships. Refers to early childhood practitioners' and families' continuity and consistency in communicating information and experiences that support children in developing a strong and secure foundation during their early years.

Family resource centres. Community-based centres that offer child and parenting programs. Resources such as play materials, parent-support materials, toy-lending libraries, and workshops are available.

Feeling tone. Refers to the way an individual takes in experiences and physical sensations, processes sounds, smells, and tastes, and how these are filtered as pleasant, unpleasant, or neutral.

Formal operational intelligence (12–13 years through adulthood). During this phase, abstract and logical thinking develop, which allows children to engage in scientific investigation.

Froebel programs. Based on the work of Friedrich Froebel, the founder of kindergartens, these programs have play as their focus, based on children's levels of development.

Head Start programs. Centre-based programs designed and implemented for children who are generally from economically deprived environments and who are deemed to have social, emotional, or cognitive delays. Family support is offered through parenting programs and community resources.

Hierarchy of being, thinking, and learning. A conceptual paradigm that outlines five levels at which children's learning can be focused to maximize the potential impact of a specific activity or environment.

High/Scope approach to programming. A constructivist approach developed by Weikart, based on Piaget's cognitive-developmental theory. Children construct knowledge through classrooms organized in interest centres that promote active learning, which broadens children's cognitive and social skills. Children use a plan-do-and-review sequence as a way to focus their learning and broaden their cognitive and social skills.

Hooking strategy. Refers to the process of placing interesting and varied materials into the play space. These materials offer children a choice of play opportunities for exploration, as well as time to make physical and cognitive connections with those materials.

Inclusive practice. Practices within the early learning and child care program that address and accommodate the individual needs of each child, regardless of developmental phase or diversity.

Infant-toddler child care. Specialized group care for children from 0–18 months and 19–30 months.

In-home child care. Refers to child care that is offered either in a child's home or in the home of a relative or non-relative.

Junior kindergarten. Half- or full-day programs, generally offered as part of the education system, for children 4 years of age. These programs focus on social skills.

Key experiences. Based on the High/Scope program model, experiences support children in participating in interaction with other children, adults, and materials. The interactions among people and materials support children's social, emotional, physical, cognitive, and language development.

Kindergarten. Half- or full-day programs for children 5 years of age, generally offered as part of the school system, although there are also privately run kindergartens and kindergarten programs offered as part of centre-based child care. These programs focus on both social skills and academic skills.

Learning community. Groups of people, such as students, who come together to examine their knowledge, skills, and visions for their learning, and set forth a collaborative plan to support themselves in gaining new knowledge that is transferable to early childhood service settings.

Locally appropriate experiences/curriculum. Program experiences (that are planned or spontaneous from a child) that are influenced by the people, culture, or events taking place in a community, such as lobster-fishing season in coastal communities.

Maturational theory. The biological process that some theorists suggest is responsible for human development.

Montessori approach to programming. Based on the philosophy of Italian educator Maria Montessori, these programs use specialized apparatus in a prepared classroom environment. Children participate in work-based learning experiences that are presented in sequential order, based on naturalistic observations conducted by teachers. The self-correcting experiences move children from simple to more complex tasks.

Motivation. A biological drive that each person is born with to live, learn, and evolve.

Multicultural programming. Early learning and child care experiences that support staff and children to learn about and be accepting of and responsive to the cultures and traditions of all children and families within the setting.

Multiple intelligences theory. Howard Gardner's concept about the different ways people interact with the world. The nine intelligences include linguistic, logical-mathematical, musical, bodily-kinesthetic, spatial, interpersonal, intrapersonal, naturalistic, and existential.

Nanny child care. Offered for one or more children in a child's home, by a trained or untrained person. This is non-regulated.

National Association for the Education of Young Children (NAEYC). The world's largest organization dedicated to improving the quality of educational and developmental services for all young children, with particular focus on children from birth through age 8.

National Children's Agenda (NCA). A comprehensive strategy set forth by federal, provincial, and territorial governments to improve the well-being of Canada's children.

Need. A lack of what is necessary for survival, health, or a feeling of well-being.

Organisation for Economic Co-operation and Development (OECD). An inter-governmental organization, made up of primarily industrialized market-economy countries, for the purpose of conducting research and being a coordinating body for policy formulation between its members.

Parent co-operative. A program operated by a volunteer parent board of directors. Parent volunteers assist early childhood practitioners during the implementation of the program. Most of the centres are not-for-profit.

Philosophical approach. One's assumptions and understanding about how children's play, environment, and people in the environment support children's learning.

Philosophy. A set of beliefs about how children learn and develop and what the role of the early childhood practitioner is in supporting children's learning.

Physiological needs. Needs such as air, water, food, and rest needed for survival.

Play-therapy programs. Play-based treatment programs designed for young children who have identified emotional or psychological problems.

Preoperational intelligence (18–24 months to 6–7 years). Children combine sensory experiences and motor movement with symbolic thinking. Children are egocentric during this phase, which interferes with their ability to see things from another perspective. Children find teasing difficult to understand because they generally take things literally.

Preschool child care. Specialized group care for children from 30 months to 4–5 years of age.

Program. A term used to describe the process for documenting the ideas or experiences that occur in early learning and child care programs for children before they enter the school system.

Program plan. A suggested plan of action that guides practitioners in planning potential experiences that will trigger children's curiosity.

Progressive education. Coined by John Dewey, progressive-education methods focus on children. The learning experiences are integrated with daily living; they preserve social values, including culture; and they are interactive with peers and adults.

Project-based programming. Children participate in in-depth investigation of an area of interest over a period of days or longer. Through the project, children engage in experiences that incorporate an array of skills, including math, science, language arts, dramatic play, and block play.

Psychoanalytical/psychodynamic theory. Erik Erikson's theory that children develop cognitively and socially simultaneously. There are eight psychosocial stages of development: trust versus mistrust, autonomy versus shame and doubt, initiative versus guilt, industry versus inferiority, identity versus identity confusion, intimacy versus isolation, generativity versus stagnation, integrity versus despair.

Psychological needs. Human needs necessary to maintain a healthy equilibrium both physically and emotionally.

Quality. Refers to early learning and child care services that are delivered within the quality framework identified by the organization, families, and government. Practitioners and families work collaboratively to promote and sustain practices that foster quality care for children. One of four early learning and child care principles.

Quality indicator. A predetermined set of criteria used to identify the degree of program excellence available to children and families.

Reggio Emilia program approach. This approach, adapted from programs in the City of Reggio Emilia, Italy, focuses on a community development model. The natural environment influences the use of in-depth projects as a way for children to learn about their environment, their community, and themselves.

Representation skills. Being able to examine an object and understand its use, and to use one object to represent another.

Responsive learning environment. Includes people, ideas, objects, and places that support children by creating a stress-free and psychologically and physiologically comfortable place to play.

Scaffolding. A fundamental principle of nature whereby one concept is built upon a previous learning structure, thereby ensuring its stable integration into the learner's knowledge or skill base.

School-aged child care. Child care offered for children from kindergarten to approximately 10–12 years of age. The care is offered before school, at lunchtime, after school, and on school holidays.

Self-actualization. The process of realizing one's full potential.

Self-concept. A term used to describe the collection of beliefs that people have developed about themselves through their experiences.

Self-esteem. The feelings of self-worth developing from an individual's beliefs about being valuable, capable, lovable, and worthwhile.

Sensorimotor intelligence (birth to 18–24 months). Children learn about their world through sensory experiences and motoric activity. The infant's sucking on her toy helps her learn through touch about things in her environment.

Social Union Framework Agreement (SUFA). An agreement, signed by nine provinces (excluding Quebec) and two territories, that commits each level of government to work together and with Canadians to strengthen Canada's social safety net, involve Canadians in the development of social programs, and strengthen partnerships among governments.

Sociocultural theory. Lev Vygotsky's theory suggests that children's mental, social, and linguistic development are influenced by interactions with other children, peers, and adults.

Spontaneous experiences. Are included in the program as a result of children's expressing an interest in a particular object, place, subject, or activity.

Success by 6 programs. Community-based programs championed by community business leaders. The programs are designed to help children by the age of 6 to be healthy and prepared for success in school and life.

Supervised-access program. Settings where children visit with a parent/parents who are required by law to see their children only in a supervised, neutral environment.

Supportive activities. Repeated experiences that affirm children's past learning and enhance their self-confidence.

Teachable moment. That point in a learner's development where a keen observer intervenes in some way to build on the learning that is occurring, thereby maximizing the learner's evolution.

Teen parent programs. Centre-based child care programs for children from infancy to school age, usually located in or near high schools. Support services specific to teen parents, including parenting classes, parent–child conferences, and program participation, may be offered.

Thematic program. Program experiences available to children are organized around an idea or topic originating from either the children or the early childhood practitioner.

Theory. As identified by Arce (2000), a theory is a collection of ideas, concepts, terms, and statements blended to illustrate behaviour.

Universally inclusive. All children, without discrimination, including children with special needs, Aboriginal children, and children with various cultural and linguistic backgrounds, have equal access to services. One of four early learning and child care principles.

Waldorf approach to programming. Based on the work of Rudolf Steiner, the curriculum draws on the natural nature of children, with emphasis on children learning through imitation. The program is arts-based, with a strong focus on image, rhythm, movement, drawing, painting, poetry, and drama. Academic content is held to a minimum.

Work tasks. Materials and experiences offered to children in Montessori programs that support children in learning about daily living, sensory, academic, cultural, and artistic domains.

A World Fit for Children. A declaration made by all countries belonging to the United Nations (except for the United States of America and Somalia) to improve the living conditions for children worldwide. *A World Fit for Children* identifies four priority areas for action: promoting healthy lives; providing quality education; protecting children against abuse, exploitation, and violence; and combating HIV/AIDS.

Zone of Proximal Development (ZPD). A concept developed by Vygotsky (1978) that suggests that children require activities that both support past learning and encourage new learning at slightly more difficult levels.

References

Arce, E.M. (2000). *Curriculum for Young Children*. Albany, NY: Delmar.

Arredondo, D., Brody, J., Zimmerman, D., & Moffett, C. (1995). Pushing the envelope in supervision. *Educational Leadership, 53*(3), 74–78.

Atheron, J. S. (2003). Doceo: Tutoring theory 1. UK: Available at **www.doceo.co.uk/original/tutorial_1.htm**

Atlas, J. & Lapidus, L. (1987). Patterns of symbolic expression in subgroups of the childhood psychoses. *Journal of Clinical Psychology, 43*, 177–188.

Auxter, D., Pyfer, J., & Huettig, C. (2001). *Principles and Methods of Adapted Physical Education and Recreation*. Saint Louis, MO: Mosby–Year Book, Inc.

Background Report of Canada (2003). Ottawa: Social Development Canada.

Bandura, A. (1977). *Social Learning Theory*. Englewood Cliffs, NJ: Prentice Hall.

Bandura, A. (1986). *Social Functions of Thought and Action: A Social Cognitive Theory*. Englewood Cliffs, NJ: Prentice Hall.

Bandura, A. (1998). Swimming against the Mainstream. Accentuating the Positive Aspects of Humanity. Paper presented at meeting of the American Psychological Association, San Francisco, August.

Bandura, A. (2000). Social cognitive theory. In A. Kazdin (Ed.), *Encyclopedia of Psychology*. Washington & New York: American Psychological Association and Oxford University Press.

Bandura, A., & Schunk, D. H. (1981). Cultivating competence, self-efficacy, and intrinsic interest through proximal self-motivation. *Journal of Personality and Social Psychology, 41*, 486–598.

Beach, J., Bertrand, J., Forer, B., Michal, D., & Tougas, J. (2004). *Working for Change: Canada's Child Care Workforce: Labour Market Update*. Ottawa: Child Care Human Resources Sector Council.

Beane, J. A. (Ed.). (1995). *Toward a Coherent Curriculum: 1995 Yearbook of the Association for Supervision and Curriculum Development*. Alexandria, VA: The Association for Supervision and Curriculum Development.

Bennett, J., Buysse, B., Lindberg, P., & Penn, H. (2004). Early Childhood Education and Care Policy—CANADA—Country Note. OECD Directorate for Education, Organisation for Economic Co-operation and Development, [OECD] Paris.

Berk, L. E. & Winsler, A. (1995). *Scaffolding Children's Learning: Vygotsky and Early Childhood Education*. Washington: National Association for the Education of Young Children.

Berkson, G. (1993). *Children with Handicaps. A Review of Behavioural Research*. Mahwah, NJ: Erlbaum.

Berner, M. M. (1992). Building conditions, parental involvement, and student achievement in the District of Columbia Public School System. *Urban Education, 28*(1), 6–29.

Berner, M. M. (1995). Buildings matter: The connection between school building conditions and student achievement in Washington, DC. In A. Meek (Ed.), *Designing Places for Learning*, (pp. 85–87). Alexandria, VA: Association for Supervision and Curriculum Design.

Bjorklund, D. F. & Pellegrini, A. D. (2002). *The Origins of Human Nature: Evolutionary Developmental Psychology*. Washington: APA.

Borgia, E. (1991). Impressions of Reggio Emilia. (ERIC Document Reproduction Service No. ED 338386).

Boss, S. (2001a). Breaking out of the box. *Northwest Education Magazine, 6*(4). Available at **www.nwrel.org/nwedu/summer01/breakingout.html**

Boss, S. (2001b). Schoolyard lessons. *Northwest Education Magazine, 6*(4). Available at **www.nwrel.org/nwedu/summer01/lessons.html**

Bowlby, J. (1969). *Attachment and Loss* (Vol. 1). London: Hogarth Press.

Bowlby, J. (1989). *Secure and Insecure Attachment*. New York: Basic Books.

Bredekamp, S. (1987). *Developmentally Appropriate Practice in Early Childhood Programs Serving Children from Birth through Age 8* (Expanded ed.). Washington, DC: NAEYC.

Bredekamp, S. & Copple, C. (Eds.). (1997). *Developmentally Appropriate Practice in Early Childhood Programs* (rev. ed.). Washington, DC: National Association for the Education of Young Children.

Brenner, Sydney. The man who made worms the workhorses of genetics. "Discover dialogue," interviewed by Duncan, D. E. In *Discovery Magazine*, April 2004.

Bronfenbrenner, U. (1986). Ecology of the family as a context for human development. Research perspectives. *Developmental Psychology, 22*, 723–742.

Bronfenbrenner, U. (2000). Ecological theory. In A. Kazdin (Ed.) *Encyclopedia of Psychology*. Washington & New York: American Psychological Association and Oxford University Press.

Bruner, J. (1972). The nature and uses of immaturity. *American Psychologist*, 27, 687–708.

Bruner, J. (1985). Vygotsky: A historical and conceptual perspective. In J. Wertsch (Ed.), *Culture, Communication, and Cognition* (pp. 22–34). New York: Cambridge University Press.

Bullough, R.V., Jr. (1994). Personal history and teaching metaphors: A self study of teaching as conversation. *Teacher Education Quarterly, 21*(1), 107–120.

Bullough, R. V. & Gitlin, A. (1995). *Becoming a Student of Teaching: Methodologies for Exploring Self and School Context*. New York: Garland.

Camp, R. (1989). Benchmarking. The search for industry best practices that lead to superior performance. Milwaukee, WI: American Society for Quality.

Canadian Child Care Federation (1991). *National Statement on Quality Child Care*. Ottawa: Author.

Canadian Child Care Federation (1994). National guidelines for training in early childhood care and education, draft document, May 1994. *Interaction, 8*(2), 6–9.

Canadian Child Care Federation (1994). *National Statement on Quality Child Care*. Ottawa, ON: Author. Available at **www.cfc-efc.ca/docs/cccf/00000111.htm**

Canadian Child Care Federation (2000). *Code of Ethics of the Canadian Child Care Federation*. Ottawa: Author.

Canadian Child Care Federation and Child Care Advocacy Association of Canada (2003). Perceptions of quality child care. Available at **www.cccf-fcsge.ca/pressroom/images/poll-full%20version.pdf#search='Canadian%20Child %20Care%20Federation%20and%20Child%20Ca re%20Advocacy%20Association%20of%20Canad a%20%282003%29.%20Perceptions%20of%20qu ality%20child%20care.'**

Caples, S. (1996). Some guidelines for preschool design. *Young Children, 51*(4): 14–21.

Capra, F. (1996). *The Web of Life: A New Scientific Understanding of Living Systems*. New York: Anchor Books.

Carlson, A. (2002). Environmental aesthetics. In E. Craig (Ed.), *Routledge Encyclopedia of Philosophy*. London: Routledge. Available at **www.rep.routledge.com/article/M047SECT1**

Catron, C. & Allen, J. (1999). *Early Childhood Curriculum*. Upper Saddle River, NJ: Merrill.

Chaille, C. & Silvern, S. (1996). Understanding through play. *Childhood Education, 72*(5), 274–277.

Chan, T. C. (1979). The impact of school building age on public achievement. (ERIC Document Reproduction Service No. ED 191138).

Chan, T. C. (1980). Physical environment and middle grade achievement. (ERIC Document Reproduction Service No. ED 198645).

Child Care Human Resources Sector Council (CCHRSC) (2004). Canada's child care workforce: Labour market update. Toronto: available at **www.ccsc-cssge.ca/english/pdf/workingfor change/CCHRSC%20MAIN-e.pdf**

Childcare Resource and Research Unit (2005). *Trends & Analysis. Early childhood education and care in Canada 2004*. Toronto: University of Toronto, Centre for Urban and Community Studies, Childcare Resource and Research Unit.

Clarkson, Her Excellency the Right Honourable Adrienne, Governor General of Canada Installation Speech, October 7, 1999. Available at **en.wikisource.org/wiki/Adrienne_Clarkson's_installation_speech**

Cleveland, G. & Krashinsky, M. (2001). *Our Children's Future: Child Care Policy in Canada*. Toronto: University of Toronto Press.

Cleveland, G. & Krashinsky, M. (2003). *Fact and Fantasy: Eight Myths About Early Childhood Education and Care*. Toronto: Childcare Resource and Research Unit, Centre for Urban and Community Studies, University of Toronto.

Cleveland, G. & Krashinsky, M. (2003). *Starting Strong. Financing ECEC Services in OECD Countries*. Paris: OECD.

Cleveland, G., & Krashinsky, M. (2005). The quality gap: A study of non-profit and commercial child care centres in Canada. Available at **www.child carepolicy.net/**

Coffey, C. In *Early Learning and Care* by Cook, M., Keating, D., & McColm, M. Available at **www.gbrownc.on.ca/earlychildhood/documents/ELCC_paper_final.pdf**

Coffey, C. & McCain, M. (2004). Final Report—Commission on Early Learning and Child Care for the City of Toronto, May, 2002. Available at **www. city.toronto.on.ca/children/report/elcc.pdf**

Cole, P. M. (1999). Culture in development. In M. H. Bornstein & M. E. Lamb (Eds.), *Developmental Psychology: An Advanced Textbook* (4th ed.). Mahwah, NJ: Erlbaum.

Cooke, M., Keating, D., & McColm, M. (2004). Early Learning and Care in the City. Available at **www.acscd.ca/acscd/public/home.nsf/a025980268 38279d852568ff007d3fd9/4b5fe0040af9d7a185256 f0200580cef/$FILE/ELCC_Aug04.pdf**

Crossley, B. (2000). The magic of motor movement. In *Young Children and Educators.* Vol II *(2)*. Quispamsis, NB: Portfolio 2000.

Crossley, B. & Dietze, B. (1996). *Designing Programs for Young Children.* Rothesay, NB: Portfolio 2000.

Crossley, B. & Dietze, B. (2003). Outdoor programming and play for young children in Canada, "Our Opportunity." In *Outdoor Play in Early Childhood Education and Care Programs.* Ottawa: Canadian Child Care Federation.

Crossley, B., Dietze, B., & Hume, J. (2001). *Staff Development Options in Early Childhood Education.* Belleville, ON: Loyalist College.

Crowther, I. (2003). *Creating Effective Learning Environments.* Toronto: Nelson.

Crowther, I. (2005). *Introduction to Early Childhood Education. A Canadian Perspective.* Toronto: Nelson.

Dahlberg, G., Moss, P., & Pence, A. R. (1999). *Beyond Quality in Early Childhood Education and Care: Postmodern Perspectives.* Philadelphia: Falmer Press, Taylor & Francis.

Darwin, C. (1979). *The Origin of the Species.* (7th Printing). Toronto: Random House Value Publishing.

Dewey, J. (1990/1956). *The Child and the Curriculum and the School and Society.* London: The University of Chicago Press.

Dietze, B. (2002). The learning community perspective. In *A Report on Staff Development in Early Childhood Education.* Belleville, ON: Loyalist College.

Doherty. G., Friendly, M., & Beach, J. (2004). *Early Childhood Education and Care Policy—Background Report for Canada—OCED Thematic Review of Early Childhood Education and Care Report.* Paris: Organisation for Economic Co-operation and Development.

Driscoll, A. & Nagel, N. (2005). *Early Childhood Education, Birth–8, The World of Children, Families, and Educators.* Boston: Allyn & Bacon.

Dudek, M. (2000). *Kindergarten Architecture: Space for the Imagination.* (2nd ed.). Independence, KY: Spon Press.

Eccles, J. S. (2001). Gender and Ethnicity as Developmental Contexts. Paper presented at meeting of the Society for Research in Child Development, Minneapolis, Apr.

Edwards, C., Gandini, L., & Forman, G. (Eds.). (1993). *The Hundred Languages of Children: The Reggio Emilia Approach to Early Childhood Education.* Norwood, NJ: Ablex.

Elkind, D. (2004). Thanks for the memory: The lasting value of true play. In D. Koralek (Ed.), *Spotlight on Young Children and Play* (pp. 36–41). Washington: National Association for the Education of Young Children.

Erikson, E. (1963). *Childhood and Society.* (2nd ed.). New York: Norton.

Erikson, E. (1968). *Identity: Youth and Crisis.* New York: W.W. Norton.

Essa, E., Young, R., & Lehne, L. (1998). *Introduction to Early Childhood Education.* (2nd Canadian ed.). Scarborough, ON: ITP Nelson.

Evans, G. W. & Cohen, S. (1987). Environmental stress. In I. Altman & D. Stokols (Eds.), *Handbook of Environmental Psychology* (pp. 571–610). New York: Wiley.

Evans, G. & McCoy, J. (1998). When buildings don't work: The role of architecture in human health. *Journal of Environmental Psychology, 18,* 85–94.

Feeney, S. & Moravcik, E. (1987). A thing of beauty: Aesthetic development in young children. *Young Children, (6),* 7–15.

Ferguson, E. (2004). What's in a Name? Discussion paper, Canadian Child Care Federation, Ottawa.

Flavell, J. (1963). *The Developmental Psychology of Jean Piaget.* New York: D. Van Nostrand.

Franklin, M. & Biber, B. (1977). Psychological perspectives and early childhood education: Some relations between theory and practice. In L. Katz (Ed.), *Current Topics in Early Childhood Education* (pp. 1–32). Norwood, NJ: Ablex Publishing.

Freud, S. (1938). *An Outline of Psychoanalysis.* London: Hogarth.

Friendly, M. (2004). Strengthening Canada's social and economic foundations: Next steps for early childhood education and care. *Policy Options.* March: 46–51. Montreal: Institute for Research on Public Policy. Available at **www.irpp.org/po/archive/ mar04/friendly.pdf**

Friendly, M. & Beach, J. (2005). *Early Childhood Education and Care in Canada 2004.* (6th ed.). Toronto: University of Toronto, Centre for Urban and Community Studies, Childcare Resource and Research Unit.

Friendly, M., Beach, J., & Turiano, M. (2002). *Early Childhood Education and Care in Canada 2001.* Toronto: University of Toronto, Centre for Urban and Community Studies, Childcare Resource and Research Unit.

Froebel, F. (1889). *Autobiography of Friedrich Froebel* (E. Michaelis & K. Moore, Trans.). Syracuse, NY: Bardeen.

Funk & Wagnall. (1976). *Standard Desk Dictionary.* New York: Funk & Wagnall's.

Gallahue, D. (1993). Motor development and movement skill acquisition in early childhood education. In B. Spodek (Ed.), *Handbook of Research on Education of Young Children* (pp. 24–41). Upper Saddle River, NJ: Prentice Hall.

Gandini, L. (1998). Educational and caring spaces. In C. Edwards, L. Gandini, & G. Forman (Eds.). *The Hundred Languages of Children: The Reggio Emiia Approach—Advanced Reflections* (2nd ed.), (pp. 161–178). Greenwich, CT: Ablex.

Gardner, H. (1999). *The Disciplined Mind.* New York: Simon & Schuster.

Gesell, A. & Ilg, F. (1949). *Child Development: An Introduction to the Study of Human Growth.* New York: Harper & Brothers.

Gestwicki, C. & Bertrand, J. (1999). *The Essentials of Early Education.* Toronto: Nelson.

Ginott, H. (1972). *Teacher and Child: A Book for Parents and Teachers.* (1st Collier Books ed.). New York: Colliers, 1993, c1972.

Glasser, W. (1998). *Choice Theory. A New Psychology of Personal Freedom.* New York: Harper Collins.

Gordon, A. & Brown, K. (1989). *Beginnings and Beyond. Foundations in Early Childhood Education.* Albany, NY: Delmar Publishers Inc.

Government of Canada (2003). *Multilateral Framework Agreement on Early Learning and Child Care.* Ottawa: Author. Available at **www.ecd-elcc.ca/en/elcc/elcc_multiframe.shtml**

Government of Canada (2004). *A Canada Fit for Children. Government of Canada Report.* Ottawa: Author.

Government of Canada and Government of Saskatchewan (2005). *Moving Forward on Early Learning and Child Care. Agreement-in-Principle between the Government of Canada and the Government of Canada.* Ottawa: Author.

Government of Saskatchewan (2005). *Our Children. Our Promise. Our Future.* Saskatchewan: Saskatchewan Learning.

Greenman, J. (1988). Caring Spaces, Learning Places. Children's Environments That Work. Redmond, WA: Exchange Press.

Han, E. P. (1995). Reflection is essential in teacher education. *Childhood Education, 71,* 228–230.

Harms, T., Clifford, R., & Cryer, D. (1998). *Early Childhood Environment Rating Scale* (rev. ed.). New York: Teachers College Press.

Harms, T., Jacobs, E. V., and White, D. R. (1996). *School-age Care Environment Rating Scale.* New York: Teachers College Press.

Harter, S. (1990). Self and identity development. In S. S. Feldman & G. R. Elliott (Eds.), *At the Threshold: The Developing Adolescent.* Cambridge, MA: Harvard University Press.

Harter, S. (1999). *The Construction of the Self.* New York: Guilford.

Hathaway, W. (1995). Effects of school lighting on physical development and school performance. *The Journal of Educational Research, 88*(4), 228.

Havighurst, R. J. & Neugarten, B. L. (1967). *Society and Education.* (2nd ed.). Boston: Allyn & Bacon, Inc.

Heathington, B.S. (1980). Needed positive reading self concepts. In T. D. Yawkey (Ed.), *The Self Concept of the Young Child* (pp 63–71). Provo, UT: Brigham Young University Press.

Heidemann, S. & Hewitt, D. (1992). *Pathways to Play: Developing Play Skills in Young Children.* St. Paul, MN: Redleaf Press.

Helgeson, S. (1995). *The Web of Inclusion.* New York: Doubleday.

Hendrick, J. (2001). *The Whole Child. Developmental Education for the Early Years.* Upper Saddle River, NJ: Prentice Hall.

Hendrick, J. & Weissman, P. (2006). *The Whole Child,* (8th ed.). Upper Saddle River, NJ: Pearson.

Henniger, M. (2002). *Teaching Young Children. An Introduction.* (2nd ed.). Upper Saddle River, NJ: Pearson.

Hildebrand, V. (1994). *Guiding Young Children.* (5th ed.). Columbus, OH: Merrill/Prentice-Hall.

Hohmann, M. & Weikart, D. (1995). *Educating Young Children.* Ypsilanti, MI: High/Scope Press.

Holt. (1969). *How Children Learn.* New York: Pitman.

Hughes, F. (1999). *Children, Play, and Development.* (3rd ed.). Boston: Allyn & Bacon.

Isbell, R. (1995). *The Handbook of Learning Centre.* Beltsville, MD: Gryphon House.

Isbell, R. & Exelby, B. (2001). *Early Learning Environments That Work.* Beltsville, MD: Gryphon House.

Ishai, A., Ungerleider, L. G., Martin, A., Schouten, J. L., & Haxby, J. V. (1999). Distributed Representation of Objects in the Human Ventral Visual Pathway. Proc. Natl. Acad. Sci. USA. Available at **www.pnas.org/cgi/reprint/96/16/9379**

Jalongo, M. & Isenberg, J. (2004). *Exploring Your Role. A Practitioner's Introduction to Early Childhood Education.* Upper Saddle River, NJ: Prentice Hall.

Johnson, J. E., Christie, J. F., & Yawkey, T. D. (1987). *Play and Early Childhood Development.* Glenview, IL: Scott Foresman.

Johnson, J. E., Christie, J. F., & Yawkey, T. D. (1999). *Play and Early Childhood Development.* New York: Addison Wesley Longman.

John-Steiner, V. & Mahn, H. (1996). Sociocultural approaches to learning and development: A Vygotskian framework. *Educational Psychologist, 31*, 191–206.

Jones, B. F., Palinscar, A. S., Ogle, D., & Carr, E. G. (1987). Learning and thinking. In B. F. Jones, A. S. Palinscar, D. S. Ogle, & E. C. Carr (Eds.). *Strategic Thinking and Learning: Cognitive Instruction in the Content Areas.* Alexandria, VA: North Central Regional Educational Laboratory.

Kameenui, E. & Darch, C. (1995). *Instructional Classroom Management.* White Plains, NY: Longman.

Katz, L. (1993). Five perspectives on quality in early childhood programs. Perspectives from ERIC/EECE. [Monograph series, 1]. Urbana, IL: Eric Clearing House on Elementary and Early Childhood Education.

Keating, D. (2004). Towards an Early Child Development System. Conference presentation, Quebec City, May 25.

Klein, T. P., Wirth, D., & Linas, K. (2003). Play: Children's context for development. *Young Children, 48*(6), 22–31.

Labinowicz, Ed. (1980) *The Piaget Primer.* Don Mills, ON: Addison-Wesley Publishing Company.

Lackney, J. A. (2000). Thirty-three educational design principles for schools and community learning centers. Washington: National Institute for Building Sciences (NIBS), National Clearinghouse for Educational Facilities (NCEF).

Larose, E., Terrisse, B., Bedard, J., & Karsenti, T. (2001). Preschool Education Training: Skills for Adapting to a Changing Society. Paper presented at Pan-Canadian Education Research Agenda Symposium: Teacher and Educator Training, Current Trends and Future Directions, Quebec City, May.

Lero, D. & Brophy, K. (2005). *QC Wellington: A Community-Wide Approach for Improving and Sustaining High Quality Child Care in Wellington County.* Guelph, ON: University of Guelph.

Lewis, S. (2004). Proceedings of Child Care for a Change! Shaping the 21st Century Conference. Winnipeg, MB: Canadian Council on Social Development (CCSD).

Lindeman, E. C. (1989). *The Meaning of Adult Education.* Norman, OK: Printing Services, University of Oklahoma.

Linder, T. W. (1993). *Transdisciplinary Play-Based Intervention: Guidelines for Developing a Meaningful Curriculum for Young Children.* Baltimore, MD: Brookes.

Malaguzzi, L. (1991). (March/April). Not just anywhere: Making child care centers into "particular places." *Childcare Information Exchange, 85*, pp. 5–9.

Maslow, A. H. (1970). *Motivation and Personality.* (2nd ed.). NewYork: Harper & Row.

Maslow, A. H. (1987). *Motivation and Personality.* (3rd ed.). New York: Harper & Row.

Mayfield, M. (2001). *Early Childhood Education and Care in Canada.* Toronto: Prentice Hall.

McAfee, O. & Leong, D. (2002). *Assessing and Guiding Young Children's Development and Learning.* Boston: Allyn & Bacon.

McCain, M. & Romonow, R. (2005). Stand on guard. *Globe and Mail*, Friday, February 4, 2005, P.A.15. Available at **atkinsonfdn.on.ca/updates/Document_1108389811561**

McClenney, K. (2003). Benchmarking best practices in the learning college. *League of Innovation*, 6(4), 1–4. Retrieved from **www.league.org/publication/abstracts/learning/lelabs0304.html**

McLean, M., Wolery, M., & Bailey, D. B. (2004). Assessing infants and preschoolers with special needs. (3rd ed.). Upper Saddle River, NJ: Merrill/Prentice Hall.

McLoyd, E. (2000). Poverty. In A. Kazdin (Ed.), *Encyclopedia of Psychology.* Washington & New York: American Psychological Association and Oxford University Press.

McLoyd, V. C. (1998). Children in poverty: Development, public policy, and practice. In W. Damon (Editor-in-Chief), I. E. Sigel, & K. A. Renninger (Volume Eds.), *Handbook of Child Psychology, Vol. 4: Child Psychology in Practice,* (pp. 135–208). New York: Wiley.

Milliron, M. & Prentice, M. (2004, February). Anytime, anyplace and the community college: Ten emerging insights. The Sloan Consortium *Journal of Asynchronous Learning, 8*(1), pp. 1–6.

Mitchell, A. & David, J. (Eds.). (1992). *Explorations with Young Children.* Mt. Rainier, MD: Gryphon.

Monigham-Nourot, P., Scales, B., & Van Hoorn, J. (with Almy, M). (1987). *Looking at Children's Play: A Bridge between Theory and Practice.* New York: Teachers College Press.

Montessori, M. (1914). *Dr. Montessori's Own Handbook.* New York: Frederick Stokes.

Morrison, G. (2003). *Fundamentals of Early Childhood Education.* Upper Saddle River, NJ: Merrill Prentice Hall.

Nash, J. M. (1997). Fertile minds. *Time, February 3,* pp. 50–54.

National Institute for Child Health and Human Development (NICHD). (2000). The relation of child care to cognitive and language development (Report of the Early Child Care Research Network). *Child Development, 71,* 960–980.

Odgen, Frank. (2005). Doctor tomorrow: Where science fiction becomes fact. Available at **www. drtomorrow.com/laws.html**

Okagaki, L., Diamond, K., Kontos, S. J., & Hestenes, L. (1998). Correlates of young children's interactions with classmates with disabilities. *Early Childhood Research Quarterly, 13*(1), 67–86.

Organisation for Economic Co-operation and Development (OECD). (2001). *Starting Strong: Education and Care.* Paris: Author.

Pacifici L. & Garrison, J. (2004). Imagination, emotion and inquiry: The teachable moment. In Rodopi (publisher), *Contemporary Pragmatism, Volume 1, Number 1,* 1 June 2004, pp. 119–132(14). Available at **www.ingentaconnect.com/content/rodopi/cpm/ 2004/00000001/00000001/art00007**

Parten, M. (1933). Social play among preschool children. *Journal of Abnormal and Social Psychology, 28,* 136–147.

Pellegrini, A. (1985). Social-cognitive aspects of children's play: The effects of age, gender, and activity centres. *Journal of Applied Developmental Psychology, 6,* 129–140.

Pellegrini A. & Perlmutter, J. (1988). Rough and tumble play in the elementary school playground. *Young Children, 43*(2), 14–17.

Pepler, D. & Ross, H. (1981). Effects of play on convergent and divergent problem solving. *Child Development, 52,* 1202–1210.

Perry, B. (2001). Curiosity: The fuel of development. Available at **teacher.scholastic.com/professional/ bruceperry/curiosity.htm**

Piaget, J. (1962). *Play, Dreams, and Imitation in Childhood.* New York: Norton.

Piaget, J. (1970). Piaget's theory. In P. Mussen (Ed.), *Handbook of Child Psychology, Vol. 1.* New York: Wiley, 1983.

Piaget, J. (1971). *The Child's Conception of Movement and Speed.* New York: Ballantine.

Pierce, K. (1990). The child in the curriculum. In I. M. Doxey (Ed.), *Child Care and Education—Canadian Dimensions.* Scarborough, ON: Nelson Canada.

Plympton, P., Conway, S., & Epstein, K. (2000). Daylighting in Schools: Improving Student Performance and Health at a Price Schools Can Afford. Paper presented at the American Solar Energy Society Conference, Madison, Wisconsin, June 16, 2000.

Pritchett, P. & Pound, R. (1995). *The Stress of Organizational Change.* Dallas: Pritchett & Associates.

Read, M. A., Sugawara, A. I., & Brandt, J. A. (1999). Impact of space and color in the physical environment on preschool children's cooperative behavior. *Environment and Behavior, 31*(3), 413–428.

Reicher, D. (2000). Nature's design rules: Leading the way toward energy-efficient schools. *Learning by Design.* Available at **www.asbj.com/lbd/2000/ 00inprint/00reicher.html**

Rinaldi, C. (1998). The space of childhood. In C. Ceppi & M. Zini (Eds.), *Children, Spaces, Relations: Metaproject for an Environment for Young Children,* 114–120. Reggio Emilia, Italy: Reggio Children.

Rinaldi, C. (2001). Documentation and assessment: What is the relationship? In Project Zero & Reggio Children (Eds.), *Making Learning Visible: Children as Individual and Group Learners,* (78–89). Reggio Emilia, Italy: Reggio Children.

Rosario, J. & Collazo, E. (1981). Aesthetic codes in context: An exploration in two preschool classrooms. *Journal of Aesthetic Education 15*(1), 71–82.

Rubin, K. H. (1977). The social and cognitive value of preschool toys and activities. *Canadian Journal of Behaviour and Science, 9,* 383–385.

Rubin, K. H., Maioni, T. L., & Hornung, M. (1976). Free play behaviours in middle- and lower-class preschoolers: Parten & Piaget revisited. *Child Development, 47*, 414–419.

Sanders, S. (2002). *Active for Life: Developmentally Appropriate Movement Programs for Young Children.* Washington: NAEYC.

Santrock, J. (2002). *Life-span Development.* Boston: McGraw Hill.

Schulz, P. V. (1978). Day care in Canada: 1850–1962. In K. G. Rolls (Ed.), *Good Daycare: Fighting for It, Getting It, Keeping It* (pp. 137–158). Toronto: Women's Educational Press.

Seagoe, M. (1970). An instrument for the analysis of children's play as an index of socialization. *Journal of School Psychology, 8*, 139–144.

Selye, H. (1952). *The Story of the Adaptation Syndrome.* Montreal: Acta, Inc.

Selye, H. (1956). *The Stress of Life.* New York: McGraw Hill.

Shiraev, E. & Levi, D. (2001). *Introduction to Cross-Cultural Psychology.* Boston: Allyn & Bacon.

Singer, J. L. (1973). *The Child's World of Make-Believe: Experimental Studies of Imaginative Play.* New York: Academic Press.

Singer, J. L. & Singer, D. G. (1980). The values of imagination. In B. Sutton-Smith (Ed.), *Play and Learning* (pp. 195–218). New York: Gardner Press.

Singer, J. L. & Singer, D. G. (1985). *Make Believe: Games and Activities to Foster Imaginative Play in Young Children.* Glenview, IL: Scott, Foresman.

Skinner, B. (1974). *About Behaviourism.* New York: Knopf.

Smilansky, S. (1968). *The Effects of Sociodramatic Play on Disadvantaged Preschool Children.* New York: Wiley.

Sobel, D. (1994). Authentic curriculum. *Holistic Education Review, 7*, 33–43.

Spodek, B. (1986). *Today's Kindergarten: Exploring the Knowledge Base, Expanding the Curriculum.* New York: Teachers College Press.

Statistics Canada (2002a). A profile of the Canadian population. Where we live, 2001 Census. Available at **www.chass.utoronto.ca/datalib/cc01/announcement/article.pdf#search='A%20profile%20of%20the%20Canadian%20population.%20Where%20we%20live%2C%202001%20Census'**

Statistics Canada (2002b). Profile of language, mobility and migration for Canada, provinces, territories, census divisions and census subdivision, 2001 Census. Available at **www.statcan.ca/Daily/English/021210/d021210a.htm**

Statistics Canada (2002c). Age groups of children at home and family structure for census families in private households. Available at **www.statcan.ca:8096/bsolc/english/bsolc?catno=95F0316X&CHROPG=1**

Statistics Canada (2003a). Census of population: Immigration, birthplace and birthplace of parents, citizenship, ethnic origin, visible minorities and Aboriginal peoples. The Day. January 21, 2003. Available at **www.statcan.ca/Daily/English/030121/d030121a.htm**

Statistics Canada (2003b). Aboriginal peoples of Canada. A demographic profile, 2001 census. Available at **www12.statcan.ca/english/census01/products/analytic/companion/abor/contents.cfm**

Szanton, E. S. (1998). Infant/toddler care and education. In C. Seefeldt & A. Galper, *Continuing Issues in Early Childhood Educaton* (2nd ed.), (pp. 62–86). Upper Saddle River, NJ: Merrill/Prentice Hall.

Tanner, C. K. & Langford, S. (2003). The importance of interior design elements as they relate to student outcomes. Dalton, GA: Carpet and Rug Institute. (ERIC Document Reproduction Service No. ED 478177).

Tarr, P. (2001). Aesthetic code in early childhood classrooms: What art educators can learn from Reggio Emilia. Minneapolis, MN: Design Share, Inc. Available at **www.designshare.com/research/tarr/aesthetic%5Fcodes%5F1.htm**

Tarr, P. (2003). Reflections on the image of the child: Reproducer or creator of culture. *Art Education 56*(4), 6–11.

Tinzmann, M. B., Jones, B. F., Fennimore, T. F., Bakker, J., Fine, C., & Pierce, J. (1990). *What is the collaborative classroom?* Available at **www.ncrel.org/sdrs/areas/rpl_esys/collab.htm**

Trawick-Smith, J. (1992). A descriptive study of spatial arrangement in a family day care home. *Child & Youth Care Forum, 2*(4), 263–276.

Uline, C. L. (1997). School architecture as a subject of inquiry. *Journal of School Leadership, 7*(2), 194–209.

Upitis, R. (2005). Architecture, Complexity Science, and Schooling in the Early Years. Paper submission for the 2005 Hawaii International Conference on Arts and Humanities.

Valsiner, J. (2000). *Cultural and Human Development.* Thousand Oaks, CA: Sage.

Van Hoorn, J., Nourot, P. M., Scales, B., & Alward, K. R. (2003). *Play at the Centre of the Curriculum.* (3rd ed.). Upper Saddle River, NJ: Merrill/Prentice Hall.

Vasta, R., Miller, S.A., & Ellis, S. (2004). *Child Psychology* (4th ed.). New York: Wiley.

Vold, E. (2003). Young children's affirmation of differences: Curriculum that is multicultural and developmentally appropriate. In J. P. Isenberg & M. R. Jalongo (Eds.), *Major Trends and Issues in Early Childhood Education.* New York: Teacher's College Press.

Vygotsky, L. (1978). *Mind in Society: The Development of Higher Psychological Processes.* Cambridge, MA: Harvard University Press.

Wasserman, S. (1992). Serious play in the classroom—How messing around can win you the Nobel prize. *Childhood Education, 68*(3), 133–139.

Winter, S. (1999). *The Early Childhood Inclusion Model: A Program for All Children.* Olney, MD: Association for Childhood Education International.

Wortham, S. (1998). *Early Childhood Curriculum.* (2nd ed.). Upper Saddle River, NJ: Merrill.

Wylie, S. (2004). *Observing Young Children.* Toronto: Nelson.

Zachary, L. (2000). *The Mentor's Guide.* San Francisco: Jossey-Bass.

Photo Credits

Index